ART IN
EDUCATION

HOWARD CONANT AND
ARNE RANDALL

ART IN
EDUCATION

Chas. A. Bennett
Peoria, Illinois

Introduction to the Visual Preface

ART would have no significant place in education, unless it had a place in the lives of everyone. Actually, the place art occupies in our lives is much more widespread and important than we can comprehend, even though some of us call ourselves art educators.

We tend to forget that art remains independent even when applied to social studies, advertising layout, or hardware design. Persons in art education who fear that their work will lose identity if it is related to other subjects might turn to Shakespeare, in his poem on beauty, Who Is Sylvia? "To her eyes Love doth repair, to help him of his blindness; and being helped, inhabits there." To say it more directly, art transforms any object or emotion. It helps even Love to see. We are moved by the grace and warmth of art creation in any form. Art makes the difference between good and bad design, and this difference cannot be "integrated," or separated.

On the next sixteen pages, which serve as the Visual Preface to ART IN EDUCATION, are shown examples of some ways art enters and shapes our lives. You will think of other examples: television settings, billboards, magazine displays, newspaper layouts, book pages, window exhibits, clothing, facial makeup and hairstyling, home plans, automobiles and aircraft, household utensils, landscaping, hardware pieces, streets, parks, community planning, and religious expressions.

The Visual Preface is divided into three parts: (1) **Art in Entertainment,** because much of our living is expressed

5

in the works of art which Entertainment represents—in fact, we spent $55,000,000,000.00 (fifty-five billion) on luxury goods and entertainment in the United States in 1957; (2) **Art in Material Use,** *because every man-made object we use must be designed by someone, and we use art every day—in the classroom, in our homes; (3)* **Art in Tribute to the Human Spirit,** *because here we meet in common understanding of man's religious, social, and personal achievements and aspirations.*

The examples of art expression shown on pages 7 to 11 include the world of self-entertainment as well as entertainment of others.

On page 7, a 3-year-old is thoroughly entertained and engrossed in manipulation of colors, using a liquid paint medium . . . . two older girls are making paper decorations and a hand puppet . . . . the boy beside them is discovering the sheer pleasure of working with clay . . . . the boy below them is deriving pleasure and true artistic growth in the manipulation of crayons . . . . and the boys at the right are using art works to express their interests and feelings.

At its inception, all art may be a form of entertainment.

ART

in

Enter-

tainment

Art in costume, in stage setting, and in the poetry of the dance—as expressed in *The Sleeping Beauty* ballet.

"Entertaining himself while he learns"—and everyone else who sees him!

A stick puppet show, prepared by primary school children.

A large mural background design for a "French" variety show—planned and executed by senior high students.

Note the drollness and the appeal of this fourth-grader's hand puppets. Only children can achieve this exact quality in entertainment.

A *Hansel and Gretel* presentation designed entirely by elementary school students.

Even in traditional entertainment such as *The Fire Bird* suite and *Romeo and Juliet,* rich originality of design can be created for successive generations. Costumes and scenery here depicted are from the finest examples in today's repertoire.

COURTESY ELLENSBURG, WASHINGTON, AND LUBBOCK, TEXAS, PUBLIC SCHOOLS

Study of natural scenes leads to artistic development in scenic design. Every member of the class will remember outdoor sketching as a true highlight in his experience.

The art of display can be used in entertainment or in a commercial way. Below it is represented by the spirit of students who have created three-dimensional works.

COURTESY PITTSBURGH PUBLIC SCHOOLS

COURTESY WILLIAM H. MILLIKEN, JR., AND BINNEY & SMITH

COURTESY PRATT INSTITUTE, BROOKLYN, N. Y.

COURTESY HERMAN MILLER FURNITURE COMPAN

COURTESY WHIRLPOOL CORPORATION, RCA

COURTESY UNIVERSITY OF BRITISH COLUMBIA,
VANCOUVER

12

ART in Material Use

The display at the top of page 12 is famous in National Art Education Association annals. It was part of a unified plan that converted a hotel display space into a well-designed setting. But the expression of student and commercial designers is equally effective when applied to furniture construction, community planning, house design, and window display.

COURTESY BALTIMORE PUBLIC SCHOOLS

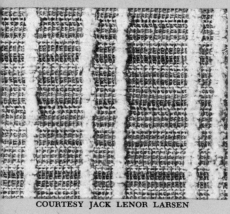

COURTESY JACK LENOR LARSEN

COURTESY KANSAS CITY, MISSOURI, PUBLIC SCHOOLS

COURTESY OKLAHOMA CITY PUBLIC SCHOOLS

"Art in Material Use" can mean texture, color, and form in textile designs; a true means of useful expression for a handicapped child (bottom, shown opposite page); and a study of communities and transportation as in the elementary classrooms represented in the illustrations on this page.

15

Learning to use a potter's wheel. Ceramics ranks among the most useful and expressive of the crafts.

A student-designed metal bowl representing great skill and an understanding of art principles.

An electric sander, beautifully designed for visual pleasure and use.

An exquisitely proportioned student-designed magazine rack that would contribute interest and distinction to a home.

ART in Tribute to the Human Spirit

Tributes to the spirit of the United Nations and to the power of religious belief: the lobby of the UN building, and the Wayfarer's Chapel designed by Lloyd Wright.

The modern sculptor Seymour Lipton fashioned *Sanctuary*, a significant personal expression, out of nickel-silver and steel.

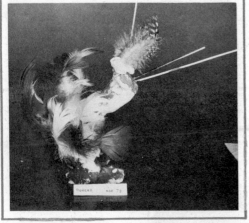

U. S. military forces crafts leaders stimulate interest in many types of art activity.

At left, a spirited construction created by a 7½ year old boy, using feathers and other natural materials.

Easily bent aluminum wire reduces risk of injury in developing this highly satisfying art form.

Carnival or circus scenes, and sport activities often induce children to express themselves in art media.

An interpretation of the power of nature which has universal appeal—a painting by Marsden Hartley.

19

An outstanding modern design by a Polish architect, Matthew Nowicki. The State Fair Arena near Raleigh, North Carolina.

At seventeen, an American student, George Nowacki, painted the opaque watercolor interpretation of the religious service, below left.

The silver wire sculpture was created by Richard Lippold and is entitled Young Venus. It formed part of a collection circulated by The American Federation of Arts.

Young St. John the Baptist, by
Piero di Cosimo. This creation
of the late 15th century has a
timeless and universal appeal.

This crayon "etching" reveals the subject interest and careful attention to detail
which is often typical of the art products of nine-year-old children.

CONTENTS

Introduction: Art in Education

ART IN EDUCATION *was chosen as the title for this book since it indicates a certain philosophic viewpoint. It implies that art should retain its identity in education as a quality of human experience which rises above the commonplace and the mediocre. It follows that learning experiences in art can be most effectively and creatively guided by the specially prepared art teacher.*

The title indicates that art is an integral part of education and life. Art education has become recognized as a field which contributes richly to the total learning experience of the child. Without art, and an art teacher to guide children's experiences, no school curriculum is complete.

One of the aims of this book is to show how historic philosophies can be fused with the most desirable aspects of more recently developed educational beliefs. This approach to the formulation of a contemporary art educational philosophy is being adopted by an ever-increasing number of art teachers who feel that their immediate predecessors were too frequently over concerned with segments of education such as the "child-centered" or "product-centered" approach.

There are several major areas in which art teachers should possess much greater understanding and facility if they are to effectively meet the needs of the children, adolescents, and adults with whom they work. The following are among the most important of these areas of need:

1. Art teachers need to understand the arts. To help people express themselves creatively through art, and to help them gain an understanding of this important aspect of our culture, the art teacher must not only participate actively and, wherever possible, significantly in some form of art expression but must possess a reasonably broad understanding of the arts as well. To understand the arts implies far more than a superficial knowledge of art history, artists' names, or their works. To understand the arts one must study and observe them deeply, over a long period of time.

A profound understanding of art is best achieved through extensive study of art works of all styles and ages as well as by continuous reading and discussion of important books in all of the major disciplines, with an emphasis, of course, on the arts. In addition, one must personally experience the joy and sorrow of personal artistic creation.

In short, art teachers need to be what their title implies instead of being just "group leaders" whose philosophic aims and conceptual understandings do not extend beyond the technicalities of processes such as silk screen printing and papier mâché construction.

They need to be as consecrated to their field as scientists are to theirs.

2. Art teachers need to understand human growth and development. To understand human growth and development, one must study psychology and other social sciences, and put this knowledge into practice. The art teacher who does not understand human growth and development cannot be as effective as one who can anticipate, understand, and cope with the behavior response of his students.

3. Art teachers need to use better, clearer terminology. One would imagine that art, because of its dominantly visual nature, would be easily understood. Yet just the opposite is often the case. This is partially due to the fact that visual symbols are difficult to translate into meaningful words. Yet the public is justified in expecting members of the art teaching profession to be able to explain their subject in understandable, intelligent terms.

If the foregoing needs, and others described in the text, are met with reasonable speed and effectiveness, it is possible for art education to make an unexpectedly significant contribution to a culturally ill, war-threatened society which has not responded favorably to treatments by scientists, politicians, and experts in other fields.

This book will attempt solutions to major cultural, social, and personal problems by:

1. Suggesting a philosophy of art education and a variety of workable school-community art programs.

2. Showing why art education must play an essential role in every school-community curriculum on every educational level so as to encourage creative expression in all people and so they may live in more satisfying, more beautiful, better designed environments.

3. Indicating how broad segments of society, instead of a limited few individuals, may deepen their understanding and enjoyment of the arts by securing worth-while art works for their homes, offices, schools, and community centers; by extending their reading to include the arts; and by attending art exhibitions, lectures, and demonstrations in the arts.

An attempt has been made to limit the contents of this book to *clearly stated philosophy, concrete suggestions,* and *factual descriptions.* Classroom observations, actual teaching experiences, and discussions among readers will supplement what is indicated and demonstrated. In this way the student is able to provide himself with direct experience references which we hope will give greater meaning to the text.

Charts and illustrations have been used wherever possible to clarify subjects which might otherwise require lengthy discussion. A conscious effort has been made *to avoid specialized terminology* in order that whatever time a person may choose to give to this book may be spent upon its contents rather than the meaning of its vocabulary.

It would be unfair, however, to give readers the impression that the profession of art teaching can be fully explained in a few chapters or that it has reached a point where further improvements are unnecessary. It is true that there are a few schools in which art programs seem ideal. This ideal will change in the future, and most schools have art programs which are inadequate now. In many schools throughout the world, art activities are non-creative or non-existent.

This book is intended for undergraduate and graduate students of art education, art teachers and supervisors, elementary and secondary education students, classroom teachers, youth group leaders, camp counselors and directors, school administrators, parents, and other interested adults. There are many people in each of these categories who, directly or indirectly, are contributing to the continued improvement of art education. To those who will not be satisfied until opportunities for understanding, producing, using, and enjoying art have been provided for everyone, this book is dedicated.

1: The Teacher of Art

IT IS NOT BY ACCIDENT *that the teacher of art is the first topic in this book. No other person, no group, no amount of art materials, no physical facility, no community exceeds in importance the art teacher as the single element of greatest potential value in art education. One must, of course, exempt the art teacher's pupils from this sweeping generalization, since individual learners are always the most important elements in their own education. But no other person, thing, or place can make such extensive and penetrating contributions to art education. A really superb art teacher can do more for the art education of individual pupils than any number of new and well-equipped art rooms, sympathetic administrators, cooperative classroom teachers, expensive art materials, top-notch communities, or educated parents.*

Although art, like any special subject, is best taught by a person with concentrated professional preparation and experience in the area, the broad field of art education is, in a sense, everyone's responsibility. Art is as integral to the life of the child as any subject area or activity. Art is becoming increasingly a participatory activity, and because of its unlimited scope, it can make a contribution to virtually every life experience of the child and the adult.

Searching self-analysis will reveal that everyone possesses a kind and degree of inherent art ability. This ability is fostered by continued creative experiences, and more significant expression and deeper understanding in art can be developed through sensitive guidance. Most art educators would agree with Herbert Read's classic statement on the subject of *creative teaching:*

Every child possesses the ability to express himself creatively through art. Competent art teachers are needed in every school to give all children this opportunity.

The good teacher is not a dictator, but rather a pupil more advanced in technique than the others, more conscious of the aims to be achieved and the means that must be adopted, who works with the children, sympathizes with them and encourages them, gives them that priceless possession which is self-confidence. *

PEOPLE WHO TEACH ART

Art is taught directly and indirectly by many people in various professional, trade, and domestic situations. Art is also, in a sense, taught by the environments in which people live.

Among the many people who teach art are art teachers, classroom teachers, pupils and students themselves, school administrators, designers, authors, salesmen, parents, and youth group leaders. When an adult gives a coloring book to a child, for example, he is teaching art and endorsing the type of learning experience which coloring books foster. Unfortunately, this type of art teaching does not serve the best interests of the child. On the other hand, when a classroom teacher encourages children to think creatively as in making three-dimensional models representing experiences they have shared—and provides them with necessary art materials and a place in which to work—he may be teaching creative art as well as reading. This type of art teaching, though indirect, is usually constructive and desirable.

The chart which follows describes some of the people who are directly or indirectly involved in art education.

---

* Herbert Read, *The Grass Roots of Art,* George Wittenborn, Inc., New York, 1955, p. 108.

An important and highly effective mode of art education is the informal teaching accomplished as students watch one another work.

28

PEOPLE WHO TEACH ART

ART TEACHERS	NON-ART TEACHERS AND SCHOOL ADMINISTRATORS	DESIGNERS, AUTHORS, AND OTHERS	PARENTS AND YOUTH GROUP LEADERS
Usually teach art creatively and constructively to meet a variety of human needs. Most art teachers have adopted sound educational practices and have eliminated copy work.	Often provide creative art experiences as a means of fostering total educational growth and to deepen pupil understanding in related subjects. Administrators affect the teaching of art by encouraging sound art educational practices.	Influence public art taste through commercially designed and produced products. Some of these people and their products help art education, while others work in direct opposition.	Sometimes, unknowingly, teach art harmfully. "Craft kits" and similar activities are not creative and are contrary to the aims of art education. Some parents and youth group leaders are beginning to realize the need for better leadership preparation for creative art activities.
elementary school art teachers (art teachers, art consultants, art resource people, art helping teachers, etc.)	nursery school teachers	advertising artists	parents
junior high school art teachers (and consultants)	kindergarten teachers	illustrators	relatives
senior high school art teachers	elementary school teachers	all types of designers, such as industrial, clothing, furniture	neighbors
junior college art instructors	teachers of exceptional children	authors of books on art subjects	religious teachers
college and university professors of art	secondary school teachers of subjects such as English, music, mathematics, home economics, industrial arts, science, social studies, and foreign languages	book and magazine publishers	camp counselors and "camp craft" teachers
adult education program art instructors		art supply store merchants and clerks	leaders of Brownies, Cub Scouts, Boy and Girl Scouts, Camp Fire Girls, clubs
TV and radio program art teachers	principals, supervisors, and superintendents	designers manufacturers and retailers of art supplies	YM and YWCA, CYC, YM and YWHA, Teen-Center, and other community agency "arts and crafts" leaders
professional art school instructors	members of boards of education and boards of trustees of school systems		
professional artists who give private lessons			
art supervisors and art directors of city, county, and state school systems			
directors of college and university art departments			

Through understanding his pupils, the art teacher is better able to contribute to their improved behavior.

Art teachers of yesterday and today. The art teacher of yesterday, like many other teachers in the past, was usually interested only in his own area of specialization and had little interest in the broad effects of education on his pupils. He was often an ardent disciplinarian, insistent upon pupils' conformance to strict rules.

Today's art teacher is interested in the total educational, emotional, mental, physical, and aesthetic growth of his pupils, not in the development of their art expressive ability alone. He is deeply concerned with bettering pupils' general understanding and behavior as well as developing their art concepts and skills.

The chart at right attempts to show some typical functions of art teachers of yesterday and today. This chart applies to art teachers on all educational levels, but obviously, no individual teacher's characteristics would fall entirely within one column or the other.

Some desirable characteristics in an art teacher. An art teacher could once receive a teaching certificate, be hired, promoted, or given tenure solely on the basis of his personal art ability or on the basis of work produced by a few of his most gifted pupils. Although an art teacher should be technically competent in one or more art media, this is not the only qualification for teaching the subject.

Before viewing the check list "Desirable Characteristics in an Art Teacher" it is important to study some general principles upon which the characteristics are based.

1. *The following characteristics are presented with the hope of encouraging future or beginning teachers of art.* No individual can excel in, *or even possess,* all elements of these characteristics. Like most check sheets, this one has been made broad in scope in order that it may be used by people of varied personality and background. A person who possesses *only a few of the characteristics listed* here might well qualify as an excellent teacher. On the other hand it is entirely possible that someone who might possess some ability in all eight would be poorly qualified for teaching art.

ART TEACHERS OF YESTERDAY AND TODAY *

THE ART TEACHER OF YESTERDAY

All available time was spent in teaching art according to a pre-determined schedule.

Not interested in "outside" work or public appearances.

Limited the teaching of art to the regular school curriculum.

Art "lessons" were often limited to "seat work," such as crayon drawings on manila paper. "Advanced lessons" included such themes as "autumn still life" or "railroad track" perspective.

Often drew pictures or examples on blackboard for children to copy.

Did not take time to secure free materials in community. Complained that "directed" teaching was the result of a limited budget.

Preferred two-dimensional media such as drawing and painting because of ease in passing out and cleaning up materials.

Prepared bulletin board displays without pupil participation.

Repeated same art lesson plans year after year.

Neglected the use of audio-visual aids.

Restricted art activities to the classroom.

Praised only those children whose work approached the teacher's concept of how it should look. Often made "corrections" directly on children's work.

Believed that art was limited to drawing and painting.

Volunteered for homeroom, corridor duty, ticket taking, janitor assistance, and other routine, time-consuming responsibilities in erroneous belief that prestige would thus be enhanced.

* Based on a portion of "How Good is Your Art Program?" by Howard Conant and Clement Tetkowski, *National Elementary Principal*, Vol. XXX. No. 5, April, 1951, pp. 13-15.

TODAY'S ART TEACHER

Personally guides children's creative growth through art; also available to teachers, children, and parents for consultation on matters related to art and suggestions for supplemental art activities not led by art teacher.

Speaks occasionally to the PTA and other community and teacher groups.

Offers courses in art to parents and other community residents through an adult education program.

Creatively teaches art activities such as painting, modeling, ceramics, weaving, and block printing. Encourages classroom teachers to guide follow-up activities in art and related subjects.

Emphasizes creative art activities rather than those which are directed or formal.

Seeks and utilizes free, native, and scrap materials for art activities, in addition to purchased supplies.

Urges the use of more three-dimensional art activities such as ceramics, leather work, cardboard construction, and weaving.

Assists children and teachers in planning the arrangement of classroom and corridor displays and stage sets.

Works together with teachers and administrators in the development of long-range art plans.

Uses motion pictures, film-strips, recordings, slides, and important works of art (borrowed, or from the school collection) to serve as stimuli for children's art expression.

Escorts groups of children on field trips to museums, local artists' studios, or other places related to art, and encourages children to paint pictures, etc., of their impressions. Takes classes outdoors to sketch.

By noting good work habits, cooperation, neatness, and indications of progress in art work, the art teacher is able to find encouragement and praise for all children in addition to constructive criticism when necessary.

Is interested in increasing children's understanding of and expressive powers in art in all areas of living.

2. *These characteristics are listed separately only for purposes of more detailed study.* Actually, the various aspects of the total makeup of an art teacher cannot be isolated, since any one characteristic may be conditioned by many others. For instance, appearance may be affected by personality, emotional stability, and physical fitness. In addition, the various elements of each characteristic are important as they relate to one another.

3. *The most important of the desirable characteristics in an art teacher are similar to those usually considered essential for teachers in other areas.* The administrator who is selecting or promoting an art teacher usually looks first for evidence of characteristics he considers desirable in all teachers.

4. *An art teacher's personality and knowledge of human growth and development are as important as technical competence in art.*

1. PERSONALITY

Teachers need to be well adjusted. They need to understand themselves as well as their subject. They need to enjoy working with people in a friendly and democratic manner. If an art teacher realizes that art is one phase of total education and not an end in itself, he will take as one of his broad educational aims the preparation of future citizens who can assume positions of responsibility in society.

The art teacher who works with students in a cooperative, polite, and respectful manner is practicing as well as teaching democracy. He is also teaching art in a highly effective way. His methods of planning with students and colleagues, and his sharing of responsibilities with them, develop democratic practices.

He should be the kind of person who can speak easily and convincingly about other subjects as well as art. In addition to developing art knowledge and ability, an art teacher should be sincere as an educator and artist. He should be willing to work patiently with others, sharing his knowledge with them as they expect to share their knowledge with him.

Pointing up the importance of the art teacher's role, Robert Cato says:

. . . every time he (the teacher) enters a class room of students to teach he will be in one way or another touching the future. Therefore, we will know how important it is for him to constantly struggle for a deeper understanding of himself and what he teaches. This struggle, or search, or finding, whatever you may call it, is never-ending.*

* Robert Cato, "Sources of Inspiration," *Print*, Vol. XI, No. 1, Feb.-March, 1957, pp. 20-22.

NEW YORK UNIVERSITY,
PHOTO BY IRWIN GOOEN

At times the art teacher checks with his students, advising on certain complex procedures, or he may work on a project of his own for students to observe without copying.

NEW YORK UNIVERSITY,
PHOTO BY IRWIN GOOEN

Even in choosing informal studio clothes and smocks, teachers and students of art education should apply their knowledge of clothing design and good grooming.

Certain extrovert characteristics are desirable in an art teacher in order that he may be able to deal effectively with a wide variety of personalities. The art teacher should not, however, be overly aggressive or vociferous. Some, in fact, who are soft-spoken, even withdrawn and somewhat introverted, have proved effective as art teachers. Concerning these exceptions to the personality characteristics described briefly above, Riesman has wisely said:

Nor will it do to assume, as American aptitude testers sometimes do, that certain jobs can be successfully handled only by a narrowly limited range of character types: that we need 'extrovert' or 'oral' salesmen and administrators, and 'introvert' or 'anal' chemists and accountants. Actually, people of radically different types can adapt themselves to perform, adequately enough, a wide variety of complex tasks.*

The art teacher should be able to stimulate interest in creative expression, and to dramatize everyday experiences in order to

* David Riesman, *The Lonely Crowd*, Doubleday Anchor, Garden City, New York, 1955. p. 46.

33

deepen their meaning for pupils. He should be able to enter into the spirit of those with whom he is working. A good sense of humor, the ability to laugh *with* people and not at them, and an understanding of subjects which concern people at various interest and ability levels are further qualifications which an art teacher should possess.

2. APPEARANCE

A teacher needs to be appropriately dressed and groomed. The art teacher's appearance should provide visual evidence of his art background and his ability to apply art knowledge to personal dress and grooming. Women in the art education profession usually wear simple, well-designed clothing. Attractive clothes and accessories need not be expensive, but they must be carefully selected and cared for. Men in this field may wear new, but not necessarily extreme, colors and textures in their shirts and sport coats.

Even as an undergraduate, the student of art education should begin to apply art knowledge to personal dress and grooming. The casual clothes appropriate for college campuses, whether or not a student's schedule for the day includes studio workshops, can be carefully chosen. Denim, for example, is sold in a variety of colors. Numerous other inexpensive but appealing fabrics and ready-made articles are widely available. A student may find a challenge in re-tailoring or dyeing a piece of clothing to enhance its design quality.

In addition to good taste shown in the color and style of clothing, the student of art education should be well groomed. Taste in clothing selection and grooming should improve as the student progresses through the program of professional preparation. By the time students are juniors or seniors they should give clear evidence of their ability to dress and groom in a manner well suited to their complexion, height, weight, personality, and profession.

3. EMOTIONAL STABILITY

An art teacher is frequently called upon to dramatize an everyday experience as a stimulus for children's creative activities. He should be able to motivate children's interest in various subjects without making them or himself overly excited. In the case of very young children, in particular, it is possible to bring them to tears or hysterical laughing by overstimulation.

Because of the numerous personal contacts necessitated by the responsibilities of an art teacher to the varied personality types with which he must deal every day, he needs to retain his emotional stability in all kinds of situations. For example, he should be able to work effectively with either first-grade children or seventh-graders.

The elementary school art teacher may deal with many children in the course of a single day, each of whom has a unique personality and differing needs and interests.

It is also important for the art teacher to be calm and efficient under pressure. As he gains experience there will be increasing demands for his services. He must be able to accept or reject these requests politely, to organize effectively those commitments he does accept, and to do one thing at a time without becoming frustrated.

4. Physical fitness

Vitality is desirable in an art teacher. An art teacher's position often requires more physical stamina than some other teaching positions. There are occasions when bulky art materials need to be transported from one room, floor, or building to another, and helping hands are not always available. Then, too, there may be several hundred boys and girls, plus teachers, parents, and administrators with whom an art teacher works each week. Both of these aspects of an art teacher's responsibilities, plus the energy it takes to teach

DESIRABLE CHARACTERISTICS IN AN ART TEACHER

Note: See important limitations suggested for interpreting this list, in preceding discussion and in elaborations of chart in section which follows.	UNSATISFACTORY	BELOW AVERAGE	AVERAGE	ABOVE AVERAGE	OUTSTANDING
1. PERSONALITY — Integrated. Friendly. Works with people, not over them. Willing to share. Sincere. Patient. Extrovert tendency. Able to dramatize. Sense of humor.					
2. APPEARANCE — Dresses appropriately. Dresses attractively. Tastefully groomed. Neatly groomed. Not "extreme" in appearance. Clothing and grooming appropriate to: complexion, height, weight, personality. Pleasant facial expression.					
3. EMOTIONAL STABILITY — Not overly excitable. Friendly without coddling. Firm but not harsh. Efficient under pressure. Calm.					
4. PHYSICAL FITNESS — Possesses physical vitality. Possesses stamina. Voice adequate in: volume, enunciation, pitch. Attends to personal hygiene.					
5. PROFESSIONAL PREPARATION — Meets national, state, or local certification requirements (depends on locality). Graduate of accredited school. Major in art education. Adequate background in: professional (education) courses, technical (painting, etc.) courses, general (academic or liberal arts) courses. Has attitude of intellectual inquiry. Possesses sound convictions. Up-to-date knowledge of child, adolescent, and adult psychology.					

	UNSATISFACTORY	BELOW AVERAGE	AVERAGE	ABOVE AVERAGE	OUTSTANDING
Understands contemporary educational philosophy. Proficient in several art media or processes. Familiar with most other media. Personal living quarters reflect art background.					
6. PARTICIPATION IN SCHOOL AND COMMUNITY ACTIVITIES *Note:* Though obviously desirable, *participation in these activities must be carefully limited to avoid excessive commitment.*	Aware of responsibilities to school and community. Advises co-curricular groups. Helps students select tasteful decoration schemes for school dances, parties, etc. Advises on interior design of school. Helps to select works of art for school. Speaks to community organizations. Active in faculty organizations. Responsible member of school and community committees. Participates in radio and TV art programs.				
7. ORGANIZATIONAL ABILITY	Well organized in thoughts. Groups students effectively. Well organized in dress and grooming. Uses efficient cleanup procedures. Has well organized lesson plans and records. Organizes effective discussion groups. Inventories and re-orders supplies efficiently. Organizes supplies efficiently. Arranges furniture for best use of room space. Keeps several activities going at one time.				
8. PROFESSIONAL GROWTH	Welcomes new opportunities. Understands and implements modern educational philosophy. Continues professional study. Continues to experiment with various art media. Maintains professional status as artist. Publicizes art program through writing and speaking. Participates regularly in community and professional conferences.				

effectively and to fulfill at least part of the extra demands made by various school and community groups, make a definite demand on physical vitality.

Numerous lesson presentations, subsequent explanations, and talks to various school and community organizations make it important for an art teacher to have adequate voice volume, to enunciate clearly, and yet to speak in a pitch which is not irritating. This demands physical control.

In order to work closely with many students, colleagues, and community residents, it is imperative that the art teacher maintain the highest standards of personal hygiene.

5. Professional preparation

An art teacher should complete four or five years of professional preparation in art education. With this background he is better prepared to teach art than one who has by chance been elected to teach it.

Excellent backgrounds are usually provided by institutions which have departments that specialize in art teacher education. In addition to a well-planned major sequence of courses in art and art education, their curricula usually include a wide variety of courses in the humanities, the social studies, and the sciences.* This well-balanced combination of professional, technical, and general education courses does more than develop individual art skills; it also gives a student insight into most of the other important areas of learning which he will use in effective art teaching, stimulates and fosters his intellectual vitality, tends to develop an attitude of intellectual inquiry, and helps him to form sound convictions.

In general, colleges and universities offering a recognized major in art education prepare better teachers than do institutions whose art teaching programs are incidental. Institutions which spe-

---

* See Chapter 2 for a more detailed discussion of art teacher education curricula.

COURTESY ARTHUR KRUK, STATE TEACHERS COLLEGE, SUPERIOR, WISCONSIN

The teacher of art should be professionally competent in at least one medium, and familiar with many others.

cialize in art teacher education usually have larger and better faculties, more varied and up-to-date art courses, better student teaching situations, and more professional-type extra-curricular activities. Many of them even have better professional courses in fields such as painting and sculpture due to the fact that they *insist upon teaching ability* as well as professional eminence in teachers of studio courses.

A qualified art teacher should have considerable knowledge of child, adolescent, and adult psychology and should keep abreast of contemporary trends in the philosophy of art education.

An art teacher should also develop satisfactory proficiency in at least one form of art expression such as painting, sculpture, interior design, or ceramics, and should be familiar with a wide variety of other art media and processes. He should be an artist as well as a teacher of art.

Although professional preparation is adequate by the time an art teacher has graduated from college, it is by no means complete and should never be considered terminated. Art teachers should continue to prepare themselves professionally through graduate study (see Chapter 3), participation in professional organizations (see Chapter 4), in-service workshops (see Chapter 8), and by reading current professional literature.

6. Participation in school and community activities

Because of his interest and ability in the field of art, an art teacher is frequently called upon to participate in a variety of school and community activities. But beyond the demand for his special abilities, the art teacher has a responsibility for understanding the general structure of the entire school curriculum and to work with certain community groups. Effective education often steps beyond the limits of the school, and is deeply concerned with overall community improvement.

School dramatic groups often seek an art teacher's advice and sometimes his assistance in the design and construction of stage sets. School organizations sometimes ask for help in the preparation of party and dance decorations. School administrators regularly seek advice from art teachers concerning color schemes for classrooms, corridors, and offices; suggestions for the landscape design of school grounds; and help in selecting reproductions of paintings and sculpture or original art works for the school.

Art teachers also receive requests from community organizations to speak about various art subjects. Among these are parent-teacher associations; Scout groups; women's church or club groups; men's service or luncheon clubs; and young people's groups such as 'teen craft centers and church youth organizations. Requests may vary from informal talks on interior design to demonstrations of painting.

In all cases, however, it is imperative that the art teacher accept no more non-art teaching responsibilities than he is able to handle effectively and without strain. It is more than easy to become over-burdened with general school and community responsibilities to the eventual detriment of the art teaching program.

Non-art subjects: Art teachers should, of course, have interests in education which extend beyond the subject of art. They should be concerned with such professional problems as faculty welfare and teaching load, and participate in faculty organizations and school committees.

School administrators and art supervisors often consider carefully the school and community activity participation of an art teacher when thinking of selecting, retaining, or promoting him. This aspect of an art teacher's responsibility may actually be doing as much for the total educational program in the school and community as regular school art teaching and consulting duties. Nevertheless, it needs to be maintained in proper perspective.

7. ORGANIZATIONAL ABILITY

Organization is an important element of all good teaching. It is essential that an art teacher possess a high degree of organizational ability.

Most school administrators recognize a need for an efficient organization. An art teacher's organizational ability is reflected in a variety of ways: in the way his thoughts are expressed and communicated to others; in his personal dress and grooming; in his lesson plans and school records; in the way he groups students according to their interest and ability; in the way he introduces new learning experiences; in the way he conducts discussions; and in the way he orders and arranges supplies, equipment, and furniture.

What the administrator sees. A quick, passing glance into a busy art workshop where several art activities are simultaneously in action might lead the observer to believe that the art teacher in charge is not well organized. The alert school administrator or art supervisor, however, realizes that an art teacher who is able to offer individual instruction and maintain interest in several art activities during a single studio period is probably better organized than one who can offer effectively only one activity per period. Encouraging children to choose an activity according to their interest and ability is usually more worthwhile than requiring all of them to do the same thing at the same time.

8. PROFESSIONAL GROWTH

Somewhere in an art teacher's credentials should appear an indication that he has grown or is likely to grow professionally. Many types of experience will give an art teacher opportunities for professional growth. The art teacher should look forward to each new experience as a learning opportunity.

If an art teacher is to grow professionally he should be aware of recent trends in educational philosophy, know how this philosophy can be implemented, and realize that only through continuous study and experimentation can he keep abreast of current educational practices. He should continue to develop his proficiency in some form of creative activity such as painting, ceramics, or interior design, and attempt to achieve professional recognition. An art teacher needs to publicize various aspects of the art education program through newspaper and magazine articles, as well as by speaking to various community groups. As a result of these writing and speaking experiences, he should have learned how to communicate effectively to various types of people. Continued professional growth is also fostered by regular participation in the conferences and committee work of art teachers' professional organizations. A detailed description of these is given in Chapter 4.

THE ART TEACHER'S RESPONSIBILITIES

There are many positions and titles for people who teach art or administer local, county, state, or college art programs. Some typical functions of various art teaching positions are described here.

The elementary school art teacher. Several names for the elementary school art teacher are now in use. The position is sometimes called "art consultant," "art resource person," "art helping teacher," or "art teacher." The development of these new names, as well as new and enlarged areas of responsibility, has raised questions as to which method of working, teaching, or consulting is best for the art education of the pupils or students concerned.

The art consultant idea, as it is understood and practiced by responsible educators, is not a substitute for art teaching, nor is it a device for spreading the services of an art teacher over two schools instead of one. It is rather a means of improving the teaching of art on the elementary school level. The term "art consultant" might be better explained as a description of one *area* of an art teacher's responsibility instead of a name for the position. The consultant aspects of an art teacher's work are suggested below, but are, of course, dependent upon the abilities, needs, and preferences of the pupils and teachers concerned.

Many art teachers have for a number of years been enriching art activities for children by working closely with classroom teachers. They have suggested ways in which classroom teachers could take a more active part in the art education of their pupils. This aspect of the art teacher's work was often done in addition to regular art teaching. It necessitated considerable after-school and evening work, and because of its "extra work" connotation the consultation idea was slow in developing.

Many of today's art teachers, having recognized consultation as a valuable practice, work with classroom teachers in planning art activities and furthering children's growth through art as part of their regular daily art teaching schedule. By combining art teaching with a reasonable amount of consulting, the art teacher is sometimes able to provide for more hours of competent, creative art teaching per child per week than was possible under the usual one-art-lesson-a-week system.

How can one implement an art teaching-consulting program? This problem is especially perplexing for the teacher who has been teaching art in the same school for several years. How can classroom teachers who have been working with a "once-a-week" art teacher be encouraged to assume their share of responsibility in a consultant art teaching program? What is the first step? Answers to these and related questions are suggested in the following chart. These steps for implementing a consultant art program are indicated in recommended chronological order.

SUGGESTED PROCEDURE FOR IMPLEMENTING THE CONSULTANT ASPECT OF ART TEACHING:

1. Read important and up-to-date literature on art, art education, education, and related fields.

2. Seek additional information: (a) from art education specialists in other schools, colleges, universities, and state education departments; (b) by attending professional conferences; and (c) by taking in-service and graduate art education courses.

3. Carefully note individual classroom teachers' interest and ability in creative art teaching (bulletin board displays in classrooms, encouragement of "free time" art activities, use of art activities in other subjects).

4. Formulate a general plan to transform a once-a-week art teaching system to one in which consultation is part of the schedule (often necessitating the addition of another art teacher).

5. Request teachers to assume greater responsibility for teaching art to children in their classrooms, assuring them that in this way the children will receive as much "specialized" art teaching as before, *plus* additional opportunity for art experiences under the classroom teacher's guidance.

6. Confer with principal and superintendent. Suggest and explain in detail the ways in which the consultant aspects of art teaching can be implemented. Provide list of names of classroom teachers who are willing to assume responsibilities for supplemental art activity guidance. Use professional literature and descriptions of successful practices in other school systems to support views on needs for an expanded and enriched program of art education.

7. Submit to administrators a definite plan for implementing the consultant aspects of art teaching. This proposal might include:

• A plan for devoting a major portion of the art teacher's time to actual teaching and the remainder to consulting with classroom teachers, parents, children, and administrators.

• A proposal to hire an additional part or full-time art teacher. In order to determine the number of art teachers needed for an effective art education program, a ratio of 1 art teacher to 500 pupils is suggested as good; 1 to 400 or less, excellent; 1 to 1,000, ineffective. Interested and qualified classroom teachers or helping teachers might be used to supplement the art teacher's work, but they should not be used as substitutes for additional art teachers because of their inability to foster art experiences of sufficient aesthetic quality and creative intensity.

• A plan for holding a series of art workshops for classroom teachers, administrators, and parents to be held during the school day (or on days prior to the opening of school on an extra-pay basis for participants.) Workshops should cover the aims and functions of art education in the elementary grades; art media, processes, and subjects recommended for the elementary grades; and suggestions for art activities which are best guided by the art teacher, classroom teacher, experienced children, or parents. (See pp. 287-289, Chapter 8 for more complete workshop itineraries.)

8. Stress the fact that recently graduated classroom teachers have often had a full year or more of art education courses. (a) These teachers use art in social studies and other subjects, as well as in connection with many co-curricular activities. (b) In every

school a few classroom teachers (already named under item 7) assume leadership responsibilities for certain creative art activities. Their influence is likely to spread throughout the school if the consultant aspects of art teaching are implemented.

9. Point out that a fully implemented program usually necessitates the hiring of helping teachers who guide classroom activities during rest periods for the regular classroom teacher. This arrangement permits classroom teachers to be present when the art teacher is guiding class activities and to have adequate consultation without having to add an additional time burden and responsibility to an already heavy load. Providing rich, varied, and frequent creative art experiences for all children is important enough to justify the addition of helping teachers in the school system.

Junior high school art teachers. The responsibilities of the junior high school art teacher are similar to those suggested for the elementary art teacher; in fact, undergraduate preparation is usually identical except for a secondary level emphasis in art teaching methods, educational psychology, principles of education, and student teaching courses.

While most states now require courses in art education for prospective elementary classroom teachers, many have not yet realized the importance of art experiences in the preparation of junior and senior high school teachers of subjects other than art. Most non-art teachers in junior high schools have had little opportunity to learn about art, even less opportunity to experiment in art media, and, in most instances, no opportunity to learn how art is taught. In some school systems, however, the teaching of junior high school art is sometimes correlated with other subjects such as English, music, drama, and social studies. Although the actual teaching is usually done by an art teacher, teachers of related subjects occasionally assume responsibility for art activities growing out of the subjects they teach, just as an art teacher at times helps youngsters learn art aspects of academic subjects. The procedures for developing and enriching a junior high school program in art are similar to those listed above in "The Consultant Aspects of Art Teaching" on the elementary education level.

Art teachers in senior high schools, colleges, and adult education programs. The emphasis in art teaching at upper educational levels is primarily on consumer education, that is, developing students' understanding of art instead of concentrating exclusively on their personal art expression. However, a great deal of actual experimentation in various art media should be included along with the study of art in architecture, painting, interior design, clothing design, and other areas. Therefore, art teachers in secondary schools need to have a broad and reasonably profound understanding of the arts as well as proficiency in art media and processes. Teachers of advanced and highly specialized art courses, such as ceramics and graphic arts, also need to have a broad knowledge of the arts, but in addition need to possess a deeper insight and technical skills which are sought by advanced art students.

Television art teachers. Although there are relatively few TV program art teachers, they reach a vast audience and their teaching has far-reaching effects. A few commercially minded TV "art teachers" have resorted to educationally unsound and stereotyped methods, but most art educators working through this mass communication medium offer highly stimulating and educational programs through commercial as well as educational TV stations. It is particularly important for people working in mass communication media to understand that *the same principles of art education apply to the teaching of art whether it is being telecast to an audience of thousands or being presented in one classroom* to a small group of pupils. Too often, TV art teachers are more interested in becoming celebrities than in teaching creatively to the best of their ability.

Professional artist teachers. Most professional art schools are staffed by recognized, practicing artists. These artists, together with others who hold private classes in their own studios, provide specialized instruction for persons who wish to prepare for professional art fields such as painting, sculpture, industrial design, and fashion illustration. Most artist instructors have been prepared as artists rather than teachers. Consequently, their teaching procedures vary from oustanding to poor. Sometimes, however, one finds a profes-

The contemporary sculptor, Chaim Gross, offers individual instruction to an adult student.

sional artist who has become an excellent teacher without having had any formal teacher education preparation. Such a person is often more effective than others in teaching advanced students in specialized art media.

Correspondence school art teaching, another phase of professional art instruction, has a unique relationship to the art teaching profession. Teaching by correspondence is questioned by some, yet the qualifications of correspondence school instructors are often comparable to those of instructors in art schools. Hence it is the *method of instruction* rather than the qualifications of the instructors which must be considered. One of the basic needs in effective teaching is *knowledge of individual students*, which is best gained through direct personal contact.

School art supervisors and art department directors. Most art supervisors and directors act as consultants and administrators to those who do actual art teaching. However, art administrators should continue to teach courses and direct activities such as in-service education for teachers. In this way they maintain a first-hand contact with the teaching process and indirectly affect the art education of thousands of people. No administrative position in art education should be permitted to grow in scope or detail to a point where actual studio or classroom teaching is precluded.

Nursery school and kindergarten teachers. Nearly every activity, ranging from sand play to paper pasting, can be a creative activity. Fortunately, teachers responsible for early childhood education are among the finest creative teachers. Almost without exception they believe in and practice a philosophy of creative teaching. Children who are fortunate enough to attend nursery school and kindergarten are likely to develop confidence in creative self-expression for at least this brief period in life.

Art activities provide important periods of quiet concentration for characteristically active four- and five-year-olds.

46

Elementary classroom teachers. Every time a classroom teacher asks children to illustrate a story they are reading, encourages them to make a model village related to their social studies unit, or gives them worksheets to illustrate, he is teaching art. Regrettably, the later type of activity is often used, and since most worksheets contain adult drawings to be filled in by the child, the "art" is non-creative. "Color-in" worksheets and other stereotyped activities cause children to become dissatisfied with their own creative work. In fact, such materials and activities actually hamper their creative growth. However, an increasing number of classroom teachers are beginning to understand the importance of creativity in every phase of their teaching. In addition to supplementing special activities taught by the art teacher, they often encourage children to draw their own illustrations on reading and arithmetic worksheets and help to develop creativity in other phases of the educational program.

Secondary school teachers of subjects other than art. Every secondary school instructor indirectly teaches English by the way he speaks, chooses words, and evaluates written work. In a like manner he indirectly teaches art by the way he dresses, arranges objects in his room, gives his opinions on various works of art, and selects materials to illustrate the subject he teaches. Perhaps the best art education in secondary schools is taught in core programs where instructors work together toward common goals. In programs of this type, teachers are aware of each others' aims; consequently, learning experiences on the part of both students and faculty members tend to complement one another.

It is particularly important for teachers of art, home economics, and industrial arts to work closely together, since an emphasis on contemporary, creative design should be made in all phases of these

Some classroom teachers supplement special instruction with creative activities in free time periods. There are enough weeks in the school year for *every* child in the class to receive special attention by having his work chosen as "painting of the week."

COURTESY JOHN WESLE,
ILLINOIS STATE NORMAL UNIVERSITY

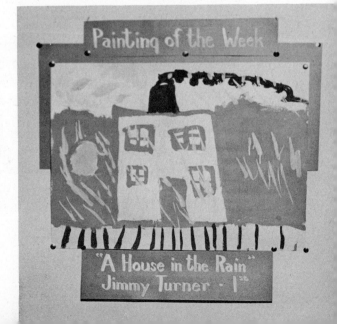

subjects. Otherwise one subject may nullify another and students will fail to grasp the essentials of this broad, interrelated area of education. Parallels also exist between music, dance, and drama.

It is important for all students to learn principles of aesthetic judgment prior to the termination of their formal education. Learning in all branches of the arts is particularly facilitated because criteria for understanding, evaluating, and enjoying them are largely the same for one as another.

School administrators and board members. Although administrators do not teach art directly to pupils, their influence upon the quality and amount of art education in a given school system can be far reaching. School administrators and board members are the ones who often decide to:

1. Initiate, broaden, or improve art education programs.

2. Include plans for art rooms in new school buildings, with studio space for the art teacher's personal creative work.

3. Plan the remodeling of the school plant, including the purchase of paintings and sculpture (originals as well as reproductions) representative of the best in contemporary and historic art periods.

4. Propose outstanding, contemporary architecture for the designs of new schools or additions.

5. Hire an art teacher or recommend additional ones.

6. Suggest educational field trips to art galleries, museums, or other places of interest.

7. Suggest assembly programs on art subjects.

8. Arrange art teachers' schedules for greater efficiency, including much-needed time for their personal creative expression and relief of routine responsibilities such as homeroom and corridor duty. Permit art teacher and advanced students to use facilities on evenings and Saturdays, if desired.

9. Encourage students on all educational levels to take art courses.

10. Establish an art major program to meet the growing need for pre-professional art preparation in all secondary schools.

11. Through careful and non-discriminatory counseling, guide qualified high school students to enter the art teaching or professional art field.

Although the initiative for such actions may come from an art teacher or an art-conscious citizen, final decisions are usually made by school administrators and board members. Consequently, it is important for them to be aware of the need for and nature of adequate art instruction at all educational levels.

By being more familiar with, and sympathetic toward, the art program, the school administrator can more easily justify the budget requirements that it demands. He knows that he must be selective in obtaining a competent art staff. By providing adequate materials and equipment, securing a resource person, and organizing art workshops and in-service courses for all teachers, he can do much to improve the quality of art instruction in school and community art programs. He also finds it advantageous to consult with art personnel on matters pertaining to building and planning in order to develop the best possible facilities for the art program.

It is obvious that the school administrator must take leadership in organizing the school program; likewise he must help in making long-range plans for the art program. He and all teachers concerned should plan together to insure the adequacy of special services such as art instruction. It is his responsibility to serve as coordinator of such services by securing outstanding special teachers, arranging suitable time schedules, providing materials, and allocating necessary space.

Designers, authors, and others. Few people realize the extent to which art education is fostered by contemporary designers and authors. Artists who design newspaper and magazine advertisements, posters, automobiles, household appliances, clothing, furniture, and various interior accessories have a far-reaching effect upon the development of popular taste in art. The increasing public acceptance of modern architecture has to a considerable extent grown from first-hand acquaintance with good design in household appliances. Now that they are somewhat accustomed to contemporary architecture and interior design, people are beginning to understand and purchase modern paintings and sculpture.

Authors of books on painting, sculpture, interior design, architecture, and numerous related subjects have also made contributions to the development of public taste in art. Television costume and scenery designers play an increasingly important role in affecting public art taste. Many books, magazines, and some newspapers illustrate, describe, and evaluate well-designed furniture, interiors, architecture, and whole communities. Designers in all mass communication media should understand their ethical responsibility in producing work which is planned at least as much for its positive aesthetic value as for its sales effect.

Playwrights such as Tennessee Williams and designers such as Donald Oenslager have visualized new treatments in stage settings which have had a revolutionary influence on theater art.

On the other hand, people who design and market coloring books, pre-cut craft kits, numbered oil painting kits, and other stereotyped devices are hampering creative art education in children as well as adults. To help designers, manufacturers, wholesalers, and retailers of such products realize their responsibility in this matter, an increasing number of art teachers are writing to them about the dangers inherent in their patterned activities. By this and a variety of other means, notably the editorial policy of *School Arts* magazine, a number of art materials firms have earned the title "partners in a profession" by refusing to manufacture kits or other devices known to be harmful to creativity. Some art teachers limit their supply orders to firms which maintain high ethical standards.

Parents and Youth Group Leaders. Of all the categories of *people who teach art,* this is probably the largest. Nearly every parent, as well as grandparent, aunt, and uncle, is interested in a child's welfare. Many of them sincerely feel they are providing children with worthwhile art materials when coloring books and stereotyped art kits are purchased. For the most part, parents and youth group leaders are unaware of the fact that these materials stifle children's creative growth.

Art teachers throughout the country are offering workshops and other sources of information planned to give adults the background necessary for guiding children's growth in creative art activities. However, the task is a mammoth one, since adults need to know that the creative *process* is as important as the *products* children produce. They also need to know that the *product of a creative activity,* however crude it may appear to the adult, *is infinitely more valuable to a child than a stock item produced through the use of adult-designed kits or drawings.*

This girl, who is making a brightly colored potato print which she has designed, is one of the fortunate few who have access to genuine creative activities at summer camps or community art centers.

COURTESY UNIVERSITY SETTLEMENT, NEW YORK

2: Art Teacher Preparation

Teaching is an important profession and its members maintain high standards. Most teachers have completed at least four years of college or university education. Many others have an additional year or two of professional preparation for which they are awarded a master's degree. Others have taken a sixth year of post-master's degree graduate study, while some have completed a total of seven or eight years of university study. In recognition of outstanding graduate work, some of the latter receive a doctor of education or doctor of philosophy degree.

Art teachers, as well as teachers of other subjects, are highly regarded in contemporary society. Like clergymen, lawyers, and doctors,they are respected by community residents, and occupy positions of considerable prestige.

Nearly every community is striving to increase teachers' salaries to a point where they compare more favorably with salaries in other professions.

Developing a professional attitude

The young man or woman who decides to prepare for the art teaching profession is embarking upon a period of intense but interesting study. College students use a great deal of personal initiative in planning and concentrating upon their studies. They are ex-

College art study requires initiative. This student spends part of her leisure time in the art workshop of her dormitory.

COURTESY THE ART SCHOOL, PRATT INSTITUTE

51

Art education students take advantage of evening "open hours to spend additional time at much-in-demand potter's wheels to enhance their experience in ceramics.

pected to do more than that which is assigned or otherwise required. They are expected to think for themselves, to ask questions, and to investigate many "unassigned" subjects. Otherwise, they are not likely to graduate.

THE COLLEGE CLASS SCHEDULE

Professional preparation requires much more intensive study than that which was required in high school. But in college schedules, one often finds two, three, or even four-hour periods during the day when no actual classes are scheduled. Primarily, these "free" periods are planned for library study, creative work, field trips, and various types of class preparation. The average undergraduate art education student needs to spend three or four hours in out-of-class study and studio work *each day, including week-ends.* Better-than-average students usually spend even more time in study and creative work. By using wisely blocks of "free" time during the day, students are often able to free some of their evening and weekend hours for participation in extra-curricular and social activities.

The semester time budget. One of the best habits a college student can develop is that of making out a time budget at the beginning of each semester, and then adhering to it as closely as possible. Included in a student's time budget (see opposite page) should be regularly scheduled class hours, study periods, time for meals, creative activity periods, art gallery visits, rest periods, time allotted for organization meetings and social activities, and (where applicable) periods for part-time employment.

THE ORIENTATION PROGRAM

Once qualified students have been admitted to a program of art teacher education, they participate in an orientation program which introduces them to the personnel, philosophy, and physical plant of their new school, as well as to the nature of the art teaching profession which they will eventually enter.

52

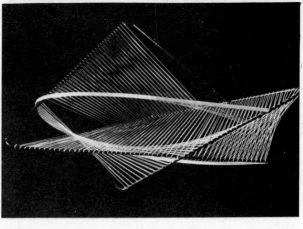

This brass, steel, and cotton string "hanging stabile" was made by a freshman. Experiences of this type early in a student's college career make it possible for him to develop reasonable professional competency in the medium of his choice by the time he qualifies for his degree.

A SAMPLE TIME BUDGET SHEET

	MON.	TUE.	WED.	THU.	FRI.	SAT.	SUN.
7 AM		Bkfst.		Bkfst.			
8 AM	Bkfst.	Eng. 101	Bkfst.	Eng. 101	Bkfst.	Bkfst.	
9 AM	SS101	Study	SS101	Study	SS101	Visit art galleries and museums	Bkfst.
10 AM	Coffee, Study	Coffee, Study	Eng. 101	Ed. 101	Convo-cation		Recre-ation
11 AM	Ed 101	Gym.	Study	Pool	Ed 101		Church
12 N	Lunch	Lunch	Lunch	Lunch	Lunch	Lunch	Study
1 PM	Art 101	Study	Art 101	Study	Art 105	Recre-ation	Dinner
2 PM	"	Art 103	"	Art 103	"	"	Rest
3 PM	"	"	"	"	"	"	Study
4 PM	Rest	Rest	Rest	Rest	Rest	Rest	Study
5 PM	Part-Time Employment.						
6 PM	Dinner	Dinner	Dinner	Dinner	Dinner	Dinner	Supper
7 PM	Recre-ation	Recre-ation	Recre-ation	Recre-ation	Recre-ation	Recre-ation	Recre-ation
8 PM	Study	Club	Study	Study	"	"	"
9 PM	"	"	"	"	"	"	Study
10 PM	"	Study	"	"	"	"	Study
11 PM					"	"	
12 M							

(Note: "Study" includes time for out-of-class creative activities)

Children at work in a Saturday morning art class sponsored by the Vancouver, British Columbia, school board. Art education students often assist or lead classes of this type.

The fascination of art teaching. Students of art education are renowned for their enthusiasm. The subject is fascinating and those who gravitate toward the arts are enthusiastic, consecrated persons. This enthusiasm is further intensified by their instructors, by undergraduate teaching experiences, and by upperclassmen. Yet orientation is sometimes difficult in the strange college atmosphere, and many students do not expect to do as much work as they encounter in the new environment.

Art education instructors are usually able to draw from a rich background of art teaching experiences in various types of educational institutions, from personal creative experiences in art, and from a deep, personal enthusiasm for art teaching. Their influence does much to encourage students to become teachers.

Students should seek actual teaching experiences prior to their formal student teaching. During evening hours, weekends, or vacation periods they can rather easily secure voluntary or part-time paid positions in church schools, 'teen centers, the "Y," and other types of community centers. The schedule of classes is usually flexible enough to permit students to pursue subjects in which they are vitally interested. The enthusiasm which a student might develop for working with children during his freshman year, for example, might be lost if he postponed additional teaching experiences for two or three years.

Upperclassmen, too, are important purveyors of enthusiasm. Their sincere interest in their chosen profession causes many freshmen and sophomores to sense more fully the pleasures and benefits which may be derived from art teacher education. By attending club meetings, working on dance decorating committees, participating in dramatic productions, and helping to hang exhibits, beginning students will have greater opportunity to meet and work with upperclassmen.

Vocational reclassification. Any student who feels lost, bewildered, or inadequate should seek immediate advice from faculty members and upperclassmen whose opinions he respects. Nearly every student who is admitted to a department of art education can, if he really tries, successfully complete his professional education and become an art teacher. However, on rare occasions a student finds he is not well suited for or not really interested in this profession. Generally he is aware of this by the end of his first or second year in college.

The reverse may also be true. A non-art education student may discover at the end of his second or third year that he is interested in teaching art, in which case he should transfer to the appropriate school or curriculum.

The responsibility for a decision to change a course of study or to leave college should always be carefully studied and should be reached jointly by the student concerned, his faculty adviser, the department administrator, and his parents. In all cases, it is essential that a constructive viewpoint be fostered, with long range planning for the student being given priority over other matters.

Although it may seem negative, the elimination aspect of orientation is actually positive. Students who lack interest or ability in their chosen profession are a hazard to their own emotional stability as well as to the educational development of the many pupils they might someday influence. There will always be a need for good art teachers, but not for mediocre or inferior ones, which the student with low interest or ability would probably become.

Freshman and sophomore art education courses are usually broad enough in scope to be of value to anyone, including beginning students who are not certain if they will become art teachers. The first two years of most art education curricula are similar to those in fields such as professional art, advertising design, or fashion illustration. The freshman or sophomore art education student who transfers to another field of study will lose relatively few credits and will not have wasted his time.

THE ART EDUCATION CURRICULUM

The courses included in an art education curriculum usually fall into three general categories:

Technical art courses such as

drawing	crafts
painting	industrial design
sculpture	clothing design
stage design and puppetry	lettering and layout
graphic arts	photography

General education courses which include subjects in the
> humanities
> science
> social studies

Professional courses such as

philosophy of art education	the art curriculum
child development	student teaching
adolescent psychology	

Technical courses. Courses in which students learn to draw, paint, print, letter, design, and construct various three-dimensional objects are usually called technical courses. These courses fulfill at least two important needs of future art teachers:

1. Develop their personal art ability by acquainting them with a wide variety of art media and by encouraging them to become proficient in at least a few.

2. Provide them with a wide background of technical information in order that they may be able to offer instructions in various art media to their own students.

Among the technical courses (plus media and activities often included therein) offered in many art education departments are:

SCULPTURE
> metal
> paper
> plaster
> scrap material
> stone
> wire
> wood

DRAWING
> charcoal
> conté crayon
> pencil
> pen and ink

PAINTING
> casein
> enamel
> encaustic
> gouache
> lacquer
> oil
> tempera
> water color

COURTESY UNIVERSITY OF WISCONSIN,
PHOTO BY ROBERT GRILLEY

COURTESY UNIVERSITY OF WISCONSIN,
PHOTO BY ROBERT GRILLEY

TWO-DIMENSIONAL DESIGN
  advertising design
  clothing design
  fashion illustration
  lettering
  rug hooking
  weaving

THREE-DIMENSIONAL CONSTRUCTION
  ceramics
  industrial design
  jewelry making
  metal
  plastic
  puppetry
  stage design
  woodworking

GRAPHIC ARTS
  etching
  linoleum block printing
  lithography
  photography
  silk screen printing
  wood block cutting
  wood and metal engraving

General education courses. Art teachers formerly received a poorly balanced education, limited almost exclusively to technical and professional (methods) courses. What was perhaps most seriously lacking in art teacher education curricula were liberal arts courses in the humanities (philosophy, music, literature), the social studies (history, sociology, geography), and the sciences (biological and physical sciences). Among liberal arts courses which are often included in art teacher education programs today are:

HUMANITIES
  Introduction to Philosophy
  Literature (world, American,
    English, European, Oriental)
  Music (combined experimentation
    and appreciation)
  Language (French, German,
    Italian, Spanish)

COMMUNICATIONS
  Speech
  Composition (written)

SCIENCE
  Biological science
  Physical science
  Health education

SOCIAL STUDIES
  History
  Cultural Anthropology
  Sociology
  Geography

Students should balance their education by electing courses which will fill gaps in their background. They sometimes choose courses at random, or elect a course on the recommendation of a friend who says it is a "snap." Such friends can be wrong! At any rate, every course should be so stimulating that the student will wish to do more than the required amount of work. He should attempt to get the most rather than the least educational returns for the effort, time, and money he and his family have invested.

Professional courses. Courses such as the philosophy of art education, methods of teaching art, the art curriculum, art teaching in elementary and secondary schools, observation and participation in art teaching, and student teaching are usually referred to as "professional" courses.

Without attempting to set forth specific course content, some of the desirable experiences which are sometimes offered in professional courses are listed below:

Frequent observations of children of all ages under as many different circumstances as possible.

Frequent observations of parents and teachers who are dealing with children in various types of situations.

Working with teachers and leaders in school, camp, church school, and recreation situations.

Teaching art to children in various types of school, camp, church school, and recreation situations.

Participating in panel discussions at meetings of parent-teacher associations, mothers' clubs, service clubs, and art teachers' organizations.

Discussing issues with leaders of art teachers' organizations in order to determine their opinions on various professional needs.

Observations of children engaged in creative art activities provide necessary supplemental information for courses in art teaching.

COURTESY KANSAS CITY, MISSOURI, PUBLIC SCHOOLS

58

Discussing professional matters with outstanding teachers and administrators in art education and other educational fields in order to become more familiar with the broad scope of educational philosophy.

Talking with experienced librarians and research workers in order to determine the most efficient means of study, research, and experimentation.

Meeting with representatives of graduate schools and educational foundations in order to determine the nature and possibilities of graduate study, travel, and research.

Reading books and magazines in the fields of art, art education, education, and the liberal arts.

Visiting art galleries, museums, planned communities, theaters, and buildings which illustrate various architectural styles.

Consumer education in art. Included in the education of today's art teacher should be courses aimed at a better understanding of all phases of contemporary art, including industrial design, music, drama, literature, painting, sculpture, and the dance, plus the interrelationships of these arts. Courses in these and related areas should attempt to provide future art teachers with some of the understandings, psychological insights, and abilities necessary to explain convincingly the role of the arts in contemporary civilization.

Long range planning. Choosing courses which are needed to round out one's education is only one aspect of long range planning. It is wise for the student to plan his entire professional course of study, including extra-curricular activities. College students are expected to assume the responsibility for completing requirements for graduation. Before a student reaches the senior year he should be certain he will be able to complete the minimum number of credits required for graduation.

One way to make long range plans and avoid possible errors in credit is to prepare a chart. It should include a listing of all required courses, electives, and extra-curricular activities. Students following a regular four year program might prepare a chart similar to the following one. Those planning a more intensive program might include space for summer session courses and activities.

See page 60.

A SAMPLE COURSE AND ACTIVITY PLAN CHART

	FRESHMAN YEAR			SOPHOMORE YEAR			JUNIOR YEAR			SENIOR YEAR		
	1st Sem.	2nd Sem.		1st Sem.	2nd Sem.		1st Sem.	2nd Sem.		1st Sem.	2nd Sem.	
	or			or			or			or		
	1st Qu.	2nd Qu.	3d Qu.	1st Qu.	2nd Qu.	3d Qu.	1st Qu.	2nd Qu.	3d Qu.	1st Qu.	2nd Qu.	3d Qu.
REQUIRED COURSES	Eng. 101 Hist. 104 Art 190 Art 193 Gym	(list all required courses here according to latest college catalog)										
ELECTIVE COURSES		(list elective courses you plan to take; make changes as you go along)										
	Art 113 Soc. 205											
EXTRA-CURRICULAR ACTIVITIES	Art Club	(list activities in which you plan to participate, starting with one or two in the freshman year)										

Such a chart has many practical values:

1. It enables a student to have an overall view of his program, and to see how one part is related to the next.

2. A posted list of possible extra-curricular activities will remind a student not to overburden himself.

3. It is helpful in budgeting costs of books, art materials, recreation, and travel.

4. It serves as a check against remotely possible errors in the registrar's office.

Juniors should extend their long-range plans to include the first four or five years after graduation. Such plans would include con-

It is important for art education students to share in planning occasional exhibitions in the college art gallery, corridors, and studios.

templated graduate study (see Chapter 3), teaching, participation in the affairs of professional organizations (see Chapter 4), and possible travel. Applications for graduate study, fellowships, assistantships and scholarships (see Chapter 3) need to be initiated at the end of the junior year. Inquiries concerning professional placement (see Chapter 3) and graduate study should begin in the junior year, and fairly definite preferences for teaching or graduate study should be known by the beginning of the senior year.

Students who are interested in securing administrative positions in art education need to plan on acquiring experience in both elementary and secondary schools, as well as the early completion of a master's (or higher) degree.

Those who are interested in fulltime employment in summer camps or city recreation programs should plan to acquire early experiences in these areas during their undergraduate summers.

Professional extra-curricular activities. Professional extra-curricular activities offer many educational, social, and personal values to students. Every high-school graduate realizes this, yet he may not understand that college activities are much more important to his professional and social life, even to his fundamental attitudes and beliefs, than were the clubs, societies, or fraternal orders to which he previously belonged.

A survey of college students' participation in extra-curricular activities* indicated a high correlation between those with the highest academic average and those with the greatest degree of extra-curricular activity participation and leadership.

Some professional activities are as well suited to informal extra-curricular groups as they are to regularly scheduled classes. Some examples are: a community teaching program; educational tours, a student-sponsored art auction; art exhibitions; parent-teacher-student open house; and art career days for high school students.

Community teaching

It is common practice for art education students to secure after-school, Saturday, or summer employment in community agencies and summer camps. This not only provides them with an excellent source of extra income but increases their likelihood of success as fulltime art teachers.

In most colleges, teaching experiences are usually limited to observation and student teaching courses in the junior or senior year. Some professors believe that students need to complete preparatory courses in teaching techniques and psychology prior to doing actual teaching. The Committee on the Function of Art in General Education has recommended that an art education student, during his freshmen year—

. . . should have contact with children under as many different circumstances as possible . . . as companion to the children or as special observer, gradually increasing his responsibility to include direction and teaching.**

An experimental community teaching program was recently established at an eastern teachers' college.*** Several junior year members of an art education club and their faculty adviser organized a voluntary educational service.

They decided to begin at a city recreational center where children gathered after school. Freshmen offered to act as observers

---

*Charles Hardaway, "From the Research Department," Teacher's College Journal, Vol. XIX (November, 1947), pp. 22-23.

** Victor D'Amico and others, *The Visual Arts in General Education*, pp. 130-131.

*** The State University of New York, College for Teachers at Buffalo.

and assistants. Sophomores offered to secure necessary materials and supplies, and to request suggestions from the club's faculty adviser and other faculty members; juniors volunteered to do the actual teaching; and seniors agreed to supervise and to give constructive criticism.

A committee of students secured permission of the recreation center director to use three second-floor rooms, a storeroom, and a sink. Since the center had no art supplies, they were furnished through funds from the club's treasury and by donations solicited by sophomores from other student members, interested faculty members, and local art stores.

Children for the art classes were recruited from neighboring schools by the director of the recreational center. After they had been grouped according to age, a waiting list was set up to provide replacements for those who dropped out of the program. Classes were thus somewhat similar in size and general structure to those found in nearby elementary schools.

The same art education club members organized other art classes for children, adolescents, and young adults in several neighborhood houses, a science museum, the Y's, a home for wayward girls, a Salvation Army house, a young people's church group, a boys' club, and several summer camps.

Reports by student participants. Some comments written by students in the community teaching program show clearly the values they derived from this extra-curricular activity.

. . . I did not teach art, but I did learn. The experience of just being with children, the kind of children I never knew existed [low economic group, mixed races], has made me more aware of my place as a future teacher . . . They asked questions and I answered them as well as I could. One little girl insisted I look at the corn on her foot, another wanted me to sew buttons on. I told one about corn plasters and sewed the other up. The rewarding smile or "HI!" when you came the next time overshadowed the minuteness of their problems—minute to me, yet ever so great to a ten-year-old. . . . They are good kids, just a bit more lonely, more repressed than usual. At the Neighborhood House they are happy and so am I. I know how to handle them, and how to cast off the crude remarks of one and reprimand another. . . . I'll remember the experience as a gift for the future. The nights I came home so tired wondering how the leaders could stand it everyday. Most of all, I'll remember the night the gang of low-teen girls who were "tough to crack" asked me to please come back; the night Myra, a colored girl older than I, asked me to be her guest at the Christmas party. . . . I have seen their treatment of others, whether they be Catholic, Jewish, Indians, or Negroes. There is no differentiation in the children's attitude toward one another. Intolerance is the fault of adults. When you see these children, true Americans, practicing real democracy, you realize this more than at any other time.—*Patricia Ann Norton.*

The remaining comments, though somewhat less dramatic than the one above, clearly show students' opinions of community teaching.

This voluntary teaching position was a valuable experience to me in many ways. It provided, first of all, an opportunity to do some actual teaching which will help me later on when I apply for an actual teaching position. It also gave me a chance to put into practice some of the teaching theories and methods which I learned in my course. Being able to work with an actual class of this sort helps make things much more clear and real to you. You get so much more out of something when actually doing it, than merely reading it from a book. It provides a fairly good idea of what to expect when you finally become a teacher. —*William Rodler.*

There are many advantages of voluntary teaching, but the most important to me is the practical experience of working with children. A criterion of a good teacher is a calm manner which is gained from circumstances and not through textbooks. I learned to expect the unexpected.—*Patricia Gilbert.*

Although I have had to contend with numerous complications and problems in my voluntary teaching, I fully realize that it is the only way to learn to work with children. Books could never express the satisfaction gained from watching a child beam over a finished product. —*Gertrude Shoolman.*

Although I came to college with only a hazy notion of actually fulfilling the training I would receive, I have developed a love for teaching which will never leave me.—*Susan Plaut.*

These freshman and sophomore students were not only enrolled in a college; they were, from the very outset of their college education, preparing themselves for the profession of art teaching. A number of school administrators have said that art teachers who come to them with previous community or summer camp art teaching experiences are better prepared than standard graduates.

EDUCATIONAL TOURS

An extra-curricular activity which is particularly popular with art education student groups is the extended field trip or educational tour. A group of students and their faculty advisers may charter a bus or arrange to use several automobiles to reach a center of

64

special interest. Some institutions excuse students and faculty members from regular class responsibilities for several days in order that they may make best use of their investment of time and money.

Educational tours might include attendance at national, regional, and state art education conferences, or conventions such as those of the National Education Association and National Parent-Teacher Association. As a planned part of their tours, many students attend major theatrical and musical presentations. One of the more important values to be derived is a better understanding of all the arts. Seeing examples of outstanding dramatic and operatic productions, the dance, paintings and sculpture, architecture, community planning, and educational institutions during a period of several days, plus talking with important artists in all fields, provides students with a background upon which they may draw for years.

ART AUCTIONS

An auction of original paintings, sculpture, ceramics, textiles, and various other art works is an excellent school-community activity. An art auction helps participating students understand monetary values, public taste, and how to implement cooperation between themselves, college staff members, local artists, and the community. Even more important, the art auction places original art works in many private homes and raises funds for art scholarships, bequests, and other worthy causes.

Among the sources of publicity for the art auction are television, radio, illustrated newspaper articles, posters in store windows and on automobile bumpers, and direct mail. All of these require careful planning and hard work, yet they are essential to a successful art auction. In addition, they contribute to the educational development of participating students by providing them with an actual, rather than artificial, learning situation.

ART EXHIBITIONS

Students often take initiative in requesting permission to select and install exhibitions of their own work as well as that of children, faculty members, students from other schools, and local artists. In addition to the more highly organized exhibition program carried on in most departments of art education, there should be opportunity for this type of informal, extra-curricular activity in which students are given a free hand to test their design ability in a practical situation. Under ideal conditions, where students are able to assume responsibility for organizing, publicizing, designing, hanging, operating, and dismantling exhibits, it is possible that for a time, at least, the department's exhibition program might be entirely operated by student groups.

PARENT-TEACHER-STUDENT OPEN HOUSE

Although they are mature and independent in many respects, most college students still enjoy showing their work, teachers, and school to their parents, and are anxious to have parental approval of the college or university they are attending. Many parents were less fortunate than their children in not having been able to attend college; hence their visits, particularly the first, are likely to be very important occasions. Whether or not parents contribute to tuition, board and room, books, supplies, and transportation, it is likely that most of them have made real sacrifices in order to send their youngsters to college. A mere acknowledgment of this sacrifice, made by the department chairman or one of the professors, does much to assure parents that their efforts are appreciated by others as well as their sons and daughters.

At least once a year, parents should be invited to a social evening or week-end on the college campus. For all students, parents, and teachers concerned, this is a valuable democratic as well as social experience. Because of their key role, students should assume chief responsibility for organizing the event, selecting an appropriate date through counsel with teachers and administrative officers, publicizing the affair to other students and their parents, arranging for refreshments and exhibits, planning an informal program, and properly introducing parents to one another, to teachers, and to other students. This type of family affair, where younger brothers and sisters may also attend, is too rare in American life today. Spending a constructive, enjoyable evening together in a wholesome, stimulating atmosphere is one of the finest ways of binding family ties. A college open house may be the beginning of a series of enjoyable activities through which the family may once again learn the nearly-lost art of effective group relationship.

ART CAREER DAYS

College students of art teacher education make excellent hosts and hostesses for groups of visiting high school students. Having recently graduated from high school, they can well remember the feelings of awe and excitement experienced during their own first visit to a college campus. Consequently, they should play important roles in college-sponsored art career days.

For purposes of local recruitment in particular, but professional welfare in general, most colleges sponsor annual art career days (or week-ends, and in some cases 1 or 2-week art workshops) where high school students interested in the arts may find out more about its many branches, requirements, rewards, and opportunities. Although the itinerary would probably be structured by the faculty, students should assist as guides, counsellors, and in arranging for meals or refreshments, accommodations, and travel. Informal conversations between high school students and college art students often prove decisive in helping a perplexed youngster to decide upon a career in the arts.

SOCIAL ACTIVITIES

A great deal has been said and written elsewhere about college social life. Many people have the impression that it is more than adequate and that if any changes are made they should be in the direction of curtailing rather than extending social activities. This is partly true, since many students have lessened considerably their professional opportunities because of overindulgence in college social life.

But the shy or retiring student needs more social life than he gets. College social activities are essential to one's professional development. What is needed is a proper balance between scheduled classes, study periods, rest, extra-curricular professional and social activities, and other elements of college life. Among the many college social activities are:

dances and proms
fraternity or sorority meetings
meetings of social organizations and clubs
film programs
art exhibit openings
theatrical, operatic, modern dance, and ballet productions
weekends at homes of college roommates or friends
weekends at the college camp
shopping tours with friends

A balanced amount of participation in varied social activities is important for all students for a number of reasons. Chief among these is the fact that much of today's teaching is based on social understanding, and a good teacher must know how to induce a friendly, informal classroom atmosphere, rather than the more rigid recitative pattern of the past. Our total psycho-physical makeup demands informal and recreational activity, especially when so much time is spent in the classroom and studio. We help fulfill one of our basic life purposes through social activities with peer groups. Students want and need to be accepted and respected by their peers.

Campus housing

Almost every college and university has dormitory or near-campus rooming facilities for its students. Campus housing offers numerous educational benefits to students in addition to clean, pleasant, and relatively inexpensive living quarters. Most educators agree that students who live on campus derive more educational benefits during their college life than do commuting students. If financial limitations make commuting a necessity, it is often wise, if possible, to plan at least a semester of residence on campus. If this is impossible, some study periods and meals should be had on the campus, plus a reasonable number of evenings for college events.

Most institutions have a director of residence halls who helps students plan their extra-curricular and social activities in addition to maintaining the highest possible living standards.

Campus housing helps students acquire responsibility for their personal conduct and welfare. It also assures parents that at least two meals a day will be well balanced and nutritious. For many students this is the first extended period of time away from their families. Vacations at Thanksgiving, Christmas, Easter, and summertime help them to make this as well as subsequent breaks in home ties without serious emotional effects on either the student or his parents and other relatives.

Since everyone living on campus is engaged in scholarly or creative art activities, studying is often less a problem than it is in a home where the student may be the only person interested in

Well-designed dormitory facilities for study and creative work in the scholarly environment of a college campus are highly conducive to regular, concentrated study.

COURTESY KNOLL ASSOCIATES

quiet concentration. At college there are study tables, desks, adequate lighting, the library, and enforced quiet hours to insure greater attention to studies than to the various distractions common at home.

For those students who cannot, for financial or other reasons, live on campus, a quiet place for concentration, with proper lighting, ventilation, and a good working surface, must be arranged. Some of the more successful of these have been located in attics, basements or garages, and spare rooms. Modestly priced electric or gas space heaters can be used where heating ducts or radiators are missing. Parents, brothers and sisters, and visiting friends and relatives must be politely but positively informed that a college student needs to spend many hours daily in study and creative work. Pre-college type social life must be radically modified in favor of increased study time if the large investment of time, effort, and money needed for a college degree is to pay dividends.

Young spirits are intensely moved by the inspiration of their environment. Colleges should try to keep up with t h e church in this respect.

3: Placement, Promotions, and Graduate Study

THE PROCESS *of securing a position in the teaching profession is called "placement." Placement services include:*

1. Securing, compiling, and making copies of credentials, transcripts of completed courses of study, records of previous work experiences, and letters of recommendation.

2. Contacting school administrators who need art teachers or supervisors.

3. Sending placement papers to interested school administrators.

4. Arranging personal interviews between candidates (teachers seeking a position) and administrators.

5. Keeping records of candidates who are placed, including school name and location, starting salary, grades taught, etc.

PLACEMENT AGENCIES

There are several types of placement agencies. Each has its advantages and disadvantages, dependent upon specialized services offered and the interests and qualifications of the individual candidate.

College agencies. Nearly every college, university, or art school preparing art teachers offers free placement services to its graduates.

When a student decides to apply actively for a position, the placement director of a college can give excellent direction. Here a college placement director discusses proper application procedure with two prospective candidates.

COURTESY DIRECTOR OF PLACEMENT, TEXAS TECHNOLOGICAL COLLEGE, LUBBOCK, TEXAS

Except in rare cases, these agencies limit placement services to alumni or students who have completed a certain number of credits.

ADVANTAGES AND DISADVANTAGES OF COLLEGE AGENCY PLACEMENT

ADVANTAGES

College agencies are usually well regarded by school administrators in area.

No placement fee is charged.

Easily accessible. No money or time wasted in mailing letters, transcripts, and credentials.

Equal treatment of all candidates. Little favoritism.

Ideal for teachers desiring placement in local area.

Can be used in addition to other agencies without any disadvantage.

College agency usually takes initiative in urging candidate to begin placement preparations early.

College placement agencies have direct contact with candidates' instructors.

Some college agencies will continue to offer free placement services for several years after graduation.

DISADVANTAGES

Outstanding candidates do not always receive extra attention they would get elsewhere.

Placement often limited to the geographic area surrounding the institution. Most alumni agencies do not advertise.

Because every graduate must be cared for, and budgets are often limited, service is sometimes slow.

Information on a position sometimes "leaks out."

A candidate would be wise to utilize college placement services unless he plans to go directly into full-time graduate study. The only reason for listing the disadvantages is to make clear that there are limitations to the services. Supplementary placement services may be desired by some candidates.

Teachers' association agencies. Some regional, state, and national teachers' associations offer free but limited placement services to their members. The type of service they render is similar to that offered by college placement agencies, but is usually not as thorough and effective. Certain professional organizations permit members and potential employers to place advertisements in their publications listing desired positions and openings, but these are very limited in scope. However, good positions have been filled and desirable candidates secured, without having to pay a placement fee beyond a nominal charge for the advertisement. Teachers desiring to make use of the services of teachers' association agencies should consult their publications to see if such services are offered, or write to the association headquarters (see Chapter 4).

State education department agencies. State education departments in some states offer free but limited placement services to teachers who are seeking positions in those states. Their services are somewhat similar to those offered by college placement agencies, but here again the services are not as inclusive. Inquiries concerning the availability of such services should be directed to the state education department in which a teacher is seeking employment.

Commercial agencies. Commercial placement agencies provide placement services in return for approximately 5 per cent of the first year's salary. This fee is payable only when *first notification* has been given by the agency and/or when *agency-compiled credentials* are used in securing a position. If a candidate has already applied for the position, it is imperative for him to notify the agency to this effect. Although an agency rarely locates the same opening, it is important for candidates and their agency to understand each other clearly because of possible legal problems. Candidates who register with commercial agencies should keep dated carbon copies of all correspondence concerning placement.

Some school administrators prefer reputable commercial placement agencies to alumni agencies because of the fast, thorough, and efficient service they receive. This is often true in the case of higher salaried positions. Experienced teachers tend to use commercial agencies.

Before registering with a commercial placement agency, inquiries should be made about its status in the alumni placement office to learn if it is fully accredited and reputable.

Candidates who seek higher-salaried positions and feel they are properly qualified would do well to register with commercial agencies. The same is true for candidates who might wish to teach in a region not serviced by their college agency.

Although the 5 per cent fee may seem excessive, it should be remembered that increment programs (see p. 92) vary in different school systems and that the *total earnings over a two or three-year period* may be greater than those earned in a similar period for a position secured through a college agency.

ADVANTAGES AND DISADVANTAGES OF COMMERCIAL
AGENCY PLACEMENT

ADVANTAGES

Preferred over alumni agencies by some administrators.

Provides placement opportunities in more regions and states.

Higher-salaried positions are usually well-serviced through commercial agencies.

Fast, efficient, specialized service.

Personal competition with fellow alumni is minimized.

Larger numbers of placement opportunities from which to choose.

Some agencies have reputations for dealing only with high-caliber candidates.

A few commercial agencies which specialize in placing teachers and supervisors of special subjects offer outstanding services in the area of art.

DISADVANTAGES

Some agencies are not accredited and may be more interested in a fee than in rendering service.

Time is lost in correspondence when agency is not in the vicinity.

5% fee charged against first year's salary results in less immediate income than from same position obtained through alumni agency.

Some agencies do not offer adequate placement services to teachers of special subjects, such as art.

Some administrators prefer to deal with alumni placement agencies.

If agency notifies candidate of position vacancy which he learns about *later* through alumni placement agency, fee must still be paid if position is taken.

National Association of Teachers' Agencies. The National Association of Teachers' Agencies is an organization of commercial teachers' agencies located throughout the United States which has formulated a highly regarded code of ethics. Included in this code, for example, are statements such as, "All advertising shall be absolutely honest, free from exaggeration, or misleading statements," and, "Candidates known to be unfit shall not be recommended." It would be wise for candidates to select a commercial placement agency from the National Association of Teachers' Agencies list, which may be secured from any college placement agency.

Personal placement responsibilities. In a sense, the individual candidate is his own "agency." Many individuals have secured good teaching positions entirely on their own initiative. In any case, it is both desirable and necessary for individuals to assume a sizable portion of the responsibility for securing a position.

Among the responsibilities for placement which all candidates should assume are:

1. Register at the proper time (six months to one year before the beginning date for a contemplated position) with an alumni agency and, if desired, with a commercial agency.

2. Complete all agency requirements, such as securing references (see pp. 78-79) and transcripts of grades, as promptly as possible.

3. Keep placement agency notified of all changes in status: desired locale, marriage, status of job inquiry, position already secured, address change, etc.

4. Write letters of application (see pp. 81-84) when asked to do so by an agency, or when otherwise informed of an opening. Write and keep carbon copies of all outgoing placement correspondence.

5. Maintain professional ethics. It is considered unethical to apply for a position learned about through conversations of candidates. It is also unethical to underbid fellow candidates. In most college agencies only three candidates are nominated for a position. In fairness to these people, a candidate should not apply for the same position unless he had learned about it previously through the school administration or through another placement agency.

6. It is advantageous to enclose an appropriate personal photograph with a letter of application. Money spent in securing good photographs is a good investment. Anti-discrimination laws in some states prevent agencies from sending photographs.

7. Appear on time and in proper attire for interviews with placement officials and prospective employers (see p. 89) for interview suggestions).

8. Make personal visits to locations of positions when asked to do so by agency or by prospective employers; or when on your own initiative, having received permission from the prospective employer, you feel a visit would be advantageous.

9. Reply promptly—affirmatively or negatively—when contracts are offered to you. Actually, contracts are not in effect until they are signed both by you and the prospective employer, unless you were offered a position verbally and accepted it verbally. In the latter case a written contract should follow. Excessive delay on your part may void the contract. It is customary to sign and return a contract within a week. Many good positions are lost by candidates who spend too much time trying to choose the better of two or three contract offers and find after several weeks of deliberation that each of them has been taken by someone else. In any event, the candidate should either: (a) sign and return the contract immediately; (b) promptly write the prospective employer a letter, acknowledging receipt of the contract and indicating when a decision will be

made; or (c) promptly return the contract unsigned, accompanied by an explanatory letter.

10. As soon as you have taken a position, notify all placement agencies with whom you have been affiliated, and all school administrators who are still considering you as a candidate. Notifications of withdrawal as a candidate should be carefully worded to maintain good standing with administrators, since at some time in the future you may again be a candidate for a position.

The failure of a candidate to assume all of the foregoing responsibilities usually has serious negative effects upon his present or future placement.

ADVANTAGES AND DISADVANTAGES OF PERSONAL PLACEMENT

ADVANTAGES

Administrators may be influenced by your personal initiative.

Candidate may select preferred geographic area instead of being "assigned" by an agency.

Position may be secured more rapidly. No delays in agency red tape.

Agency fee is saved on positions secured entirely on your own initiative.

You can emphasize your own qualifications and may not have to compete with as many others for a position.

You may send a personal photo to prospective employers. Antidiscrimination laws in some states prohibit agencies from doing this.

Honest and sincere personal statements may be more effective than routine agency statements.

DISADVANTAGES

This procedure used exclusively is seldom effective, since most administrators give advance notice of vacancies to agencies or college placement bureaus.

Poor typing, spelling, or application letter format may disqualify you even though you are an otherwise excellent candidate.

A few administrators deal exclusively with agencies.

You may take a position for less salary than you might have received through agency placement.

You must assume costs of telephoning, stationery, typing, and postage which agency would otherwise assume.

Personal placement may not be as systematic and effective as agency placement.

Optional placement responsibilities. Among the additional responsibilities which are not required of all candidates, but which individuals may wish to assume, are:

1. Write letters of inquiry to administrators of schools or geographic areas in which you would like to teach, asking if position vacancies are expected in the immediate or near future.

2. Enclose in such letters a photograph along with brief statements of interest and qualifications, mentioning that complete credentials will be sent upon request, and offering to visit the school.

3. Compile a portfolio of representative personal art work to be submitted to interested prospective employers.

Federal government agencies placement services. Actually, the federal government does not maintain a placement agency, but it does offer limited placement services as part of the functions of several government bureaus. The placement services offered by the federal government deal with certain teaching positions in government schools in the United States, its possessions, and in foreign lands. Necessary information and addresses may usually be secured from your local post office.

Army arts and crafts program. A limited number of civilian positions as directors of craft activities in U.S. armed services installations both here and abroad are available for qualified persons. Requirements for government service positions vary from a minimum of a degree from an accredited institution with major work in art plus a limited amount of teaching experience to a master's degree and six years of paid teaching experience in the art field. More detailed requirements, plus current salary schedules, may be obtained by writing to:

For positions in the United States:

> Department of the Army
> Office of Civilian Personnel
> Washington 25, D. C.
> Attn: Special Services Recruitment Section

For positions abroad:

> Department of the Army
> Office of Civilian Personnel
> Overseas Affairs Division
> Washington 25, D. C.
> Attn: Special Services Recruitment Section

Exchange teaching and university lectureships. A limited number of exchange teaching and university lectureship positions in foreign lands are available to specially qualified, experienced teachers. Inquiries concerning this program should be directed to:

> Office of Education
> Department of Health, Education, and Welfare
> Washington 25, D. C.

BEGINNING PLACEMENT ACTIVITIES

Making early personal inquiries. It is advantageous to begin making inquiries regarding art teaching positions as early as the beginning of the junior year in college. This is especially true when the candidate has selected a particular geographic area in which he wishes to teach; but, it is also true for candidates who seek a better than average position.

There are several reasons for making early inquiries. Perhaps the most important is the fact that school administrators are well impressed by candidates who make early plans and thus show sincere interest in their professional futures. Nearly every school system today contemplates continued growth, both in size and quality. Most school administrators and boards of education have made long-range plans concerning the addition or replacement of teachers. They may be able to tell a prospective candidate that in two or more years they plan to add another art teacher to their staff, or that their present art teacher will be retired at that time and will need replacement. Most schools which do not yet have an art teacher, plan to add such a person to the staff in the immediate future. Another reason for making early inquiries is that administrators are likely to give such candidates greater consideration than they will to those who make application at the last minute. It is frequently true that the pressure of other responsibilities will cause a school administrator to limit his consideration of candidates to those who have made previous personal inquiries, rather than go to the trouble of contacting a placement agency. Applying early in the senior year gives an administrator an opportunity to suggest alternate or additional courses a student can take in preparing for a particular teaching assignment.

Techniques in making inquiries. Although personal inquiries regarding placement may be made by telephone, mail, or visiting a school, a combination of the latter two is usually the best procedure. One technique which has proved to be very effective, as well as systematic and timesaving, is for an entire junior or senior year art education class to work at this problem cooperatively under

77

the guidance of their department head and placement officer. A duplicated letter may be developed, informing the addressee that: "Next September the following people will be available for art teaching positions in your area." It may go on further to state that "a year from next September other people will be graduated in art education and have expressed an interest in teaching in your locality." The appropriate letters are then sent to every school administrator in the region. The collecting of "preferred teaching area" data, the addressing of envelopes, etc., may be shared by all students whose names appear on the letters; thus an otherwise burdensome procedure may be simplified and rapidly accomplished. Where this technique has been used, it has been found effective, not only in time saved but in positions secured.

Carrying this procedure one step further, it is possible to make cooperative plans for personal visits, especially when the schools to be visited are some distance away. One car can drop off and pick up as many as six candidates who are visiting schools in a certain geographical area. By sharing expenses, costs are kept low.

Registering with a placement agency. The best time to register with a placement agency is at the beginning of the school year preceding the year in which a candidate plans to start teaching. This will give both the candidate and the agency ample time in which to gather various credentials.

Each agency has unique procedures which should be carefully followed. It is of utmost importance to be prompt and neat in filling out all papers, since negligence or carelessness may cause the agency to feel you would be negligent or careless as a teacher. Even commercial agencies, which receive a fee for securing a position for you, will not place someone they feel may reflect poorly on their recommendations.

In addition to filling out forms, a teacher placement agency will expect the candidate to secure, or to make arrangements for them to secure, written references. They will also expect the applicant to keep them up-to-date on the status of positions for which he has been recommended, on address changes, and current telephone numbers. In many instances, prospective employers want to make immediate contact with candidates, who, if they cannot be reached by telephone or letter, may miss a placement opportunity. Most agencies will provide an applicant with a pamphlet describing full procedures pertaining to letters, references, and forms.

Securing references. Prospective employers want to know more about a candidate than is told by a transcript of grades and a brief personal interview. To provide prospective employers with additional information concerning personality, appearance, emotional stability, professional preparation, successful experience, and other items of interest, candidates are expected to secure letters of reference or recommendation.

Letters of reference are an important part of placement credentials. Candidates should carefully consider the people they would like to have write letters of reference for them, rather than merely suggesting people who "might do" because of their professional positions or reputations.

The candidate should bear in mind that letters of reference are confidential affidavits from one professional person to another. Regardless of how much a reference writer may like a candidate personally, he is professionally obligated to state honestly the strengths and weaknesses of the person involved. Persons who are casually chosen for this important responsibility might do the candidate more harm than good.

Some of the people to consider as reference writers are:

college instructors from whom the candidate received grades of A or B

college advisers

the department head

clergymen

civic leaders

Some of the people who should probably not be considered as reference writers are:

relatives

personal friends

persons who have not known a candidate since high school

persons who have known a candidate for less than one year

Most placement agencies require several references. Some of these should describe a candidate's personal character, and the others his professional ability.

While personal placement is a possibility, a combination of personal and agency placement is more desirable. It is because of letters of reference that agency placement becomes almost a necessity, for in order to send complete credentials to all prospective employers, duplicate copies of references must be made. Since letters of reference are not to be seen by the candidate they describe, they can only be duplicated by an agency. Asking a reference writer to perform this service more than once is an imposition.

People should be asked in advance if they will be willing to write a letter of reference, or if their name may be used as a reference. Some agencies provide candidates with forms to be given to reference writers who accept the request, in which case the candidate should also provide the writer with a stamped envelope properly addressed to the agency. Other agencies prefer to have the candidate submit a list of people who have given their consent for reference writing, and they in turn send the proper form together with a return-addressed, stamped envelope.

Securing application photos. Personal appearance is one of the most important of the desirable characteristics in an art teacher. It is obvious that a good application photograph will be desired by a prospective employer.

There are a few general "rules" regarding an application photograph. It should be:

a good likeness

attractive (unlike stark passport photo)

head and shoulders portrait, not entire figure

application photo, not casual snapshot

about 2½ x 3½ inches in size

rubber cemented or stapled in place indicated on application form

If no place is indicated, the top left edge is usually preferred.

In some states, laws against discrimination prohibit the enclosure of application photos with placement agency credentials. This is designed to prevent employers from discriminating against candidates on a racial or religious basis. Unfortunately, the law sometimes works to the disadvantage of the candidate, since employers often say jobs are "filled" or "unavailable" when they call in a well-qualified candidate who turns out to be a member of a race or religion against which they discriminate. If the candidate has traveled some distance at his own expense, the injustice is even greater. Discrimination laws have had some positive effects, but in view of the limited status of racial and religious integration today, it would seem wise for candidates, whether or not they are members of minority groups, to submit application photos to prospective employers. If agencies are prevented by law from enclosing photos with credentials, candidates may, if they wish, send them directly with letters of inquiry or application. Very few positions are filled before candidates have been seen and interviewed; therefore, good application photos would seem to be a necessity.

Many art teacher education centers have reported 100% placement for several years, including those graduates who are members of minority groups. More and more, progressive communities are not only willing but determined to integrate members of various races and religions in their school faculties.

Letters of application. A letter of application is written to a prospective employer after notice of a position vacancy has been received. However, a letter of inquiry is sometimes considered a letter of application by employers who happen to have position vacancies. Therefore, we will deal with both types of letters in this section.

LAYOUT

Most school administrators pride themselves on the neat and attractive letters which originate from their offices. They are well impressed by applicants who submit well-planned letters. Candidates for art teaching positions can go one step further. With their knowledge of design, they can develop a letter format which is not only neat and attractive, but well arranged.

In any event, letters of application should be typed or neatly lettered on only one side of good quality paper. They should be brief, with items listed to make for greater clarity and easier reading.

When a photograph of the candidate is to accompany the letter, it should be incorporated as a part of the design of the letter, and not placed on top of written material.

SPELLING AND GRAMMAR

Every candidate should have mastered basic spelling and grammar, and letters of application should bear this out. Those who are uncertain should have an English teacher or college adviser read letters of application before they are typed in final form to check them for contents, brevity, perfect spelling, punctuation, and grammar. Many books are available on letter writing. It is also important to have the full name and correct title of the addressee, properly spelled.

CONTENTS

Although letters of application can vary considerably in format, they should give prospective employers at least the following information:

• The fact that you are sincerely interested in teaching art.
• Your belief that you can be of real service to the school and community, describing the areas in which you feel you will make your greatest contribution.

Men's Dormitory
Centerville State Teachers College
Centerville, New York

March 10, 19___.

Dr. Kenneth Schultz,
Supervising Principal,
Morris Central School,
Morris, New York

Dear Dr. Schultz:

I would like to apply for the position of
elementary art teacher at Morris Central
School. The placement agency of Centerville
State Teachers College has notified me of
this position opening, and has sent you my
credentials.

This position interests me a great deal,
since I have learned from two of your graduates, John Stoddard and Henry Marshall,
who are now students at Centerville State,
that Morris is a progressive, growing community with a fine school. It is the type
of community in which I would like to live,
and the type of school in which I might
make a real professional contribution.

I am particularly interested in helping
classroom teachers offer more than the
once-a-week art lesson to their children by
showing them ways that art can enter into
nearly every curriculum subject. You will
notice in my credentials that my student
teaching experiences in the elementary
grades gave me ample opportunity to gain
background in this type of work.

I would appreciate an opportunity to learn
more about your school and community. If
you wish, I would be happy to come there
for a personal interview at a time which is
convenient for you.

Very truly yours,
Robert A. Smith

Example of a letter of application.

82

- Your age, sex, height, weight, and appearance. (photo is helpful here.)
- Your marital status. In the case of a woman, administrators are anxious to know how long she plans to teach before becoming married; or if married, how long she plans to teach before raising a family; or if she has children, if she plans to continue teaching while the children are being cared for by someone else.
- How long you plan to stay in the position for which you are applying. If you would definitely like to stay in the position for two years or more, it is wise to tell this to the prospective employer, since he is eager to hire such people.
- Your qualifications for the position. You should objectively list what you feel to be your chief assets as a teacher and artist. (See Chapter 1, pp. 30-41). Include previous employment references (paid or voluntary), special schooling, and a brief record of art exhibitions and awards.
- A self-addressed, stamped envelope included with a letter of application is an expected courtesy, and will encourage the addressee to reply more quickly.

APPLICATION FOR POSITION: TEACHER OF ART,
SECONDARY SCHOOL LEVEL

ROBERT A. SMITH   age 22
height 6'
weight 180
single

recent
photograph

Permanent Address:
190 Beecher St.,
Mount Pleasant, N. Y.
Phone: 3180
Available: September, 19__.

ROBERT A. SMITH
(date of photo)

EDUCATION   B.S. in Art Education, New
York University, 19__.
Graduate study in ceramics,
Alfred University, Summer,
19__.

EXPERIENCE   Assistant Scout Leader, Mt.
Pleasant, N.Y. 19__-__.
Taught art classes for chil-
dren, ages 14-17, Greenwich
Village Community Center,
New York, N.Y., 19__-__.

	Playground Assistant, Mt. Pleasant, N.Y., art and craft classes, 19__.
	Student Teacher, Music and Art High School, New York, N.Y., Feb.-June, 19__.
CO-CURRICULAR	Secretary, Art Club, New York University, 19__-__.
	Art Editor, Lines and Letters, New York University, 19__-__.
ADDITIONAL INTERESTS	Coaching basketball, playing piano, bowling
AWARDS	Art League Scholarship, New York University, 19__.
	Second Prize, Student Art Exhibition, New York University, 19__.
REFERENCES	Professor Hale Woodruff, New York University
	Rev. Emmett Sanders, Congregational Church, Mt. Pleasant, N. Y.
	Miss Peggy Knowland, Director, Greenwich Village Community Center, New York 3, N.Y.
COMPLETE CREDENTIALS	Filed in Education Placement Office, New York University, New York 3, N.Y.

Example of a Statement of Qualifications which might be used for initial inquiry or as a supplement to a letter of application.

A "Personal Profile" application letter. The placement idea which follows was developed by an industrial arts teacher when he was seeking his first professional position. The value of this procedure is amply proved by the statistics presented in his conclusion.

THE GRADUATE JOB SEEKER*
By EDWARD BARTEL
New York State College for Teachers, Buffalo, N. Y.

June—graduation—job hunting. Within a short time this will be the theme of thousands of young men and women prepared to teach industrial arts. The most difficult thing will be to find a desirable job. Most

Industrial Arts and Vocational Education Magazine, Milwaukee, Wisconsin, May, 1954.

teaching positions are gained through school and state placement centers, private teacher agencies (at a fee), civil service examinations, and by the method of individual efforts. I chose the latter.

The scheme was to advertise myself through the use of a "personal profile" booklet. The method itself is not original, but the product is. I felt that by contacting a prospective employer through a sample of my own work he would gain a closer insight into my personality and ability.

The plan called for a 5½ by 8 inch booklet and a printed letter with space allotted for a typewritten inside address. Both would be placed in an envelope and mailed at a total cost of six cents each including postage.

The first step in the actual composition was to put down in words all pertinent personal data of the past, present, and future. This information was then *tailored* to fit the particular job desired; namely, a position as industrial-arts teacher. The underlying thought was always "What information would the employer want to know about me?"

The data was then grouped under convenient headings. The copy was placed with equal weight on all four pages. It was set in Roman style type, printed upon a platen press, and stapled into booklet form. A half tone placed on the cover gave an added sense of individuality.

Personal Data:

Age:	26 years. Born June 23, 1924 at Buffalo, N. Y.
Height:	6 Feet.
Weight:	195 Pounds.
Marital Status:	Married, no children.
Wife:	Mary Strodel Bartel. Employed as billing clerk by the Buffalo Forge Company.
Appearance:	Neat and clean.
Health:	Excellent. Have not been absent a single day from either high school or college.

Vocational Background:

June 1942-Feb. 1943	Art Stained Shingle Co. Fabricator of shingle panels. Good wages. Fast, skillful work. Reason for leaving: Shutdown.
March 1943-Feb. 1946	United States Marine Corps. Radar technician. Corporal rating.
Feb. 1946-Jan. 1947	Fetch Co., Buffalo, N. Y. Fabricator of shingle panels. Reason for leaving: Shutdown.
Jan. 1947-Aug. 1947	Colonial Radio Corp., Buffalo, N. Y. Punch press operator. Promoted to die setter. Reason for leaving: Enter college.
Sept. 1948-June 1950	N. Y. State College for Teachers at Buffalo. Student helper in Graphic Arts Shop.
June 1950-	Harold Wood Co., Buffalo, N. Y. Part time work. Very valuable experience for Industrial Arts.

College Courses and Grades:

Course	Grade	Course	Grade
Mechanical Drawing 1	A	General Mathematics	B
Mechanical Drawing 2	A	Essentials of In. Arts 1	B
Electrical Shop	A	Essentials of In. Arts 2	B
Physics 1	A	English Literature	B
Physics 2	A	Psychology	B
Applied Mathematics	A	English Composition	B
Graphic Arts	A	Chemistry 2	B
American Government 1	A	Industrial History	B
American Government 2	A	Algebra	B
English Speech 2	A	Ceramics	B
Chemistry 1	A	Textiles	B
Small House Planning	A	Geology	B
Plane Trigonometry	A	Science Teaching	B
Physical Science	A	General Shop	B
Wood Shop	A	Astronomy	B
Transportation Shop	A	Driver Education	B
Contemporary History	A	English Speech 1	C
Metal Shop	A	Principles of In. Arts 1	C
Principles of In. Arts 3	A	Principles of In. Arts 2	C
Biology	A	Practicum in Teaching	

Other Experiences Helpful in Teaching:

U. S. Marines: Three years of service. Honorable discharge. Developed responsibility and leadership.

Hobbies: All sports, especially golf, bowling, and hiking. Home workshop. House planning. Science study. Kodachrome slides.

Travel: My travels have included visits to all areas of the United States, parts of Canada, and overseas to Panama, Los Negros, Guadalcanal, Hawaii, and Guam.

Responsibility: Have a small bank account, no debts or liabilities, excellent credit rating, own a late-model light automobile, and am now saving up money for a home which I hope to build by myself in the near future. Can move immediately.

Educational Background:

High School: Seneca Vocational High School, Buffalo, N. Y. Graduated June 1942. Electrical course. Average 89. Obtained a New York State diploma. Won a sports letter in baseball.

Service School: Camp Lejeune, New River, N. C.
Radar technician school.

Correspondence: Practical Telephony Course. I.C.S. Taken while in the Marine Corps.

College: New York State College for Teachers at Buffalo, New York. Will graduate in January, 1951. Industrial Arts curriculum. I am at present student teaching at the Amherst Central High School, Snyder, New York. Have been on the Dean's honor roll every semester in college. Am a member of Epsilon Pi Tau, honorary Industrial Arts fraternity, and Kappa Delta Pi, honorary educational society. Will have completed the four-year course in three and one-half years and have 137 hours of credit, nine more than necessary for graduation. I have worked part time throughout college. Extracurricular activity included service as a Junior Counsellor, membership in Psi Phi Fraternity, editor of the "Psi Phi News," Epsilon Pi Tau conference work, dances, interfraternity sports and social gatherings.

References:

Dr. Marvin Rapp
History Instructor
New York State College for Teachers
Buffalo, New York.

Mr. Donald Brossman
Graphic Arts Instructor
New York State College for Teachers
Buffalo, New York.

Mr. Owen Harlan
General Shop Instructor
New York State College for Teachers
Buffalo, New York.

Mr. Irving Perkins
Head of the Industrial Arts Department
New York State College for Teachers
Buffalo, New York.

Mr. Richard Wood
Employer at the Harold Wood Company
225 Rodney Street
Buffalo, New York.

Future Intentions:

If I am unable to secure a teaching position for January, 1951, I shall immediately start work on a Master's degree at the University of Buffalo. By the end of August, I will have most of the requirements completed and still remain available for a position in September.

This Personal Profile was
designed, composed, and
printed by the author.

Three hundred and thirty-seven of these profile booklets were distributed to school superintendents as follows:

State	Profiles Sent	Replies	Per Cent Replies
Maine	26	2	8
New Hampshire	18	2	11
Vermont	54	3	6
New York	192	45	23
Rhode Island	15	3	20
Connecticut	32	8	25
Total	337	63	18

It should be noted that Maine, New Hampshire, and Vermont have teacher placement agencies (unknown to author at the time) and that the best statistical interpretation would be gained by an analysis of the New York State data.

Of the 63 replies, nine job possibilities resulted which eventually led to several interviews and finally to a teaching contract. Practically all of the returns included statements that the credentials would be kept on file for future reference. Many letters were extremely complimentary and I was pleased that not one disparaging reply was received.

Yes, June is coming and so is graduation, but, as for job hunting, that's a settled matter.

Personal interviews. Very few positions are filled before the candidate has been interviewed by a school administrator, an art supervisor, a member of the board of education, or a combination of these. The personal interview is a very important part of placement activities. It has been known to be the chief factor in determining the selection of a candidate whose credentials were near the bottom of the list compared with others. Conversely, the personal interview has eliminated some candidates whose credentials were otherwise superior.

PREPARATION FOR THE INTERVIEW

Although one can never predict what may happen during an interview, and though unexpected questions may be asked, the candidate can take certain steps which will improve his acceptability:

- Be on time for the interview.
- Get plenty of sleep the previous night. If you have had little sleep it will probably show up in your facial expression, your poise, and your verbal responses.
- Attend to personal hygiene. Offensive body odors or bad breath are certain to lessen your chances for placement. Dress neatly and tastefully. Clothing should be clean, well-pressed, and carefully selected in advance. Candidates for art teaching positions should always show evidence of good taste in their choice of clothing. Personal grooming should be impeccable. Unkempt hair will make the best clothing look shabby.
- Be up-to-date on current issues in the field of general education, as well as your own special area.
- Check over your personal weaknesses and strong points. Are you a good listener? Do you respect the opinions of "lay persons" or do you consider yourself a distinguished authority on art and art education?
- Review the chart "Desirable Characteristics in an Art Teacher" (see pp. 36-37) and attempt to rate yourself.

The interview

Personal interviews between candidates and prospective employers are usually informal and pleasant. Most administrators remember their experiences as candidates for positions, and thus are sympathetic and understanding. They are, nevertheless, seeking the best one of several good candidates, so their informality and friendliness should not be mistaken for a lack of penetrating evaluation.

Here are a few points to remember:

• As you enter, shake hands with reasonable firmness, introduce yourself unless otherwise greeted, and wait to be asked to be seated.
• Be yourself. Let your personality emerge. Individual qualities make people interesting, so let yours be known without exaggerating them.
• Be good natured; smile when appropriate. Be brief, frank, modestly confident, and sincere in your response. Most administrators prefer intelligent dissenters to meek "yes" men. However, do not enter into an argument, and if a discussion of modern art is introduced, be careful to state your views clearly, reasonably, and honestly.
• Ask questions concerning opportunities for professional growth, the community, beginning salary, increments, opportunities for additional income through community service, and the nature of your position.
• When the administrator rises, or gives evidence that the interview is over, make your departure promptly and courteously.

Accepting a position. Eventually it becomes the responsibility of the candidate to make a firm decision about accepting or rejecting a position offer. Because of the great importance of this decision, several factors should be considered.

Age level of pupils

A teacher should enjoy working with his pupils. He should make certain he really enjoys working with a certain age group, since he will be spending most of his time with them every day. Before making a final choice, it may be helpful to reread Chapter 5, "Interest and Ability Levels in Art Education," to review the characteristics of various age levels.

Opportunities for professional growth

The community, school, administration, and faculty should be considered carefully, since these are factors in one's potential professional growth. A nearby college, university, or professional art school may offer an art teacher opportunities for graduate study on Saturdays, evenings, or in summer. A large community offers cultural activities. A small town or village may offer the quiet and privacy many art teachers prefer for personal creative work. A well-regarded school is apt to make advancement more likely, whereas one with a poor reputation may hamper a teacher's growth. A faculty with advanced degrees and professional ethics can do much to supplement the art program, round out the art teacher's education, and enrich his social life.

A good art teaching position offers certain tangible opportunities for professional growth. Among these should be opportunity for salary increases (automatic as well as merit increments—see p. 92 for details) and opportunity for promotion to the position of department chairman or supervisor of art.

The following chart was developed by teachers doing graduate work at the University of Alaska during a summer session.

OPPORTUNITIES FOR PROFESSIONAL GROWTH

This is a list of possible ways in which communities provide opportunity for professional growth of teachers.

	DEGREES OF USAGE		
	None	Some	Extensive
Professional courses			
(other than correspondence)			
Availability			
Bonus			
Increment			
Committees			
Curriculum			
Textbook			
Other			
Meetings			
(Only those directly promoting professional growth)			
Faculty			
Departmental			
Grade level			
Are these on school time?			
Workshops			
During school year			
After school			
Summer			
For academic credit?			
On paid time?			

	None	Some	Extensive
Study groups			
Conferences			
Research			
Forum			
Idea exchange			
Conventions and institutes			
Sponsored by school system			
Sponsored by teacher groups			
on paid time?			
Professional Library			
Observations			
Inter-school visitation			
Demonstrations			
Other teachers			
Commercial			
Publishers			
Manufacturers			
Administrative assistance			
Supervisors			
Coordinators			
Primary			
Elementary			
Junior High School			
High School			
Music			
Art			
Reading			
Other			
_____			
Bulletins			
Teachers manuals			
Counseling and guidance			
Orientation of new teachers			
Conducted tours			
Big-sister program			
National and international education			
organizations			
American Childhood Education Intl.			
National Education Association			
Classroom Teachers' Association			
Associated Public Schools System			
Others			
_____			
Outside Agencies			
Mental Health Team			
Public Library			
Universities			
Individual Resource People			
General atmosphere			
Are you encouraged to experiment in your			
classroom to put new ideas into practice?			

SALARY

For too many years, teachers have been grossly underpaid. But the argument that members of other professions spend a longer period of time in professional preparation than do teachers is becoming less valid. Teachers once began teaching after a two-year period of study at a normal school, but now they have bachelors' degrees and many have advanced degrees.

For these and many other reasons, teachers should earn as much money as people in other professions who spend equivalent periods of time in professional preparation and service. Teachers must be well paid if competent professional people are to be attracted and retained. Fortunately, many communities have raised teachers' salaries to a point where there is competition for available positions.

INCREMENTS

Most school systems today have salary schedules which list the minimum and maximum salaries for teachers at various degree and experience levels. Within each salary level there are usually several automatic yearly increments ranging in amount, depending on the school system, from about $100 to $400. To be promoted from one salary level to another, after having received the final increment on the previous level, one must usually have completed an additional degree or a certain number of years of service and graduate credits. In some school systems, promotions from one level to another are decided on the basis of individual merit. A number of schools now follow a policy by which qualified teachers receive automatic annual increments for 12 to 18 years in succession. In the latter case, there are no merit promotions as such, but only degree, service, and graduate study requirements.

SOURCES OF EXTRA INCOME

It should be remembered that art teachers' salaries are paid on a nine-to-ten-month school year. They deal only with daytime employment on a five-day-week basis, with paid vacations at Easter, Thanksgiving, and Christmas. The summer months are not a paid vacation, although some schools pay their teachers on a twelve-month basis, dividing the nine-plus months' salary over the year. The ten or twelve summer weeks provide art teachers with an opportunity to earn supplemental income, to do graduate study, or to travel. The evenings, week ends, and paid vacation periods provide additional opportunities for earning supplemental income or, in some cases, for graduate study. Some of the means by which art teachers may supplement their regular income are:

92

Extra work in school:

>   Directing the audio-visual education program
>   Coaching an athletic team

Summer employment:

>   Camp counseling
>   Teaching art at a summer camp
>   Directing art activities at a summer camp
>   Directing a summer camp
>   Commercial art work
>   Special art classes for children or adults
>   Writing or illustrating books and articles
>   Designing greeting cards

Evening employment:

>   Teaching adult education or private art classes
>   Commercial art work
>   Writing or illustrating books and articles
>   Decorating department store windows

Week-end employment:

>   Teaching special classes for children or adults
>   Commercial art work
>   Religious education
>   Writing or illustrating books and articles
>   Decorating department store windows
>   Saleswork in department stores

Holiday employment:

>   Decorating store windows
>   Wrapping gifts in department stores
>   Designing greeting cards
>   Saleswork

It should be noted that part-time and summer employment is suggested for art teachers only until such time as their salaries have reached a level where out-of-school time may be spent exclusively in creative activities, scholarly research, recreation, and travel.

FREEDOM OF THOUGHT AND ACTION

Closely related to the opportunities for professional growth, yet more broad in its implications, is the teacher's freedom of thought and action. In contemporary society where boys and girls are taught to cherish the freedom for which our predecessors gave so much, it is essential that teachers, like all other responsible citizens, enjoy freedom of thought and action within the bounds of accepted moral, professional, and legal principles. If teachers do not possess freedom of thought and action, they cannot effectively help to develop future citizens who will be free men. Many teachers avoid important controversial topics, fearing they might be discharged or called before an investigating committee for so doing. This is unfair to oneself as well as to one's pupils and country. Teachers should not take positions in schools or communities which restrict freedom of thought and action, unless there is reason to believe that more good can be done within than outside of the system.

CONTRACT ETHICS

In most cases, a position has not been officially secured until the candidate and the prospective employer have both signed a contract. Actually, a verbal agreement between an employer and a candidate is considered binding and legal, but to avoid controversy it is wise to put the agreement into written form as soon as possible. Once the contract (which usually covers the academic year from early September to late June,) has been signed and returned to the employer, the candidate is legally and ethically bound to fulfill it. As a rule, contracts for the second and following years are issued about the first of April. They should be signed and returned promptly if a teacher wishes to continue in the same position the following year.

Those who do not wish to return or who are still undecided about plans for the following year should promptly inform the administrator of their plans. Administrators are well aware of the fact that teachers occasionally take other positions to better themselves professionally, or decide to take a year's leave of absence to do graduate study or travel. Usually a teacher may discuss his plans with the administrator and benefit from his advice.

Another element of contract ethics in the teaching profession is known as the "two-year minimum." It is generally felt that during the first year of teaching in a new school system, the teacher learns many new things: the names and personalities of pupils and other teachers; new teaching and administrative procedures; and the nature of the community. By the second year he has become better adjusted, and begins to make contributions to the school program which are on a par with those made by more experienced teachers. A teacher who leaves at the end of the first year has not had an opportunity to fulfill all of his professional obligations, and has in a sense broken the code of professional ethics. There are, of course, certain exceptions to this ethical principle. An individual may terminate his employment after the first year of teaching in cases of:

1. Personal health problems.
2. Health problems in family which necessitates moving to another locality.
3. Decision to leave teaching profession because of lack of ability or interest.
4. Decision to seek position on different age and ability level because of lack of success with or interest in present age and ability level.
5. Failure of administration to fulfill terms — and other basic employment factors.
6. Military service.
7. Unusual opportunity in another system.
8. Pregnancy.

If a first, second, or third year teacher does not receive a contract after all the others have been issued, it is likely that:

1. His services are no longer desired because of professional incompetence (see details under "Tenure," below.)
2. The faculty number has been reduced and as a junior member he is automatically eliminated.
3. The contract may have been misplaced or lost.

A teacher who is uncertain about the reason for not having received a contract may inquire about it to the administrator. Usually a teacher whose services are to be terminated will be informed about it prior to the date when contracts are issued.

TENURE

The term tenure is often misunderstood, probably because it sounds so much like "ten year." Actually it refers to the relative permanence (from the French *tenir*, to hold) of a position *after* the third year of successful teaching in the same school or school system. If a teacher receives a contract for the-fourth year of teaching in the same school system, he is in most cases being granted tenure. This means that after the third year he cannot be arbitrarily released from his position for unknown reasons. Of course anyone, at any time, may be released from his position if he is proved in-

95

competent to teach. Some of the bases for incompetence in teaching are: excessive drinking of intoxicants out of school; any drinking of intoxicants during school hours; violations of moral principles in or out of school; committing a crime more serious than a misdemeanor, and in some cases committing a series of misdemeanors; refusal to attend faculty meetings or chaperone student activities; failing to make adequate preparations for classes; and continuous inability to foster desirable behavior in students. Although very few in number, some teachers have been released for one or more of the above reasons; thus the contents of this section should not be taken too lightly.

RETIREMENT, SABBATICAL LEAVE, AND DEATH BENEFITS

Among other factors to be considered in accepting a position are the provisions for retirement, sabbatical leave, sickness, and death. Not all school systems provide such benefits, but in most cases adequate provisions are made for retirement and sabbatical leave, and in some situations provisions are made for sickness and death.

By provisions for *retirement*, we mean a procedure set up whereby the school system and the individual teacher regularly contribute similar amounts of money to an interest-earning savings account. After a certain number of years, this account grows in size to the point where it will provide the teacher who retires with a monthly income for the remainder of his life. In some school systems, teachers may, if they wish, contribute up to about 10 per cent of their gross salary toward retirement benefits, and the school system in turn adds an equal amount of money to the account. When a teacher leaves the school system (or in some cases, the state) prior to retirement, all money he has contributed, plus the compounded interest it has earned, is returned to him. However, the money which the school system has contributed, plus the interest it has earned, is not given to the teacher unless he stays in the system until retirement.

Many states have adopted the Old Age Survivors' Insurance (Social Security) plan. This, in many instances, is in addition to the state or local teachers' retirement program or it may be the only form of retirement that a teacher has.

Sabbatical Leaves are specified periods of time during which full or part-time salary is continued while a teacher travels, does graduate study, writes, or engages in creative work. Sabbatical leaves of one semester or one year are usually granted after six years

96

of continuous meritorious service. Most school systems which grant sabbatical leaves to qualified teachers require the teacher to return to teaching in the same school or system the year following sabbatical leave. To receive sabbatical leave, a teacher is usually required to submit a proposal for study, creative work, travel, or a combination of these, which shows how the leave period will benefit the teacher professionally. A sabbatical leave is not a paid vacation, but an arrangement whereby a teacher may attain certain professional goals which might not otherwise be reached on a part-time, after-school, or summer basis.

Some school systems allow teachers a certain number of days per year (or per month) of *paid sick leave*. In some cases the days of sick leave are cumulative so that teachers might be able to receive salary during periods of extended illness. Although the sick leave procedure has not yet been widely adopted, it is highly desirable.

Death benefits are usually linked with or function as alternatives to *retirement benefits*. In many school systems, provisions are made for teachers' beneficiaries to receive the balance of their retirement fund. In most school systems, the bulk of all money contributed to a retirement fund by the teacher and the school system, plus earned interest, is paid to beneficiaries in the event of his death, whether this occurs before or after retirement.

It should be noted that the clerical costs of deducting contributions for the above benefits, plus other deductions for government bonds, health insurance, and income tax, are borne by the school system. This not only saves the teacher money which would otherwise be spent for personal checks and postage, but encourages personal thrift habits and balanced budgets. On the other hand, the teacher's *net* (after deductions) salary is considerably less than his *gross* (total, before deductions) salary after all of these deductions have been made, and beginning teachers should not be misled into living beyond their means.

CONTINUING PROFESSIONAL ADVANCEMENT

A teacher has a responsibility to the school in which he takes a position to continue for at least a second year in order to repay his many professional debts. However, during the second and following years he should consider the possibility of professional advancement. Positions in other localities or on other educational levels may offer him greater challenge and a considerably higher salary, provided he is properly qualified. However, teachers should think carefully before accepting a position for its prestige value alone. A position which requires greater service (such as a supervisory position) should also pay a higher salary. Increased professional challenge and increased salary should go hand in hand, as they do in business and industry.

Advancement through initiative

Leaders in education search continuously for teachers who are ready and qualified to accept greater responsibilities in the profession. However, despite their efforts, a number of highly qualified teachers are overlooked. In these cases, teachers who could advance professionally, and who would really enjoy the additional responsibilities such advancements entail, continue to work at a responsibility level far below their capabilities because they hesitate to work actively in behalf of their own advancement. Teachers must realize that the profession needs more leaders, put aside professional modesty and actively seek to improve their status.

Individual advancement procedures

There are a number of means by which individual teachers may help to advance themselves professionally. Some of these are:

• Work actively in professional organizations to increase teachers' salaries and to improve the status of teachers in society. Active participation in the work of professional organizations will foster acquaintances with educators in other parts of the country and will thus increase opportunities for professional advancement.

• Urge local teachers' associations and community organizations to work in behalf of bettering teachers' salaries.

• Maintain active registration in at least one highly regarded placement agency.

• Continue to work on advanced professional degrees (see pages 99-102). Better positions in the teaching profession today require at least a master's degree; in many cases a master's degree plus thirty additional hours of graduate study; and in some cases a doctor's degree.

• Build a sound professional reputation through diligent, high-quality work. In filling better positions, employers will consult a candidate's previous and present employers, and the reports received must be excellent.

Certification

A teacher's certificate to teach is like a doctor's license to practice. It indicates to parents, school administrators, and other interested persons that a teacher has been approved for teaching. Although certification requirements vary somewhat from state to state, completion of work at an accredited institution which prepares teachers is usually all that is required for an initial teaching certificate.

Some states call this certificate a provisional, probationary, or limited certificate. After a teacher has completed an additional number of credit hours, he is given a permanent, continuing. or standard certificate. Some states specify that in addition to a certain number of college credits a teacher must also have completed a specified number of years of teaching in order to receive a permanent certificate.

Professional certification is important as a safeguard for qualified teachers as well as for children, their parents, and society in general.

GRADUATE STUDY

College or university courses taken *after the bachelor's degree has been received* are classified as graduate study. A person might be permitted to enroll in a graduate course on a non-credit or audit basis prior to the receipt of a bachelor's degree, but this can seldom be counted for credit toward a graduate degree. However, it is possible to have such non-credit or audit courses counted toward salary increments in school systems where every additional 30 credit hours of college courses completed qualifies a teacher for a salary increase. If proper course sequences are followed and a

Master's or doctor's degree courses offer the art teacher excellent opportunity for advanced study and personal experimentation in specialized areas such as graphic arts and other creative work.

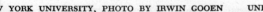 
YORK UNIVERSITY, PHOTO BY IRWIN GOOEN   UNIVERSITY OF WISCONSIN, PHOTO BY ROBERT GRILLEY

"B" or higher grade level is maintained, graduate study may eventually lead to the master's and doctor's degrees.

Graduate study for persons who teach art is highly desirable. Together with individual creative activity, study and teaching experience, graduate study is one of the best means for helping teachers keep up-to-date on desirable educational philosophies and practices. Realizing the importance of continuous learning experiences, a large percentage of persons who teach art engage in part- or full-time graduate study following their graduation from college. This keeps them abreast of current educational practices and often leads them to better teaching positions with higher salaries. It also helps them maintain the standards of an increasing number of school systems which urge (or require) their teachers to complete a certain number of credit hours of graduate study (usually 30) within a specified number of years (usually 10) following graduation from college. Actually, the average art teacher today is well ahead of graduate study requirements made by school systems. A teacher who seeks opportunities provided by institutions of higher learning betters himself as a person, a teacher, an artist, and a citizen.

The master's degree. Many institutions of higher learning offer graduate programs in the arts. Usually, they require about 30-34 semester hours of credit for the master's degree, which would necessitate at least two semesters of resident study or several years of work in part-time or summer session study. Master's degree programs include various courses, a few required, many elective, including: art studio courses; art education philosophy, methods, and workshop courses; and courses in art history, education, science, social studies, and the humanities. Some institutions prescribe the number of credits in certain of these areas which are required for the degree; others help students plan courses of study which are geared to their individual interests and needs. One development in master's degree programs in art education has been the optional substitution of a creative art project in place of the usual thesis requirement, a change widely acclaimed by art educators.

Several different master's degrees may be earned today, dependent upon the type of institution which awards them. Most university schools of education and teachers' colleges offer an M.S. (Master of Science); an M.S. in Ed. (Master of Science in Education); or an Ed. M. (Master of Education) degree. Most liberal arts colleges and nearly all universities offer an M.A. (Master of Arts). Some of them also offer the M.S., M.S. in Ed., or Ed.M.

100

degrees. M.F.A. (Master of Fine Arts) degrees are offered by a number of universities, colleges, and art schools.

Most universities and many colleges offer full-time, part-time, and summer session art education programs for graduate students. All institutions offering graduate art education programs are listed in Patterson's *Educational Directory,* which is available in major libraries. Another suggestion which has been found helpful and more personal is to consult the staff members of one's alma mater or any nearby college or university. By polling a number of them on recommended graduate schools an interested student may determine the school of his choice more effectively than by limiting his source of information to college catalogs. However, it should be remembered that institutions do change and might be quite different from the time when the people you consult attended them. In general, it can be said that art teachers should complete at least one degree in an institution and community noted for its stress upon and activities in the arts.

Professional art-school training. Also to be considered are professional art schools, most of which have on their faculties well-known contemporary artists. Many of these artists are also excellent teachers who can deeply stimulate mature students who work conscientiously under their guidance. Some of these schools are affiliated with universities for credit purposes; thus completed work may be counted toward college degrees and salary increments. Some school systems will accept non-credit courses toward salary increments if they are secured at recognized professional art schools. It would be advisable to check possibilities of transfer credit, where desired, prior to enrollment in a professional art school.

The doctor's degree. At present only a few institutions of higher learning offer a doctor's degree in the field of art education, yet their number is gradually increasing. It is possible for a qualified student to earn one of the following doctor's degrees and to relate the work he does for it to various fields of art education in which he may be interested.

The Ph.D (Doctor of Philosophy) degree is obtainable at some major universities in fields of specialization such as art studio work, art education, art history, educational administration, higher education, and teacher education. It is, of course, also offered in other subject areas such as the humanities (philosophy, literature, music, and others), science, and social studies.

The Ed. D. (Doctor of Education) is a newer degree than the Ph.D., yet it has already won its recipients, as well as the institutions which offer it, very high respect. Like the Ph. D., the Ed. D. is obtainable in a variety of special areas such as art education, elementary education, secondary education, educational administration, and teacher education.

Credit requirements for the Ph. D. or Ed. D. degrees vary from 65 to 90 hours beyond the bachelor's degree or 35 to 60 hours beyond the master's degree.

The requirements for the doctor's degree extend far beyond the mere completion of a given number of credit hours and minimum resident study. The reputation of a university depends to a great extent upon the quality of its graduates. To protect itself and to improve its reputation, but, even more important, to improve the professions which its graduates enter, universities require its doctoral candidates to maintain superior academic status. For example, most universities will not record for credit toward the doctorate a course grade less than "B." In addition they may require students to complete a certain number of credit hours of graduate study before they may even be accepted as candidates for the doctor's degree. Once they are admitted to candidacy, preliminary graduate work may be counted toward the total credit hours which are required. Only persons who possess outstanding personal and professional qualities are considered for admission to candidacy. The student interested in working toward the Ph. D. or Ed. D. degree should realize that every aspect of his undergraduate, graduate, and professional work will be carefully studied in determining his suitability for admission to candidacy. This point should be understood by art education students as early as their first year of undergraduate study, since a poor freshman or sophomore year is likely to exclude even the most able student from possible graduate study.

4: Professional Organizations in the Arts

Professional organizations are tremendously helpful in fostering the growth and quality of the arts in education as well as world culture. They encourage people with similar interests to join together to study mutually important matters. An art teacher should hold membership in art associations, as well as in certain non-art professional and community organizations. By associating with colleagues, he will make his professional life more fruitful and improve his educational service potential. Everyone in a professional group benefits as members share ideas, experiences, and problems with one another.

MEMBERSHIP FOR THE COLLEGE STUDENT

Students usually secure information about professional art organizations through college art education courses. Many institutions encourage their students not only to participate in local activities but to attend state, regional, and national conferences as well. Chartered transportation arrangements for both students and faculty members, as well as plans for parallel cultural and social activities in the metropolitan centers where these groups usually meet, do much to stimulate students' professional organization membership and conference attendance.

There are a number of reasons why students should belong to professional art organizations:

1. It enables them to become better acquainted with current problems in art education and the general field of education.

2. It offers them an opportunity to add current periodical literature to their professional library through publications which are sold at reduced rates or are included as part of their membership fee.

3. It affords them valuable sources of personal contact with possible future employers and leaders in their chosen professional field.

4. It gives them an opportunity to discuss professional problems with experienced teachers of art, artists, and educators in other fields.

MEMBERSHIP FOR THE BEGINNING TEACHER

Many problems face the beginning teacher. Joining an art organization can help him in his new assignment, since most members are experienced teachers who are familiar with school and community problems. If as a student he did not become a member of an organization, he should join early as a beginning teacher, for he has now entered the profession.

CONTRIBUTIONS TEACHERS CAN MAKE
TO A PROFESSIONAL ORGANIZATION

It is not enough that a teacher merely join an organization and pay annual dues. He will only derive from an organization what he puts into it. Each member needs to participate actively in order to build an effective organization. Each member should:

1. Attend meetings regularly.

2. Think carefully before contributing to discussions. Express points as briefly as possible and discuss the subject under consideration rather than unrelated items.

3. Be aware of problems confronting the organization.

4. Keep informed on activities of the organization.

5. Hold office and serve on committees, when asked to do so.

6. Encourage other members to participate more actively in the organization.

7. Encourage desirable non-members to join the organization.

8. Attend in-service art courses that may be offered.

9. Help to eliminate unwholesome personal competition between members.

The Functions and Purposes of Contemporary Professional Organizations in the Arts

THE AMERICAN FEDERATION OF ARTS
1083 Fifth Avenue
New York 28, New York

The American Federation of Arts was founded in 1909 by the statesman Elihu Root, as a national, nonprofit organization dedicated

Yellow Sky, an oil painting by the contemporary American artist, John Hultberg, was circulated in the American Federation of Art's "Fifty Years at the Corcoran" exhibition.

to the development of art in America. It has a national membership of over 1,000 individuals and nearly 500 chapters.

The American Federation of Arts is devoted to:

1. Servicing the art needs of the American people, particularly in areas not favored with large public art collections, art galleries, and art museums.

2. Broadening the knowledge and appreciation of the arts of the past and present.

3. Fostering a better understanding among nations through the international exchange of art.

The AFA originates and distributes traveling exhibitions which represent many periods and cultures through painting, graphic arts, sculpture, architecture, design, crafts, and photography. In the belief that international understanding can be fostered through improved and extended cultural exchange, the Federation conducts an active foreign program, whereby shows are circulated to many parts of the world, and exhibitions from abroad are brought to the United States.

As a clearing house for facts and opinions relative to art, the AFA plays an important role in assisting various governmental and professional agencies. The Federation is one of some sixty organiza-

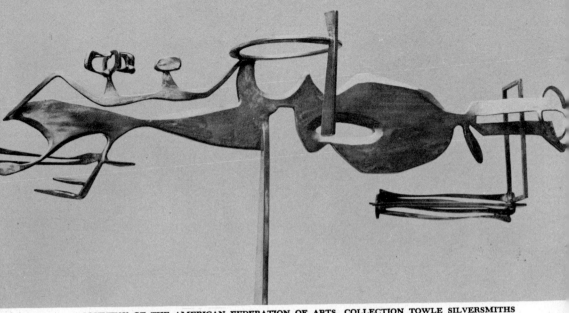

David Smith's *Birthday* was included in the "Sculpture in Silver" exhibition circulated by the American Federation of Arts.

tions which send delegates to the United States National Commission for UNESCO.

Other AFA activities include an annual national convention which brings together museum representatives and leading personalities concerned with art and art education. From time to time, regional conferences are held.

Also important are the AFA's publications, which serve every branch of the professional art world and reach many other readers as well. The American Art Directory is published every three years. It lists museums, art organizations, universities, and colleges having art departments, art schools, and private classes in the United States, Canada, and Latin America. In addition, there are sections listing art magazines; newspapers carrying art reviews, and the names of art critics; museum publications; and traveling exhibitions which are currently available. Among its other publications are: the "AFA Newsletter," which covers important events of the art world, and reference books such as "Films on Art" and "Who's Who in American Art."

ARTISTS EQUITY ASSOCIATION
13 East 67th Street
New York 21, New York

Artists Equity Association was established in 1947, to further the economic interests of artists and to give strength and effectiveness to their united voice. It is a professional, non-exhibiting, aesthetically non-partisan and non-political organization representing the artists of America. It operates a placement service for artist teaching positions and artist-in-residence appointments. Artists Equity Association also contributes to the general bettering of artists' roles in contemporary society. It publishes a quarterly "Newsletter." Regional chapters have been established in several major metropolitan centers. Artists Equity has a national membership of approximately 1,500 professional artists.

COLLEGE ART ASSOCIATION OF AMERICA
432 Fourth Avenue
New York 16, New York

The College Art Association of America was established in 1912 by a group of American professors who wanted to raise the standards of art scholarship and teaching throughout the country. The Association stands for superior qualities in education and research and promotes discussion of the function and methods of instruction in art. It maintains an active bureau for the placement of college teachers, and provides a discount book-buying service for members.

The excellent publications of the College Art Association include the *Art Bulletin,* the *College Art Journal,* and a series of monographs on art and archaeology. Individual membership is in the neighborhood of 2,000. In addition, there are about 800 institutional memberships, some of which are located in foreign countries.

INTERNATIONAL DESIGN CONFERENCE IN ASPEN
22 East Illinois Street
Chicago 11, Illinois

The International Design Conference in Aspen is a non-profit organization of designers, architects, art directors, artists, educators, executives, corporations and consumers, the purpose of which is:

• To implement the distribution, discussion, development and application of ideas in all fields of design among individuals, organizations and agencies concerned with, benefiting from, or in a position to benefit from the significant use of design;
• To plan and hold an annual international conference to further this objective;
• To publish reports of the proceedings of the annual conference and other reports of significant design interest.

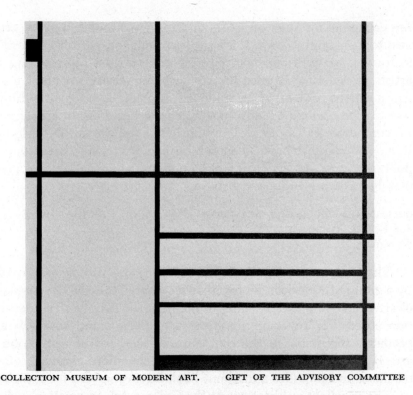

Scholarly analyses of the aesthetic bases of such important masterworks as Piet Mondrian's *Composition in White, Black and Red* are published regularly in the *College Art Journal.*

The purpose of the IDCA is to provide a forum for the study and discussion of design in its larger concept as one of the important distinguishing features of our civilization—a social and cultural technique as well as a technological one. For that reason the individuals who comprise the membership of the IDCA and who meet annually in Aspen, Colorado, to study design represent three groups: 1. The creative professions—individual designers, architects, artists, city planners, writers, scientists, engineers, musicians, sculptors, designers and writers for the theater, motion pictures, radio, and TV. 2. Educators—professors, scientists, philosophers, librarians, museum directors, art teachers, and trainers of apprentices. 3. Executives—representatives of management from great and small corporations; from municipal, state and national governments; from cultural foundations.

Members who attend the Aspen conference, benefit in several ways, among them:

• Clarification of the relationship of design in our technological civilization to all the areas of daily life.

• In an era in which time and space are shrinking, a realization of the importance of clear thinking about design and the direction of design efforts toward cultural progress.

• A clearer concept of design in its professional applications—of the distinction between true design and mere technical facility—of design as a method of thought leading to more effective solutions to creative problems.

• Deepening awareness of the integration of design with the social sciences—with the fine arts—with music—with literature—with education.

• Broadening of vision, freshening of ideas, sharpening of thinking, and stimulation of creative ability—brought about by the ideas discussed in the conference sessions and through personal contact with the thinkers responsible for them.

• Growth in professional standing—growth in knowledge—growth in confidence, strengthened by meeting designers from other cities, discussing similar problems and exchanging information.

• Additional technical knowledge, obtained incidentally from discussions with other individuals, from ideas expressed by speakers, from exhibits displayed, etc.

• Receipt of published reports of the Aspen conferences and other news and bulletins of design interest.

Membership in the organization consists of individual members, corporate members, and student members. The present membership is in the neighborhood of 500.

INTERNATIONAL SOCIETY FOR EDUCATION THROUGH ART
INSEA Secretariat,
Centre International d'Etudes Pedagogiques
Sevres (Seine-et-Oise), France

Through the combined efforts of The United Nations Educational, Scientific, and Cultural Organization (UNESCO) and a number of interested art educators throughout the world, the International Society for Education Through Art (INSEA) was established in 1951. Its aims and functions are well described in its brief and well-phrased constitution:

Preamble: The members of the International Society for Education Through Art, *believing* that: ART is one of man's highest forms of expression and communication;

that: CREATIVE ACTIVITY in art is a basic need common to all people;

that: EDUCATION THROUGH ART is a natural means of learning at all periods of the development of the individual, fostering values and disciplines essential for full intellectual, emotional and social development of human beings in a community;

that: ASSOCIATION on a world-wide basis of those concerned with education through art is necessary in order that they may share experiences, improve practices and strengthen the position of art in relation to all education;

that: COOPERATION with those concerned in other disciplines of study and domains of education would be of mutual advantage in securing closer coordination of activities directed to solving problems in common;

that: INTERNATIONAL UNDERSTANDING would benefit from a more completely integrated design and permanent structure for the diffusion of beliefs and practices concerning education through art, so that the right of man "freely to participate in the cultural life of the community, to enjoy the arts" and to create beauty for himself in reciprocal relationship with his environment, would become a living reality;

Resolve: TO SUPPORT an INTERNATIONAL SOCIETY FOR EDUCATION THROUGH ART in accordance with the foregoing statement of principles and beliefs . . .

The International Society for Education Through Art (INSEA) will sponsor the following activities:

1. Assemble and disseminate information concerning art education activities on a world-wide basis.

2. Publish a periodical journal which would include articles, book reviews, notes on sources and supplies of materials, notices of exhibitions; directory of persons, schools and organizations wishing to arrange exchanges of exhibits and materials.

3. Organize exchanges of materials, exhibitions, teaching portfolios, publications, visual aids.

4. Initiate research projects on special themes, in collaboration with national societies for art education.

5. Stimulate the formation of national societies for education through art in countries where these do not exist.

6. Support measures to improve facilities for art education in educational and cultural institutions and to improve the training and professional status of those responsible for art education.

7. Encourage and assist the organization of exchange visits and study abroad for art teachers.

8. Organize the periodical conferences of the members of the Society and cooperate with other organizations as necessary in the planning and preparation of meetings and manifestations, such as seminars, summer schools, conferences, and festivals, devoted to or related to education through the arts.

9. Cooperate with UNESCO in the execution of its programme for education through the arts, and with such other organizations as might engage in activities of a nature akin to the aims and purposes of the Society.

Membership in the International Society for Education Through Art is approximately 300.

NATIONAL ART EDUCATION ASSOCIATION
N.E.A. Building
1201 16th Street, N. W.
Washington 6, D. C.

In the late 19th and early 20th Century, several professional organizations were founded in different parts of the United States to provide service to art teachers and to encourage the exchange of ideas. These groups are now known as the Western Arts, Eastern Arts, Southeastern Arts, and Pacific Arts Associations, respectively. In 1947, members of these four groups formed the National Art Education Association which is now one of about thirty departments of the National Education Association. The first president of NAEA was Dr. Edwin Ziegfeld. Beginning in 1951, annual conferences of the four regional organizations were discontinued in favor of even-year conventions, in order to encourage attendance at the biennial conventions of the National Art Education Association held on the intervening, odd-numbered years. The NAEA met for the first time in New York in 1951, in St. Louis in 1953, in Cleveland in 1955, in Los Angeles in 1957, and again in New York in 1959. The NAEA's policy of holding its national biennial conventions in different parts of the country on a rotating basis has several distinct and important advantages:

1. It stimulates new local membership, many of whom will thereafter attend national meetings.

2. It develops leadership ability in local members who are catapulted into positions of responsibility by the mere fact that they are members of the host group. Many of these individuals continue to serve the organization in various positions of responsibility.

3. It awakens local interest in art education and brings extensive publicity to the state and city in which it is held.

The National Art Education Association also includes a number of individual members from foreign countries and a sizeable number of institutional members including museums, libraries, and art schools. The creed, adopted by its members, states:

Art experiences are essential to the fullest development of all people at all levels of growth, because:

They promote self-realization of the whole individual by integrating his imaginative, creative, intellectual, emotional and manual capacities and foster social maturity and responsibility through cultivating a deepened understanding of the problems, ideals and goals of other individuals and social groups.

Art is especially well suited to such growth because it encourages freedom of expression, emphasizes emotional and spiritual values, integrates all human capacities and universalizes human expression.

Art instruction should encourage exploration and experimentation in many media, sharpened perception of aesthetic qualities, increased art knowledge and skills, creative experience in significant activities and the realization that art has its roots in everyday experience.

Art classes should be taught with full recognition that all individuals are capable of expression in art, individuals vary markedly in motivations and capacities, and art is less a body of subject matter than a developmental activity. This is because art experiences are close to the core of individual and social development and because they pervade all phases of living. The National Art Education Association believes that *all* teachers should have basic training in art.

The functions and activities of the NAEA do not vary measurably from those of its regional affiliates, except in scale. The NAEA and its four regional affiliates issue publications which contain news of the organizations and list various services and research projects which have been performed in the field. One of the NAEA's most important functions is its role as "official" spokesman for the thousands of art teachers throughout the United States, many of whom are members.

A significant forward step was taken by the NAEA in 1958 when it established its first executive secretariat, naming Dr. Ralph Beelke, formerly of the U. S. Office of Education, to the post. Thus, in a little more than a decade after its founding date the NAEA rose to a professional status equivalent to other branches of education with offices in the National Education Association building in Washington, D. C.

Membership in the National Art Education Association is achieved through joining one of its four regional groups. The membership fee varies from one group to another, and includes subscriptions to all books and periodicals published by the national association as well as the regional group of the member's geographic area. The membership of the National Art Education Association is approximately 5,000, or about one-fourth of the 21,000 art teachers, in the United States.

The NAEA's regional associations are listed below in the order of their founding dates. (For application blanks and current business office address of a regional organization, write National Art Education Association, 1201 16th St., N.W., Washington 6, D. C.)

Western Arts Association. Office: 2304 Oxford Rd., Nashville, Tenn. The Western Arts Association includes members living in Arkansas, Colorado, Illinois, Indiana, Iowa, Kansas, Kentucky, Michigan, Minnesota, Missouri, Nebraska, New Mexico, North Dakota, Ohio, Oklahoma, South Dakota, Texas, and Wisconsin.

The Columbian Exposition held in Chicago in the summer of 1893 attracted educators from all parts of the country. On August 10th of that year, at a meeting held in the Chicago Manual Training School, "The Western Drawing Teachers' Association" was organized.

Eighty members, representing many sections of the United States, assembled for their first convention in the State Normal School at Milwaukee, May 3-5, 1894.

A sample of the ideals held by the charter members is indicated in the following extract from an address by Ada M. Laughlin, first president of Western Arts.

We meet hoping by mutual interchange of thought and experience to broaden our own horizon, free ourselves from all that is petty and uncharitable, stimulate our energies, elevate our individual ideas, and gain some knowledge of how we may concentrate our forces in that unity of action which shall tend to produce symmetrical development in the characters of those we teach. We recognize the divine right of childhood to the freedom which we so highly prize, to the privilege of learning obedience and self-command through voluntary self-mastery, gained by the proper training of natural instincts, and to utilize the abounding activity of childhood in our several ways and lay the foundation for natural healthy growth and a broad and liberal education.

Manual training teachers, appreciating the benefits that were accruing to members, were joining the organization in such numbers that the name was changed to the "Western Drawing and Manual Training Teachers' Association."

In 1907, the Western Drawing and Manual Training Association met in Cleveland, in joint session with the Eastern Arts Association and the Eastern Manual Training Association. This proved to be a meeting of epochal importance, taking on the character of a national organization. Here leading art educators of the east and west were brought together and the mutual exchange of ideas was recognized as of telling importance.

With the expansion of industrial and vocational education, the value of art education became more and more apparent to those engaged in these fields. Other departments were added to the organization, and the constitution again demanded a revision embracing the activities of all its membership. This was accomplished at the 25th annual convention, held in Chicago in 1919, when the Association became known as the Western Arts Association.

The "Ship." At a Western Arts meeting in Dayton, Ohio, the "Ship," a group composed of commercial exhibitors and their representatives, held its first joint meeting with the Association. The "Ship" had been "launched" at a Western Arts meeting in St. Louis in 1923. All members of the "Ship," representing manufacturers and distributors of art materials, equipment, and professional books and magazines, pledged themselves to promote the best interests of the Western Arts Association, socially and educationally. The "Ship" parties—and exhibit booths containing art materials, publications, and equipment—are always popular at national and regional conventions. The "Crew" now elects representatives who serve on the councils of all regional art associations as well as the NAEA.

The present membership of the Western Arts Association is approximately 1,500.

Eastern Arts Association. Office: State Teachers College, Kutztown, Pa. While the area officially covered by the Eastern Arts Association is east of Ohio and north of Virginia, it includes over 100 members from other states and countries.

The earliest record goes back to 1897 when the organization was known as the American Manual Training Association. In 1902 the organization's name was changed to the Eastern Manual Training Association. In 1906 it became the Eastern Art Teachers' Association and Eastern Manual Training Association. Conventions of the two groups are indicated as joint events with reports issued as one unit. At the Boston meeting of 1910 the name was changed again, this time to Eastern Art and Manual Training Teachers' Association. This is the date usually considered as the beginning of the Eastern Arts Association. At the time there were 640 members under the leadership of Henry Turner Bailey, educator and first editor of *School Arts* magazine. Since 1910, under the leadership of many outstanding art educator-presidents, the membership has grown steadily and the organization has become professionally strengthened.

The name Eastern Arts Association did not appear until 1915; however, the 1916 convention was announced as the "7th Annual Convention."

Of special interest to art education historians is a "Report of the First Meeting of the Eastern Art Teachers' Association," held in Brooklyn, New York, dated May 25, 1899. The report includes 82 *pages* of program events, covering three days of addresses and reports of committees. Listed in the program is a directory of 208 members, as well as an announcement (without dates) of the next meeting to be held in Boston at the Massachusetts Normal Art School. Apparently this group was entirely separate from the early Eastern Arts Association and did not continue to exist.

The present membership of Eastern Arts is approximately 3,000. Its biennial meetings in major eastern cities make it possible for members to familiarize themselves with the art collections of major art museums and galleries, as well as to discuss important professional matters.

Pacific Arts Association. Office: Arizona State College, Tempe. The Pacific Arts Association includes members living in Arizona, California, Idaho, Montana, Nevada, Oregon, Utah, Washington, and Wyoming. Its first meeting was held in San. Francisco in 1925. Professor A. B. Clark of Stanford University was the first president. Through the years, the Pacific Arts Association has kept abreast of up-to-date professional developments in the arts as well as art education and education in general. This group was one of the first to invite leading professional artists, architects, and designers to participate in art education conferences, utilizing them as speakers, exhibitors, demonstrators, workshop leaders, and resource people. At Los Angeles in 1957, PAA acted as host for an outstanding National Art Education Association convention. Among prominent architects and designers speaking at the convention were Richard Neutra and Charles Eames. The brilliantly conceived commercial exhibitors' booths at this conference were unified in style. They were devised and installed by students of Immaculate Heart College, under the supervision of Sr. Magdalen Mary. For examples, see the Visual Preface of this book.

The present membership of the Pacific Arts Association is in the neighborhood of 600.

Southeastern Arts Association. Office: 542 C Goldsboro Rd., N.E., Atlanta 7, Ga. The Southeastern Arts Association covers nine states: Alabama, Florida, Georgia, Louisiana, Mississippi, North Carolina, South Carolina, Tennessee, and Virginia.

This group was organized in 1930 at Spartanburg, South Carolina, and elected E. E. Lowry its first president. The second meeting was held in Atlanta in 1932. While the Southeastern Arts Association is only 25 years old, it has grown rapidly to a membership of approximately 400. SEAA members have an unusual opportunity to play a key role in fostering and strengthening the arts in all of the schools of the south.

In recent years the Southeastern Arts Association has issued increasing numbers of publications intended to strengthen art programs in the membership area.

NATIONAL COMMITTEE ON ART EDUCATION
21 West 53rd Street, New York 19, New York

The National Committee on Art Education is made up largely of a forward-looking group of artist-teachers and students, including representatives of every educational level from nursery school through college, and from professional art schools, art galleries, and museums. Sponsorship by The Museum of Modern Art provides the National Committee on Art Education with expert guidance and resource material from outstanding leaders in all the fields of the visual arts, as well as limited financial assistance to preclude the necessity of turning to commercial interests for subsidization. The members of the National Committee on Art Education are interested in developing a deeper understanding and broader implementation of creative art education and in improving instructional methods and the quality of students' aesthetic experiences from pre-school through college and adult education, includ-

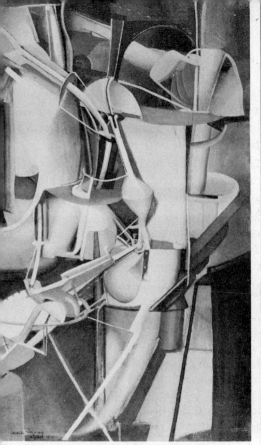

Marcel Duchamp's *The Bride*, one of many modern art works with which art teachers should become familiar during conventions in major cities.

The Museum of Modern Art, designed by Edward Stone, Philip Goodwin, and Philip Johnson, site of many National Committee on Art Education meetings.

ing the educational programs of art museums. Most members are also concerned with what they can do for the Committee as a whole and the aims it hopes to accomplish rather than what the Committee can do for them individually.

The National Committee on Art Education does not campaign for members, and hopes to hold its membership to a size which makes it possible for participants to think and work together effectively. Membership is, however, open to anyone who wishes to join.

The National Committee on Art Education is not only dedicated to the support of the arts in education, but is actively opposed to any educationally unsound trends to the misuse of art, and to those interests which undermine the individual's creative integrity through so-called "easy teaching" methods, fill-in color books, and inferior art materials.

At its annual spring conferences, the NCAE brings together people who teach at all age levels in all parts of the United States and Canada. Here they can exchange their ideas and be stimulated by outstanding speakers, exhibitions, and field trips. Its Newsletter publishes philosophic statements, new ideas, and activity reports. The NCAE issues publications, exhibitions, and visual aids which it prepares both independently and in cooperation with the Department of Education of The Museum of Modern Art.

As a result of a series of intensive professional meetings held during 1956-57, the Council of the National Committee on Art Education, under the leadership of Victor D'Amico, proposed that the Committee dedicate itself to the fulfillment of the following aims:

1. to give moral and practical support to art teachers in helping them provide creative opportunities for all children by

> opposing dictatorial or laissez-faire approaches, and the fallacy that anyone can teach art

> reaffirming the need for art teachers as those best qualified to foster continuous creative growth in the visual arts

> helping the art teacher find effective ways to foster creative growth through art

> encouraging the continuing education of classroom teachers in order to make them more aware of the concept of creativity as basic to all human experience and learning

2. to cooperate with institutions of higher education in improving the preparation of art teachers

3. to help attract qualified persons to the teaching profession

4. to stimulate young people to recognize the challenging role of teaching as a career and as a service to society

5. to contribute effectively to meeting the needs of our contemporary world by making parents, administrators, and the general public more aware of the importance of creative experience as a vital factor in the education of the individual

6. to point out the shortsightedness of so-called economies of time and/or money which curtail creative experiences in the schools at any age level

7. to promote significant study and research in the field of art education through individual efforts, study groups, and seminars

8. to join in organized opposition to the encroachment of art education by commercial enterprises offering products or activities damaging to the objectives of creative art education

9. to provide guidance, stimulation, and leadership for art experiences and programs outside the school.

The membership of the National Committee on Art Education is approximately 1,000, made up predominantly of art teachers and students of art education, but also including many professional artists, art museum personnel, classroom teachers, school administrators, interested parents, and other adults.

TRAVELING ART, INCORPORATED
Box 104
Bryn Mawr, Pennsylvania

Traveling Art, Incorporated, was established in 1954 by a group of Philadelphia-area artists, headed by Mr. Dolya Goutman, who were interested in showing their works to a broader segment of the public. At this writing, artist-participants pay a $5.00 membership fee, number about fifty, and include nationally-known artists such as Benton Spruance, Hobson Pittman, and Emlen Etting. Group exhibitions of members' work are circulated extensively through the United States and Canada, particularly to colleges and universities, and are now being extended to Europe. This nonprofit organization in its first three years of existence circulated exhibits free of charge, except for one-way transportation costs. Rising costs, plus an expanding program have made it necessary to add a nominal fee of $10.00 to each exhibit, for which T.A.I. furnishes twenty medium-sized paintings in simple frames. Some T.A.I. exhibits are: Contemporary Trends in American Art; Artists of Philadelphia; New Directions in Art; Painters Who Teach; and Contemporary Graphics (thirty drawings and prints).

State art organizations. Art educators in many states are now building strong art education associations with stimulating meetings and informative publications. State organizations provide opportunities to combine problems of local urgency with those which are more broadly professional. In addition to annual conventions, state art education organizations sponsor workshops, conferences, and seminars conducted by individual school systems and educational institutions within the state. In states such as New York, California, and Illinois, where the art teacher population is unusually large,

COURTESY KARL SCHLICHER, STEPHEN F. AUSTIN
STATE COLLEGE, NACOGDOCHES, TEXAS

Art education students participate in production of multicolor silk screen print covers for state art teachers association publication, *Texas Trends*.

it has been found desirable to form regional or zone groups within the framework of the state art teachers' association.

Other Organizations Which Influence Art Education. There are hundreds of educational and social organizations, clubs, societies, labor unions, guilds, and leagues which devote some of their time and money to the art interests of their members and members' families.

Art educators are fortunate in having the professional support of organizations such as the Association for Childhood Education International, whose credo calls indirectly for improved and extended art education:

1. To work for better understanding of children and better guidance for every child in the school, the home, and the community.

2. To strive for better conditions and facilities that contribute to the continuous growth and development of children.

3. To urge the improvement of existing educational services for children under six, and the extension of these services to more children.

4. To seek more well-prepared teachers and encourage pride in the profession.

5. To publicize the needs of children and the school program to parents, community workers, legislators and the general public.

Many national education associations recognize the necessity of the arts in the lives of all human beings and recommend that the arts become an established part of every curriculum. Obviously, art teachers should become active members of non-art as well as art organizations to the extent that their time, interest, and money will permit. In fact, an art teacher's comments and actions at a meeting of a non-art organization may have more positive effects than those made at a meeting of an all-art group.

5: Interest and Ability Levels in Art

FEW INDIVIDUALS are wholly typical of their age. In like manner, there is no one experience or medium in the arts which is perfectly suited for a person of a particular age; nor is there any group of experiences or media which we may say is the ideal combination for a certain age range. Concerning this, Frances Wilson has said:

A medium that is good in one situation may not be at all suitable in another. The total situation in which a medium is used is made up of many factors such as (1) the person using it, his experience, immediate mood and degree of integration (his personal environment) and what he wants to express, (2) the art teacher, his personality and skill and the degree to which he can identify with and contribute to the creativity of the person using the medium, (3) the total group and the degree to

Crayon has been used as a medium of art expression by professional artists. In *Abstraction,* Lee Drechsler brushed India ink over crayon and blotted the excess to remove all but the desired textural effect.

121

Creating three-dimensional constructions with toothpicks, balsa wood, and various other materials, joined with airplane cement, is an activity well suited for children in the eight to eleven year age range.

which they are contributing or opposing him and the degree to which they are making demands on the teacher at the moment the person needs help, (4) and the physical setting, what it contributes to or detracts from the person using the medium.*

Most of us are aware of the limitless variations in personality, social adjustment, art ability, size, and appearance, to name but a few characteristics found in any group of people of a given age. One should not expect two or more children of the same chronological age to react identically, perhaps not even *similarly*, to a given experience. *Yet there are certain general, broadly distinguishing characteristics of various interest and ability levels in art.*

As we examine some of the characteristics of art experiences for various age ranges, we should not lose sight of these principles:

1. The "ability levels" of art experiences *vary* from one individual to another:

A. *Current ability level.* Experiences performed on the current ability level are those with which the individual is already familiar and enjoys, but which do not unduly challenge him.

B. *Frustration level.* When the individual is expected to do far more (or much less) than he is able to do, he sometimes becomes frustrated.

C. *Instructional level.* Experiences which take the student beyond the current ability level, challenge him and deepen his interest and awareness within the general scope of his ability, without inducing frustration, are on what is known as the instructional level.

2. *No individual can be expected to fit exactly the characteristics of a given chronological age level.*

3. *If an individual possesses characteristics of a slightly younger or older level than his own, this does not necessarily mean he is retarded or specially gifted.*

4. *Variations in response should be encouraged and no one should be made to conform to a particular pattern.*

---

*Wilson, Frances, "Art Experience or Experience in Being," mimeographed pamphlet, Ithaca, New York, Cornell University College of Home Economics, May, 1955, p. 43.

To take further precautions against rigid classification of art experiences into specific chronological age categories, the various age ranges discussed here are overlapped, such as 2-5, 5-8, 8-11. Anyone familiar with five-year old children, for example, realizes that some look, behave, and create like four-year-olds, whereas others seem more like six or seven. The same is true of every age level, through adulthood, except that the range of variability increases rapidly on a chronological basis.

We should not attempt to classify, but rather encourage maximum individual growth through art by consistent and progressive emphasis on creativity and the deepening of aesthetic sensitivity in every year of a person's education and adult life.

Most of the materials and processes suggested here are common to all age levels and educational areas. Our aim is not to claim them as the exclusive property of art, but to show how they may be used creatively as part of the total development of the individual. We are concerned with *all* experiences with materials and processes which can be used in a creative manner.

PRE-SCHOOL AGE   2-5 YEARS

ART-EXPERIENCE NEEDS

Art experiences help young children develop more fully as individuals and prepare them to become members of social groups. They also prepare the child for the many creative art activities he will encounter as he progresses through school.

Art experiences are enjoyable as well as educational. As early as two years of age most children enjoy working with materials such as paint and clay. Through art, pre-school children can express personal experiences, thoughts, and feelings about people and things, or they may merely play with paint, clay, and various construction materials.

Parents find that art activities are ideal for rainy days, for children who are ill, and for active children who need physical rest periods. Teachers find that children become deeply absorbed in art activities, that they can be calmed as well as excited by them depending on the medium or activity used, and that through continuous study of a child's art expression a great deal can be learned about him.

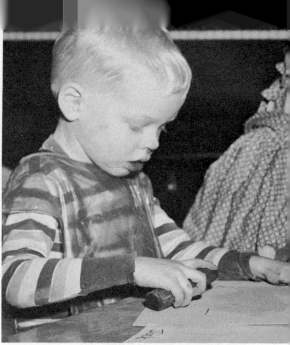

Even the selection of material is an art activity for very young children.

This three-year-old can achieve rapid, satisfying results by using a large stick of chalk which he can easily grasp.

Cleanup is an important activity. The child should not be rushed. If necessary teacher should set the faucet to avoid hot water burns.

The young child's natural interest in manipulating materials, plus occasional suggestions from a teacher, usually provides adequate motivation.

Suggested stimuli—2-5 years

As a child becomes interested in some object or activity he often needs to *express* his feelings by painting, modeling, or constructing. The means by which a child's interest may be aroused is called a "stimulus." For the very young child the stimulus may be unknown to him as well as to his parent or teacher, since his work often expresses feelings which he cannot put into words. Merely placing several jars of brightly colored paint, brushes, and paper before the young child may prove to be an adequate stimulus. The resulting art work may be no more than strokes and splashes of color but it will probably be satisfying to the child. Later on, recorded music, story telling, trips, telling about his own experiences, and some encouragement from the parent and teacher may prove to be effective stimuli.

Coloring books and adult drawings hamper rather than help a child to develop his creative abilities. These substitutes are not part of a child's normal experience, as they exceed his understanding and perceptual ability, and stifle rather than stimulate creative growth.

Suggested activities—2-5 years

Since some art activities require more coordination and intelligence than young children possess, it is important that those offered to children in this age range be within their current ability or instructional level. Among the art activities which are well suited to the pre-school child are: clay, paper pulp, or dough modeling; water painting on blackboards; drawing with large crayons and chalk; tempera painting; playing with blocks; torn and pasted colored paper work; finger painting; and stick printing.

Creative guidance—2-5 years

Well-planned but very little technical instruction is given the pre-school child. He needs the opportunity to express himself freely by experimenting with tools and materials which are within his interest and ability level. He should receive adequate encouragement during and following the activity. *But pre-school children should not be shown how to draw animals, faces, houses, or any object or person.* Such instruction only tends to confuse the child of two or three whose drawings and clay models are usually non-representational. "How-to-do-its" also harm the child of four or five whose changing symbols for objects and persons bear little resemblance to adult work.

There is, however, one form of technical instruction the parent or nursery school teacher may give; but only if *after considerable*

This is the first painting made by a boy aged two-years, two months. On several previous occasions he had made scribble drawings with crayon.

uninhibited experimentation the child has not discovered it for himself. Suggest (but don't demonstrate) other ways of working with materials, such as making spots of color with a brush, or "welding" clay by pressing pieces together with the finger tips, or pasting bits of paper, cloth, and wood on sheets of paper or cardboard.

The symbols for human figures developed and used by some children as they emerge from the 2-5 year age range are uniquely delightful, sometimes mystical, and often highly promising in quality. This shaded pencil drawing by a girl of four years, eleven months possesses design qualities and a feeling of fantasy. There is, of course, a vast difference between the child's inherent design sense and the professional artist's studied ability to produce paintings of significance.

THE NATURE OF ART WORK—2-5 YEARS

The child of one, two, or three does little more than play with art materials which are made available to him. Yet we know that this playing is important to his total growth and is expressive of his feelings about things as well as the nature of his personality. His swirls and scribbles in tempera paint afford him considerable pleasure. He scribbles for the sheer joy of scribbling, yet on occasion he will name a completed scribble to describe (or supplement) what he has been doing. His concentration upon and absorption in art activities, even for brief moments, is delightful to observe. The pre-school child should not be expected to draw something recognizable, nor should a search be made for traces of reality in his work. He should not be asked, "What is that?" Questions of this type would probably cause him to look at his work and try to think of something it suggests in order that he may satisfy the inquisitive parent or teacher. He might even be led to believe he has represented something that is actually not present in his concept or work.

Although no single art work can be said to be "typical" of this age range, it is known that between the ages of three and five most children learn to control their scribbles, can produce series of horizontal lines, spots of color, circular shapes, and sometimes (of their own accord) name some of these shapes "Mommy," "Daddy," or "me." By the time they are five or six, sometimes earlier, most children are capable of drawing, painting, or modeling objects which can be identified by adults. The development of such ability is a normal characteristic of child growth and should not receive undue attention.

PRIMARY SCHOOL AGE   5-8 YEARS

ART-EXPERIENCE NEEDS

Art offers one of the earliest means of personal expression and satisfaction for the child. He can learn to paint, model, and build before he learns to write. Through art the child gradually develops an understanding of the nature of things he has observed, touched, smelled, heard, or otherwise experienced. Creative art experiences are particularly important to his early educational development.

Visualizing one's experiences through art is a means of expressing more complex ideas and reactions than can be expressed through words. Subjects of current interest to the child in this age range are

127

This third grader's interpretation of a class field trip to the conservatory conveys an atmosphere of color, fragrance, dampness, and abundant growth.

understood and remembered more fully when he organizes the various elements into a two- or three-dimensional art work. Most primary classroom teachers realize, and every parent should know, that art expression is as natural for the young child as eating and sleeping.

Suggested stimuli—5-8 years

Many art materials, usually new to the child at this age, are stimulating in themselves. Once the child has developed satisfactory proficiency with them, however, additional stimuli become necessary. Among the stimuli which are well suited for children of primary school age are: recorded music (listening and imagining things to draw, paint, or model); story telling, pantomime, play acting, puppet shows, television programs, movies, slides, and filmstrips; and trips to places like the zoo, farm, firehouse, factory, or park. Children of this age are also deeply stimulated by unusual objects or animals brought into the classroom for study and observation.

Primary school children should not be encouraged to draw

directly from objects, to use coloring books, or to trace drawings made by others. However, *they should not be forbidden* to do these things, as it may call undue attention to harmful, stereotyped activities which are best quietly ignored. One might offset them with a comment such as, "I really think your own paintings are much nicer." Over a period of time, this approach usually proves effective.

Most children of this age form mental and emotional concepts based on their personal experiences. They should be encouraged to express these concepts (their own ideas) in a wide variety of art media.

SUGGESTED ACTIVITIES—5-8 YEARS

As the child grows older, he enjoys art activities which are more complex. In the primary school age range the child is anxious to explore all types of tools and materials, such as making applique designs on cloth, painting one color on another, mixing different media, building with cardboard boxes and wood, and brushing tempera color over lines and shapes drawn in crayon on paper.

Children in this age range also become interested in expressing and re-living their experiences rather than merely experimenting with materials. Since new processes and materials usually induce

Children are actively stimulated by brightly colored, variously shaped, textured collage materials, many of which are new to them. They enjoy pasting, stapling, sewing, tearing, and bending cellophane, pipe cleaners, colored paper, raffia, sandpaper, feathers, metal foil, and other materials.

Several important aims are achieved through crayon drawing on unbleached muslin chair back covers. These primary grade children have expressed themselves creatively and *personally*, used a combination of materials new to most of them, and have experienced the discipline of working on a surface which necessitates strength and motor coordination.

First grade children enjoy the freedom, rapid results, ease of application, and physical movement of potato and cellulose sponge printing. These activities serve as excellent foundations for later experiences in graphic arts.

people of any age to manipulate and experiment prior to making things or expressing ideas, a certain amount of preliminary scribbling should be expected.

Among the many art activities which seem to have special appeal to children in this age range are potato printing, chalk or tempera painting, simple stencilling, pasted paper construction, crayon etching, scrap material sculpture, drawing with sticks and ink, making collage pictures, and simple weaving. Numerous other art activities can be effectively used by modifying them to suit the interests and abilities of primary age children.

CREATIVE GUIDANCE—5-8 YEARS

The need for creative guidance at this level ranges from little in the early years to encouragement, precautions, and suggestions in the use of certain tools and materials in the later years. It should be remembered that technical suggestions are offered only after the child has experimented fully and indicated a need for help, except for the use of tools, such as pointed scissors, which might cause in-

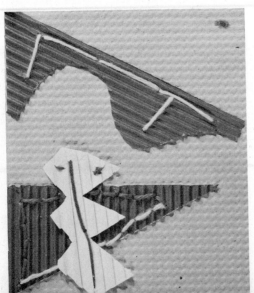

A cutout and sewn design created by a primary grade child. Made from yarns, corrugated paper, and a molded papier mâché packing sheet.

At any age, the use of actual or live subjects as stimuli and teaching aids is preferred to pictures or films. They have more interest and call for greater expression of movement.

jury. Sometimes it is helpful to have an experienced classmate demonstrate and describe the proper use of a tool.

Children should not, however, be told or shown how to draw trees, houses, faces, or other objects, by either their classmates, parents, or teachers. Instead, they should be encouraged to do original, creative work in which they can take personal pride, and for which they should be adequately praised and encouraged. The child asking, "Will you draw me a dog?" should be asked to look at and touch a dog, observe a dog in action, and compare dogs with other animals. If this does not help, the child should be encouraged to model, construct in paper, or otherwise create the dog which he cannot seem to draw. The child's symbols for dogs, or anything else, grow out of his personal experience. Any "dog" which an adult draws for a child grows out of the adult's personal experience, which is probably very different from the child's. An imposed, stereotyped symbol should never be substituted for a rich, personal experience at any age.

THE NATURE OF ART WORK—5-8 YEARS

Wide variation is typical of the work children produce during this age range. Primarily, they progress from the use of simple symbols for persons and objects, through stages of more or less definite concepts, such as the repeated use of horizontal ground and sky lines in the pictures of six or seven-year-olds, to wider interpretations of objects seen and drawn which are characteristic of the child of eight or nine. This three or four-year age range usually involves greater change in the nature of a child's art expression than is found in any other period of his development.

The transition period from scribbling through varied interpretations of subject matter is rapid for most children, but slow for others. For example, one cannot say that a given seven-year-old should have developed the *base line* type of symbol, since it may

Picasso's mural, *Guernica,* symbol of Nazi ruthlessness. Compare the child's drawing of a human head (below, upper right) with the thrown-back heads in *Guernica* (far left and right), and her horse's head (lower right) with Picasso's (upper left center).

Five-year-olds often reveal the "pure" feeling for movement and design found in famous works by great artists. This pencil drawing makes us think of certain elements in Picasso's *Guernica,* although the child had not seen it prior to the creation of this drawing.

develop much earlier, or later, or in rare cases not at all. The interested reader should study numerous examples of children's works of a given age range in order to understand better the variety in modes of expression at identical chronological age levels.

ART-EXPERIENCE NEEDS

Art provides one of the most effective means of helping children of this age level to understand better the relationship between things they see or experience and the way they express their reactions to these experiences. Careful guidance and adequate encouragement are needed because the child often feels that his interpretations of experiences are inadequate. He may feel that his paintings or models do not properly represent the subject involved in sufficient detail, in "correct" proportion, or in "proper" color. A child in this age range needs more technical instruction and specific encouragement than he has had before. He wants to model or draw things as he sees them, which is still quite different from the way things look to the adult. It is important, therefore, that the teacher or parent know how much help to give the child, what kind of help to offer, and when to offer it. Various group activities, such as crafts which require fewer representational skills, appeal to the child of this age because of his desire to be an active member of a "gang" of children of similar age and sex. Successfully produced art objects give him status in his "gang," and help him to bridge the temporary gap between representational skill and perceptual ability.

SUGGESTED STIMULI—8-11 YEARS

As a rule, stimuli which appeal to the "gang" are more effective than those which appeal to the individual. Discriminately chosen

CLARENCE, N. Y., PUBLIC SCHOOLS

During the 8-11 year age range children desire more instruction from their art teacher, yet they still wish to do their own work. Clay modeling is often helpful.

OKLAHOMA CITY PUBLIC SCHOOLS

Sixth graders, emerging from the "gang age," enjoy cooperative contacts with members of opposite sex, and find that sewing techniques suit boys as well as girls.

A spring field trip such as this provides a most vivid kind of experience, one which will not be forgotten because it is intensified through painting. This activity fosters deep thought and careful observation.

COURTESY VANCOUVER, B. C.,
SCHOOL BOARD

films, television and radio programs, slides, recordings, and group activities such as outdoor painting, field trips, games, and plays are usually good stimuli for children in the 8-11 year age range. Children of this age are more likely to become interested in an art activity demonstrated or described on television, radio, or film than one suggested by their teacher or parent. They have a strong urge to do things which children of their own age and sex are doing. They like activities which are somewhat complex, adventurous, and thrilling.

Boys and girls should be encouraged to use familiar media in a variety of ways and to interpret different subjects. If this fails to arouse them, they should be urged to try a new medium. Crayon etching or crayon batik, for instance, due to their complexity and startling results, are usually enjoyed even though someone might say, "I've already done that!"

Intermediate grade children also enjoy illustrating, modeling, or constructing things discovered in other learning areas such as social studies. The slow reader's teacher is always gratified when, having hesitated to let him give up much needed reading time to build an Indian village, he finds the art activity has stimulated the child to do more (and sometimes faster and better) reading than he had done before.

Suggested activities—8-11 years

More creative craft projects, with fewer drawing and painting activities, should be encouraged when a child is encountering difficulty in making things appear as he thinks they should. During this age range the child enjoys complex art activities which challenge his ability to construct, to remember steps in processes, and to produce useful as well as purely decorative objects.

The chart on pp. 136-137 suggests a few of the ways materials can be used in creative activities well suited to this and other age levels.

A periodic study and discussion of paintings, sculpture, crafts, architecture, and works in other media by artists of the past and present may be successfully carried out in the upper grades. Children can become conversant with an artist's technical and aesthetic problems as well as the content of his works and the characteristics of the society in which he lived. Early and continuing study of the arts, in addition to personal experimentation, is the best way to educate people in this important and too-often neglected aspect of our culture.

CREATIVE GUIDANCE—8-11 YEARS

Although the principle of not showing an individual how to draw or paint an object applies to all age levels, the child of 8-11 needs and often asks for technical assistance in making things look as they appear to the eye. The child also needs help in complicated processes such as construction, printing and casting.

An extensive library of visual aids is needed in order that children may see films, slides, filmstrips, photographs, and other illustrations of various subjects of current interest. This is particularly important when the actual object such as a lighthouse, locomotive, or circus is not readily available. If neither the actual object nor an illustration

Upper grade children prefer a certain amount of freedom in the use of tools and materials. They also like to produce objects which may be used at home, either as gifts for their parents or for their own rooms.

COURTESY DEPARTMENT OF ART, BOARD OF EDUCATION, CITY OF NEW YORK

Children appreciate such art studies as *The Painter's Daughter* by Thomas Gainsborough (1727-1788) because of the age of the subject and the relationship of the oil painting technique to the era in which it was used.

COURTESY METROPOLITAN MUSEUM OF ART, NEW YORK

	PAPER AND CARDBOARD	CRAYON AND CHALK	CLAY AND PLASTER	TEXTILES
tools and techniques	Cut with 　scissors 　knife 　paper cutter tear crumple fold weave roll paste model 　(papier mache) assemble 　(cardboard 　boxes)	draw 　(point, 　side) etch melt rub over 　textured 　surfaces combine 　with other 　media: 　water color 　tempera	squeeze punch pull press cut in strips (attach with slip) glaze fire carve model pour in self- 　designed cast 　of plaster 　or sand	sew by hand 　or machine stencil with 　crayon 　tempera 　lacquer 　shellac 　textile 　paint
types of activities or objects	puppets paper sculpture booklets masks shoe box 　"theater" murals painting printing Christmas 　ornaments mache 　modeling cleaning bag 　costumes party hats pasted strip 　construction 　of figures, 　animals, 　rhythm in- 　struments, 　totem pole 　miniatures	designs figures sketching murals posters stenciling 　greeting 　cards, place 　mats crayon etching chalk or wet 　bogus paper	animals figures bowls candle 　holders pin trays dishes earrings pins ash trays vases plaster-string 　spheres 　(over in- 　flated 　balloons) plastic (oil 　base) clay 　modeling	wall hangings toys puppets doll costumes purses boat sails wigwams rag dolls decorative 　banners for 　school festi- 　vals, parades kites (with 　wood or 　aluminum)

or model is available, the teacher or parent might make several varied sketches of the objects to satisfy the child's curiosity, urging him strongly to create the object in his own way without copying the examples. Making drawings or models for children to look at, but not copy, should be the *rare exception* rather than a common practice. *They should never be left on display after they have been drawn or constructed.* Some teachers carry a sketch book from pupil to pupil which they use to illustrate various points visually. Following the discussion, they close the book and carry it away.

136

STRING, YARN, ROPE	TEMPERA, WATER COLOR, CASEIN, OIL	WIRE AND METAL	WOOD	PRINT MEDIA

weave with
  spools
  tongue
    depressors
  looms
    Navajo
    box
    cardboard
knit
crochet
hook rugs
	paint with
	  flat
	  pointed
	  bristle
	  sable or
	  camel hair
	  brushes
	stencil
		cut
		bend
		pinch
		twist
		solder
		fasten
		pound
		turn
		polish
		heat
		cool
		weld
		braze
			saw
			build
			nail
			carve
			turn
			use in collage
			assemble
			  with
			  other
			  scrap
			  materials
				linoleum
				  and wood
				  cut tools
				craft,
				  sloyd, or
				  paring
				  knife
				hammer and
				  tacks
				celluloid,
				  copper,
				  zinc,
				  (acid)

weaving
  scarves, rugs,
  mats
knitting
  scarves, socks,
  sweaters
hooking
  rugs, wall
  hangings
	finger
	  painting
	murals
	designs
	pictures
	portfolio
	  covers
	stenciling
	tempera-over-
	  crayon
	  (batik)
		wire sculpture
		mobiles
		stabile
		scrap
		  material
		  sculpture
		dishes, trays
		spatter
		  printing
		  (with wire
		  screen,
		  toothbrush)
		sculpture in
		  iron, steel,
		  brass, copper
			furniture
			toys
			wheels
			masts for
			  boats
			looms
			armatures
			sculpture
			  carved,
			  toothpick,
			  scrap wood,
			  drift wood
				linoleum or
				  wood cut
				  printing
				vegetable,
				  stick, or
				  inner tube
				  printing
				monoprinting
				etching

This list of art materials and activities represents only a portion of those which are appropriate for this and certain other interest and ability levels. Although children in the 8-11-year-age range are able to handle sharp tools, they need very close supervision, in small groups of six to eight.

The proper use of tools, in potentially dangerous processes like linoleum block cutting and stenciling, should be carefully demonstrated either by an experienced pupil or teacher. In other processes, such as crayon resist and scrap material sculpture, children should be encouraged to experiment with or "invent" various working processes, since they may quickly discover useful techniques. In this way, children not only learn standard processes and techniques but actually devise new and improved ones as well.

THE NATURE OF ART WORK—8-11 YEARS

During this age range there is less rapid change than in prior years. However, children usually progress from the use of symbols (example, same symbol for house appears in numerous drawings or paintings) through the use of varied symbols for objects due to an increased awareness of environment and sharpened perceptual abilities, to a stage of development where they are dissatisfied with childlike symbols for things. Many children at the age of nine are interested in drawing, painting, or modeling objects as they seem to appear, using simple perspective, correct proportion, and true color.

Some children, however, indicate a subjective or non-realistic rather than an objective or realistic reaction to things perceived or otherwise experienced. This is usually evident in their work. The parent or teacher should therefore not expect all children to produce increasingly realistic work, and should expect to find some children at this and older age levels who prefer designs or abstractions and who may actually possess greater design sensitivity than the child who has greater representational ability. As Lawrence K. Frank and other responsible psychologists have shown us, however, it would be a serious mistake for teachers or parents to classify children into "types" who do or do not possess representational ability. All children are both objective and subjective, possess representational as well as "design" abilities, are extroverted and introverted, and can show love as well as hate, strength as well as weakness, and boldness as well as fear. In short, they are intricate, complex human beings, whose many sidedness makes classification into "types" a foolhardy enterprise. Even in rare cases where tendencies toward one or the other of these extremes are indicated, children are still educable and their personalities can be modified by elements of their human and physical environment.

Figure modeling and sketching directly from posed models or classmates is well suited to the interests and needs of junior high school students.

Outdoor sketching adds the professional touch to art activities often enjoyed by junior high school pupils who are anxious to participate legitimately in adult type activities. They are deeply stimulated by the challenge of sketching actual objects.

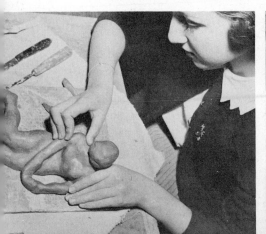

ART-EXPERIENCE NEEDS

The adolescent is anxious to achieve the characteristics as well as the pleasures of adulthood. It is understandable that he is interested in activities which will help him achieve these goals. A number of art activities not only serve these purposes but also tend to stabilize the youngster's irregular emotional development. In addition, they help him to adjust mentally and physically to his present age, give him status with his peers, and may even indicate for him a possible vocation, profession, or worth-while and enjoyable hobby.

The early adolescent's normal interest in his own bodily changes, as well as those of the opposite sex, may be satisfied to some extent through figure modeling and sketching in a way that is wholesome and normal. Drawing, painting, ceramics, jewelry making, working in wood, plastics, leather, and other craft activities afford the early adolescent means by which he can produce objects which are not childish or trivial (as some of his verbal and written expressions often seem to him) but which are high in quality and praised by members of his peer group whose opinions he holds in high esteem.

SUGGESTED STIMULI—11-14 YEARS

Care must be taken to select stimuli which have genuine appeal to the early adolescent, avoiding anything which might be considered childish. Fashion shows of boys' as well as girls' clothing, demonstrations by professional artists, movies or slides showing youngsters of this age or older engaged in sports, art activities, and hobbies, movies or illustrated talks on the lives and works of contemporary artists or old masters, and popular and classical music can be effectively used. Early adolescents are particularly impressed by people who can demonstrate competence in sketching, painting, ceramics, metalwork, and fashion designing. They are also motivated by field trips, movies, slides, and demonstrations having to do with interior design, architecture, and community planning as it relates to the improvement of their rooms, homes, and cities.

SUGGESTED ACTIVITIES—11-14 YEARS

Early adolescents are chiefly interested in art activities which are detailed in process and which involve skill. They seldom enjoy

A competent art teacher encourages each 11-14 year-old pupil to express his own personality in activities such as paper hat construction. Although children in this age range like to feel and act grown up, they must have lighter activities as well.

activities which *seem* childish, such as crayon drawing on paper, since they are interested in developing sophistication. Craft and construction-type activities are especially well suited to youngsters in this age range because:

1. they eliminate to some extent the youngster's tendency to impress others with subject matter and pictorial representation; and

2. they are sufficiently complicated to require skills which youngsters of this age are anxious to acquire and demonstrate.

Some of the creative activities well suited to this age level are: paper sculpture; marionette making (with stage, scripts, etc.); clay modeling of figures and animals; pasted-paper construction of figures, animals, or abstract shapes; wood and plaster carving; silk screening; and building scale models of "ideal" rooms, homes, or communities in which the youngster would like to dwell.

Also satisfactory are activities such as figure and portrait sketching, outdoor drawing and painting, fashion illustration, dream inter-

Observing and discussing works by important artists, initiated in the lower grades, is intensified during the 11-14 year age range. A good example is this sculpture by Kenneth Armitage, a semi-abstract interpretation of *Family Going for a Walk*.

pretation paintings, drawings or paintings interpreting popular or classical music, and murals depicting elements of school life such as sports or social affairs.

A knowledge of historic and contemporary art masterpieces by famous painters, sculptors, designers, and architects will provide cultural information needed by all adults plus a certain amount of deserved prestige for the young teenager. "Picture of the Week," "Industrial or Motor Car Designer of the Month," and other features selected by the class, help to dramatize and personalize various art areas being studied.

CREATIVE GUIDANCE—11-14 YEARS

Because of their interest in achieving realistic likenesses or good designs, adolescents frequently ask for technical assistance. In this case, the teacher should attempt to describe the appearance of the object in question by referring to examples of the actual object, either in life or in films, slides, and reproductions. Should this not suffice, different methods of working (i.e., gesture and scribble methods of sketching) in a given medium might be suggested or demonstrated.

Suggesting a different medium of expression such as clay, plaster, wood, wire, yarn, fabric, or cardboard, may also help the youngster to solve problems of appearance and design which he cannot seem to overcome in drawing or painting. The importance of personal integrity in the production of art works should be understood by the adolescent, and in turn he should receive proper praise for every creative idea and product. It is a great opportunity for the instructor who is dedicated to improving the art program. Serious development is needed in many communities.

THE NATURE OF ART WORK—11-14 YEARS

Whether the art work of the adolescent is realistic and representational or designed and abstract, it is usually produced with careful regard for technique and detail.

Youngsters consciously begin to incorporate principles of design such as rhythm, balance, and emphasis into their art works, and become progressively more critical of design qualities in the work of their classmates as well as professional artists. Their drawings and paintings often give evidence of the needs and characteristics of early adolescence: awareness of awkwardness, interest in personal appearance and members of the opposite sex, participation in adult-type activities, and demonstrations of individual skill.

Craft-type activities are more likely to reveal the young adolescent's understanding of detailed processes and design principles. In drawing and painting, he is likely to use familiar stereotypes to represent faces, hands, trees, which he knows will turn out all right and will appeal to, or draw a sympathetic laugh from, his classmates.

HIGH SCHOOL AGE   14-18 YEARS

ART-EXPERIENCE NEEDS

This is one of the most vital spans of years for developing lasting interests. Although high school art courses have traditionally been elective, there are a number of art experiences which *all* girls and boys should have prior to the termination of their formal education. Some high schools require all students to take at least one year of art.* Other schools have solved this problem by providing superior art instruction, thus increasing numbers of students in elective art courses. Whether art courses are required or elective, most high school administrators and teachers clearly recognize the importance of creative expression and aesthetic judgment. But because many institutions of higher education do not recognize pre-college art courses for entrance credit (although, paradoxically, they require art in their own curricula!), it is difficult to include art courses in many high school students' schedules.

Two of our most fundamental needs, clothing and shelter, can be more fully, pleasurably, met through skills and understanding acquired in a high school art course. Through art, students can learn which clothing styles are best suited to their personality and appearance, and in many cases they can learn to design some of their own clothes. Through art they can also acquire vitally important information concerning contemporary architecture, interior design, community planning, modern painting, and sculpture.

Beyond the obvious and urgent need for "consumer" art experiences, there is also a need for *actual creative experiences* in painting, drawing, crafts, and jewelry making, to name but a few. Only a few students will become art teachers or enter the professional art field,

---

* One year of art is required of all students in the public academic senior high schools of New York City and Chicago.

142

In addition to a required year of art for all high school students, there should be available elective courses in oil painting, sculpture, graphic arts, and crafts.

but all will utilize art knowledge every day of their lives. In addition, many students will join the growing ranks of adult art hobbyists.

Suggested stimuli—14-18 years

Although most high school youngsters are still in the midst of the critical adolescent period, they tend to become more cooperative and accept greater responsibility. They have begun to acquire some of the adult characteristics for which they have been so diligently striving. Keeping these factors in mind, one should select stimuli which are well suited for this age level.

An appropriate stimulus might be a demonstration or illustrated talk by a competent fashion designer, interior designer, ceramic sculptor, or architect. Students can see the relationship between these demonstrations and their personal needs. With adequate guidance, further study, and by personally designing for their own wardrobes or environment, students can develop a lasting interest in art.

Also excellent stimuli are: field trips to model homes, planned communities, and art galleries; writing "career information" letters to famous fashion illustrators, artists, interior designers, and architects; educational movies; slides; filmstrips; and personalized discussions of good design in furniture, dress, jewelry, painting, sculpture, photography, and architecture.

Suggested activities—14-18 years

Youngsters like art activities which are purposeful as well as creative. Consequently, they enjoy designing and making their own clothes and jewelry; designing their future homes, apartments, kitchens, hobby shops, and automobiles; learning about (and producing) paintings and sculpture they would like to own; learning

143

about the design qualities of various industrially produced utensils, appliances, and vehicles; and visiting communities planned for better living.

Adolescents also continue to enjoy art activities such as sketching each other, painting out-of-doors, producing murals for the school, making three-dimensional posters for co-curricular activities, making greeting cards, printing drapes and clothing fabrics, and weaving. Every youngster in this age range can learn to produce artistically satisfying objects in at least one art medium. The alert teacher provides a wide variety of art experiences in order that the student may develop this proficiency and the subsequent satisfaction which it provides.

CREATIVE GUIDANCE—14-18 YEARS

The relative maturity of high school students permits the instructor to discuss openly with them the need for being original and creative in their expression. Their understanding of this need permits the instructor to demonstrate occasional processes and techniques without the usual danger of copying. This should not, however, be taken to mean that students should be shown how to draw, paint, model, or construct various objects. Here, as on all other age levels, the individual student should be encouraged to experiment with each new medium, and be urged to try other media when a certain one proves unsatisfactory.

Following group experimentation with a given medium, such as cardboard for the construction of a model kitchen or workshop, students who have developed different techniques might be asked to demonstrate them to class members. Other techniques might be suggested or demonstrated by the instructor. By techniques we mean ways of handling materials and tools, and not short cuts to use in portraying the appearance of subjects. The actual appearance and design of any subject chosen by the student should be developed individually, in a creative manner. Advice on how to hold and manipulate tools or join and finish materials may help him better to express his original idea.

THE NATURE OF ART WORK—14-18 YEARS

An essential aspect of the consumer type of art education advocated for this age range is actual creative activity in a variety of media. A real understanding and appreciation of the various art ideas included in consumer art education (clothing design, interior design, contemporary architecture, industrial design, painting, and sculp-

1 DRAPERIES, LIGHTPROOF, CAN BE EXTENDED TO CENTER OF DOOR
2 GAS OUTLETS
3 MASTER GAS VALVES
4 FILE CABINET; BUILT-IN RECORD PLAYER ON TOP
5 15 FT. BY 35 FT. PATIO FOR SKETCHING PAINTING, SCULPTURE
6 CORRUGATED TRANSLUCENT FIBER GLASS OVER 10 FT. BY 15 FT. AREA AT ONE END
7 TEACHER'S WARDROBE AND PERSONAL ART SUPPLIES
8 FILE CASE FOR SMALL MOUNTED REPRODUCTIONS
9 MOUNTED REPRODUCTIONS BIN BELOW, CABINETS ABOVE (ENTIRE WALL)
10 OIL AND TUBE TEMPERA STORAGE, STORAGE CASE FOR TRIPOD EASELS AND ALUMINUM AND MASONITE DRAWING HORSES
11 TACKBOARD
12 CORRIDOR DISPLAY
13 EXTENDED DISPLAY CASES, TACKBOARDS ALONG ENTIRE CORRIDOR HALL
14 DEEP DISPLAY CASE FOR MANNIKEN, LARGE SCULPTURE, ETC.
15 BOOKS AND MAGAZINES
16 CABINETS OVER WORK COUNTER
17 SMALL REFRIGERATOR FOR FILMS, CHEMICALS
18 SINK
19 OPEN STORAGE
20 PROJET SHELVING, THREE SECTIONS
21 SLIDING CHALKBOARD AND STORAGE ASSEMBLY, PROJECTION SCREEN OVER

22 RESERVE SHELVING MODIFIED TO BE 18 INCHES DEEP, THREE SECTIONS
23 PORTABLE POWER TOOL STORAGE CAS, HAND TOOL STORAGE RACKS OVER
24 RESERVE SHELVING
25 HAND TOOL STORAGE
26 LUMBER STORAGE 12 FT. LENGTHS
27 DAMP BOX, CLAY PROJECTS SHELVING, THREE SECTIONS
28 LARGE PAPER CUTTER ON COUNTER
29 SLIDE PROJECTOR, AND PROJECTION TABLE ON
30 CUPBOARDS
31 FILES
32 TEACHER'S BOOKS
NOTE— ONE EASEL, CRAFT SPACE, GRAF SECTION OR SCULPTURE STAND SH BE RESERVED FOR TEACHER
32-A 2'X2' SLIDE STORAGE CABINET
33 SWIVEL-TYPE PLASTIC ARM CHAIR
34 CONFERENCE CHAIRS
35 CONFERENCE AND TEACHER'S DESK
36 TABLE AND FOUR CHAIRS
37 TRIPOD EASELS
39 TABORETS FOR HOLDING PALETTES
40 MOLDED PLASTIC ARM CHAIRS AND SUSPENDED WALL LIGHT
41 WEATHERPROOF TURN-TOP TABLES
42 MOVABLE MARBLE INKING SLAB

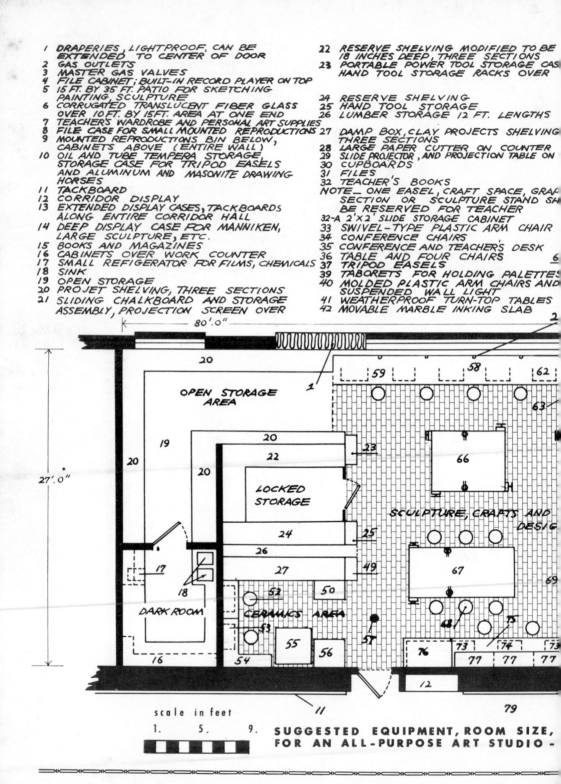

80'.0"

27'.0"

OPEN STORAGE AREA

LOCKED STORAGE

DARK ROOM

CERAMICS AREA

SCULPTURE, CRAFTS AND DESIG

scale in feet

1.   5.   9.

SUGGESTED EQUIPMENT, ROOM SIZE,
FOR AN ALL-PURPOSE ART STUDIO -

For discussion of this plan, see A

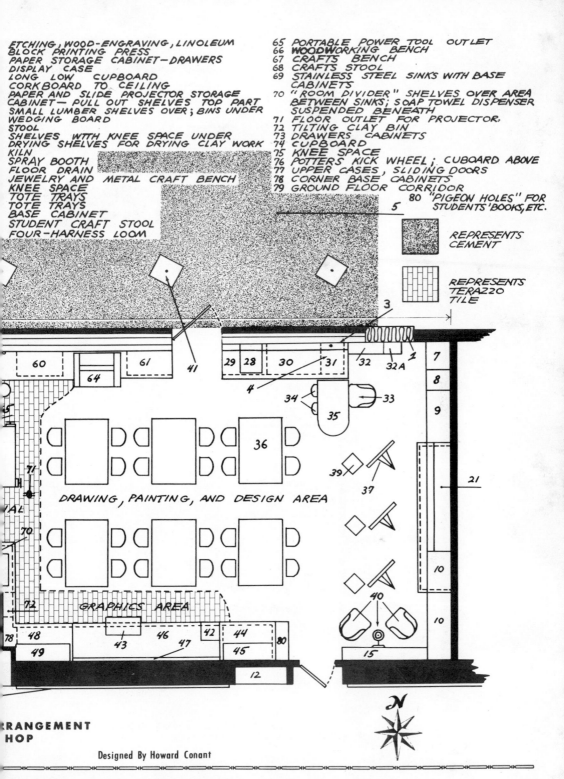

ETCHING, WOOD-ENGRAVING, LINOLEUM
BLOCK PRINTING PRESS
PAPER STORAGE CABINET—DRAWERS
DISPLAY CASE
LONG LOW CUPBOARD
CORKBOARD TO CEILING
PAPER AND SLIDE PROJECTOR STORAGE
CABINET— PULL OUT SHELVES TOP PART
SMALL LUMBER SHELVES OVER; BINS UNDER
WEDGING BOARD
STOOL
SHELVES WITH KNEE SPACE UNDER
DRYING SHELVES FOR DRYING CLAY WORK
KILN
SPRAY BOOTH
FLOOR DRAIN
JEWELRY AND METAL CRAFT BENCH
KNEE SPACE
TOTE TRAYS
TOTE TRAYS
BASE CABINET
STUDENT CRAFT STOOL
FOUR—HARNESS LOOM

65 PORTABLE POWER TOOL OUTLET
66 WOODWORKING BENCH
67 CRAFTS BENCH
68 CRAFTS STOOL
69 STAINLESS STEEL SINKS WITH BASE
CABINETS
70 "ROOM DIVIDER" SHELVES OVER AREA
BETWEEN SINKS; SOAP TOWEL DISPENSER
SUSPENDED BENEATH
71 FLOOR OUTLET FOR PROJECTOR.
72 TILTING CLAY BIN
73 DRAWERS CABINETS
74 CUPBOARD
75 KNEE SPACE
76 POTTERS KICK WHEEL; CUPBOARD ABOVE
77 UPPER CASES, SLIDING DOORS
78 CORNER BASE CABINETS
79 GROUND FLOOR CORRIDOR
80 "PIGEON HOLES" FOR
STUDENTS' BOOKS, ETC.

REPRESENTS
CEMENT

REPRESENTS
TERAZZO
TILE

DRAWING, PAINTING, AND DESIGN AREA

GRAPHICS AREA

RRANGEMENT
HOP

Designed By Howard Conant

This semi-abstract opaque water color interpretation of buildings at night painted by 15-year-old Gail Duncan shows the quality level which high school students are capable of attaining.

This liberal arts college student has become deeply interested in three-dimensional design as a result of introductory courses in art. She is working on a cellular-type construction probably derived from a study of the work of Buckminster-Fuller.

ture) is brought about by *combined* study and experimentation, not by reading, visiting, looking, and listening alone.

The designs which high school age students create as part of their study of art areas vary from poor to superior in art quality, depending to some extent upon their preference for representational or abstract modes of expression as well as their previous experience in art expression and their native ability. Students with little representational skill may produce an unsatisfactory architectural pencil sketch for a model house, for example, but yet may produce excellent models made of balsa wood, celluloid, sponge, and other materials.

The teacher of art is often able to identify some of his students' emotional, intellectual, and physical needs by carefully studying the subject matter they select and the degree of craftsmanship they employ in expressing it. In so far as he is able, the good teacher attempts to meet those needs which are within the scope of his program. He refers special problem cases to the proper guidance, psychological, or medical personnel. All high school students should be encouraged to develop to the *fullest* extent any special interests or abilities in art, since it is from this age group that the artists of the immediate future will come. Early identification and encouragement of art talent in a majority of secondary schools could strengthen immeasurably the culture of contemporary civilization.

COLLEGE AGE: GENERAL EDUCATION AND LIBERAL ARTS

ART-EXPERIENCE NEEDS

Nearly every area of living is affected by art. Cooking utensils, automobiles, homes, even entire communities are designed by artists. The paintings, fabrics, and furniture with which we supplement the bare essentials of dwellings are designed by artists. Through the study of art one learns to exercise critical judgment in the selection of these objects. *Every young man and woman can put to immediate and practical use the understandings and skills acquired through experiences in art.*

Krevitsky has set forth reasons for offering art at the college level:

1. to provide for lifetime habits of participation and enjoyment.
2. to continue the cultural training initiated in the lower grades, or to compensate for gaps in cultural experience.
3. to provide direct experience of an appreciative as well as creative nature.
4. to provide for proper personality development through normal use of one's senses and capacities.
5. to provide release from tensions created by fact-finding and memorization.
6. to provide a means of using the senses as well as the intellect, the body as well as the mind.
7. to provide an atmosphere conducive to the reactivation of original experiences of childhood wonder, and to create new experiences.*

SUGGESTED STIMULI—COLLEGE (GENERAL EDUCATION AND LIBERAL ARTS)

One of the most effective stimuli for people of college age is the *demonstrated* usefulness of a given activity or area of study. However, they are also interested in art activities which are purely creative such as oil painting, sketching, two- and three-dimensional designing, clay modeling, and plaster or wood carving.

Some stimuli which often interest college students in further study and experimentation in art are illustrated lecture-discussions on contemporary architecture and interior design, sculpture, paint-

---

*Krevitsky, Nik, "Art in the College Program: Theory vs. Practice," *Art Digest,* Dec. 1, 1952, p. 21.

ing, and clothing design. They are also stimulated by movies such as: *Birth of a Painting; The Photographer; Alexander Calder, Sculpture and Construction; Frank Lloyd Wright, California Architecture;* and *The City.* They enjoy and profit from field trips to interior design shops, contemporary homes, art galleries, museums, and planned communities. A college youth is mature enough to study the stage design, figure grouping, costuming, and script structure of television shows, stage productions, and motion pictures.

SUGGESTED ACTIVITIES—COLLEGE (GENERAL EDUCATION AND LIBERAL ARTS)

Activities which combine purely creative experiences with practical applications are perhaps the most satisfactory.

One of these activities is ceramics, in which nearly every student can develop satisfactory proficiency. After he has experimented with moist clay in a purely experimental fashion and has learned its characteristics and limitations, he proceeds to the construction of useful objects such as ash trays, vases, dishes, and lamp bases.

Another excellent activity is linoleum block cutting or silk screen printing, where the pleasures of becoming familiar with the necessary tools and materials usually precede the designing and reproduction of greeting cards, draperies, and articles of clothing.

Among other art activities of interest to college men and women is the construction of mobile and stabile sculpture. In this somewhat complicated activity students are confronted with fascinating problems of balance, motion, and space, and they learn the characteristics and use of a wide variety of materials such as wire, cardboard, various adhesives, bits of driftwood, plastic, tin, glass, and wood. Following their initial experimentation, a surprising number of people become interested in creating mobiles and stabiles to be placed in their own homes.

CREATIVE GUIDANCE—COLLEGE (GENERAL EDUCATION AND LIBERAL ARTS)

College students usually prefer to experiment and thus become acquainted with tools and materials prior to making something. But these young adults soon tire of purely manipulative activity with paint or any other medium of expression. They want to know how to hold a brush—and how to use it to blend colors into one another. They want to know how to place clay on a potter's wheel—and shape it into an attractive, sometimes useful shape. Non-art college stu-

Technical instruction, such as the first steps in reed basket weaving, can greatly encourage students without making them imitators. The size, shape, color and texture of the objects they produce, however, can be as much their own as are their interpretations in painting and sculpture.

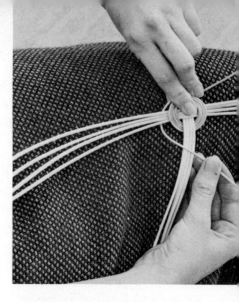

dents need to be shown certain ways of working with materials, yet they should be encouraged to develop personal techniques through experimentation. The amount and type of technical instruction given varies, depending upon the medium or process being used. In water color painting, for example, little, if any, technical instruction has to be offered until students encounter problems requiring help.

Prior to student participation in linoleum block cutting, instructors often demonstrate effective and safe ways of working with tools. The same is true for stencil knives, ceramic kilns, and gas torches. Students need to be warned in advance about the dangers inherent in careless handling of tools and pieces of equipment.

THE NATURE OF ART WORK—COLLEGE (GENERAL EDUCATION AND LIBERAL ARTS)

College slide lectures and gallery tours which were once concerned chiefly with memorization of names, dates, and places, are now less rigid and fact-laden and are supplemented by studio experiences so that students may better understand the underlying aesthetic qualities and meanings of art works. In these lecture-studio classes non-art students are encouraged to work out their own designs and techniques in a variety of media. These personal experiences are planned to enrich the student's understanding of the art productions of others, and are not intended primarily for the development of professional art skills. The art instructor does not expect non-art students to produce works of art, nor does he expect non-art history majors to memorize the footnote data of the arts. His chief concern is in developing a sincere, deep, and lasting interest in the subject. Occasionally, as a result of consumer-type lecture-studio activities, unusual interests and advanced abilities are discovered, and the student is encouraged to take advanced courses or even to consider some branch of art as a career.

Because most students taking art as part of a general education or liberal arts program are far from being talented artists, the emphasis in studio activities is placed upon the enjoyment and understanding of various art media. The fact that a student cannot develop the ability to draw or model artistically should *not* be the basis for a low grade! Experience in teaching art to non-specialist college students has shown that if they are encouraged to work in a wide variety of art media, most of them will probably develop satisfactory proficiency in at least one. They will develop a much deeper understanding of the aesthetic problems confronted by professional artists if they personally experiment with media used by these artists. Most important of all, however, is the fact that a well-taught lecture-studio art course will give non-art majors a sound basis for a lifelong interest in and understanding of the arts.

Among other art activities of interest to non-art students at the college level is *interior design*. Students enjoy making model homes as well as miniature furniture pieces, rugs, drapes, and other household items. This activity is often immediately useful in planning the interiors of dormitory rooms, apartments, or homes, and in purchasing well-designed furniture and appliances. But as in all art activities for non-majors, great care must be taken not to let model making monopolize the entire course.

COLLEGE AGE: ELEMENTARY TEACHER EDUCATION

ART-EXPERIENCE NEEDS

Today's elementary school teacher is theoretically responsible for every aspect of his pupil's education, including reading, writing, arithmetic, social studies, science, physical education, music, literature, spelling, industrial arts, homemaking, and art. In school systems that have special teachers and consultants, this responsibility is shared. Nevertheless, the final responsibility to see that each child participates to the extent of his ability in a complete and well-balanced educational program rests squarely on the shoulders of the grade teacher.

Like most active experiences, art is as much fun as it is work,

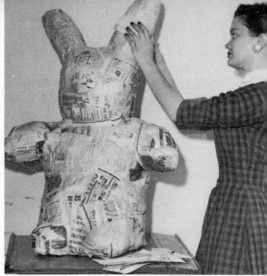

COURTESY KARL SCHLICHER, STEPHEN F. AUSTIN STATE COLLEGE, NACOGDOCHES, TEXAS

Papier mâché construction is well suited to the elementary education student's need for expression and an understanding of an art medium future pupils will use.

The padding has been covered with several layers of pasted newspaper strips. When completely dry, it will be painted with tempera colors. Later, it may be coated with shellac.

and being responsible for certain aspects of art teaching is a pleasure, provided the elementary school teacher has an adequate art education background. An adequate background for supplemental art teaching would take at least the equivalent of 8 college semester credit hours to accomplish. Included in the elementary education student's courses in art education should be an opportunity to express his own feelings in a variety of art media and develop satisfactory personal proficiency in at least one. Secondly, he needs to know how to foster creative art experiences for his future pupils. Finally, he needs to know as much as possible about the subject of art in order that he may lay the important foundation for later "consumer education" learning experiences in art.

Suggested stimuli—college (elementary teacher education)

Nearly every college student has an interest in art activities. In the freshman and sophomore years this interest is usually centered about personal expression in the arts, rather than in working with children. Since the teacher education curriculum is crowded with many important courses, it is necessary to arouse student's interest in children's art education as well as their own personal expression.

Among the more effective stimuli for arousing such an interest

150

are: visiting classrooms where children are engaged in art activities and observing their relaxed demeanor yet intense interest; discussing means by which art activities are effectively introduced to children of various ages; viewing films which are known to be effective, such as *The Beginning of Picture Making, Understanding Children's Drawings, Children Are Creative,* and *Picture Making at the Gang Age;* and, perhaps most important, engaging in actual teaching, which gives one first-hand experience with the deep pleasures children derive from art activities as well as the satisfaction of guiding them in their work.

For developing elementary education students' interest in personal art expression, several stimuli are useful: mere contact with a college art teacher who will encourage each student to develop to the maximum of his individual interest and ability, yet *not* expect professional work; art films such as *Braque* or *Matisse;* sketching trips; visits to art museums or galleries; and membership in clubs where art activity and discussion periods are regular features.

SUGGESTED ACTIVITIES—COLLEGE (ELEMENTARY TEACHER EDUCATION)

Until secondary education includes a wide variety of producer and consumer-type art activities for all youth, it will be necessary for college students majoring in elementary education to elect art courses which will provide them with consumer and producer art experiences as well as a knowledge of art activities suitable for the children they will teach. They will need to have firsthand experiences in many two- and three-dimensional art activities such as painting, sculpture, and construction in wood and cardboard; experiences in designing clothing, buildings, interiors, and engaging in other consumer education art activities. They must also have experiences working with children engaged in art activities. Obviously, such a broad introduction to personal art expression, art in everyday life, and the teaching of art to children requires a considerable block of time, certainly no less than the equivalent of four class hours per week over a two year period, or a minimum of eight college credits.

Most of the art activities previously listed in this chapter are desirable on the college level as well. In addition, certain others might be added, such as: studying examples of child art; preparing exhibitions and displays; collecting reference materials which will stimulate rather than inhibit creativity in children; making murals with two- and three-dimensional materials; and making puppets, building sets, writing scripts, and giving shows for children.

151

CREATIVE GUIDANCE—COLLEGE (ELEMENTARY TEACHER EDUCATION)

The creative teaching of future elementary teachers is very important. Since they probably come in contact with more children than do other adults, their potential influence upon the creative development of large numbers of children is far greater than that of persons in any other category. Students of elementary teacher education, like other young adults, can quickly be brought to an understanding of the importance of creativity in art as well as many other areas of living. This understanding will lessen the dead-end temptation to copy sometimes found at earlier education levels.

Because many teachers teach as they have been taught, it is of special importance for the college art instructor of elementary education students to maintain the highest standards of creativity. If it is difficult for a student to represent a tree which is personally satisfying to him, this may be due to the medium in which he is working and not the subject. Therefore, he should be encouraged to experiment in as many different types of media as possible. When he finds the medium that is satisfying to him, he may also find the solution to the problem of representing the trees. But he, as well as his future pupils, should also understand that after the age of eight or ten only a few individuals are able to draw or model things in a personally-satisfying representational manner.

THE NATURE OF ART WORK—COLLEGE
(ELEMENTARY TEACHER EDUCATION)

Elementary teacher education students enrolled in art courses were once expected by their college art instructors to produce art work of professional calibre. If they did not they failed the course or received a low, at least mediocre, grade. Fortunately, most art instructors now realize that individual psychological differences affect the nature of art work students produce. As in junior high school, some students produce works which are more or less designed in appearance, while others tend more toward the realistic. Some non-art college students can draw, paint, or model with fair representational skill. Others cannot grasp the essentials of perspective, color, or proportion because their psychological constitution is such that they react more emotionally than intellectually to various stimuli. Today's college art instructor does not expect the same type of art work from all of his students. He permits them a wide choice of media and processes and assumes that various individuals will spend varying lengths of time in art activities, dependent upon their interests and abilities.

This should in no way be construed as an excuse for low-quality or careless work. Nearly all college-level, non-art students can produce high quality work if they have adequate and suitable art materials and a good place in which to work; if they have ample opportunity and time for experimentation; if they have received adequate (but not stereotyped) stimuli and technical assistance from competent instructors; if they have chosen art activities and media on the basis of personal interest; if they have sufficient time; and if they are free from worry about final grades based on professional competence.

COLLEGE AGE: ART TEACHER EDUCATION

ART-EXPERIENCE NEEDS

The primary reason for offering art experiences to future art teachers is to help them prepare as fully as possible for their responsibilities to the children or adults with whom they intend to work. This requires a combination of experiences in creative art activities, in the philosophy of teaching, and in general education, to name but a few broad areas. No single area of experience, such as the development of art skills in drawing, painting, and sculpture, has been found to be adequate for the preparation of art teachers.

Shown here is *Balanced Sculpture* by Lynn Chadwick, constructed of iron and composition metal. Original art works should be available for study in the college art gallery.

Even highly skilled and imaginative professional artists are often unable to communicate effectively with their students. On the other extreme, the person who knows only the methods of teaching is seldom able to inspire his pupils to creative output because of his lack of personal ability and experience in any medium. The person with a rich general educational background probably realizes more clearly than others the need for cultural regeneration through the arts. However, unless he has an adequate art education background he is unable to contribute effectively because of deficiencies in personal creative development and a lack of understanding of how art is taught to others. Most art education departments today offer combinations of experiences in creative activities, the philosophy of teaching, and general education courses as the best known means of preparing teachers of art.

Suggested stimuli—College (Art Teacher Education)

Because of the complexity and scope of contemporary art education, it is necessary that stimuli be of intensity sufficient to cause students to engage voluntarily in related activities for which instructional time is not available. The intensity of these stimuli is further necessitated by the art specialist's need for continuing creative experiences and study when he has entered the profession.

Some of the more effective stimuli for students of art education are: observation, participation, and intern teaching experiences with children and adults beginning in the freshman year and continuing throughout the college career; frequent, extensive, and intensive study of important art works; instruction from competent artist-teachers, followed by sufficient opportunity for personal creative experiences; and introduction to the fascinating subjects of the humanities, the social studies, and the sciences. Here, as on other interest and ability levels, it is always more desirable for students to discover and investigate certain activities and areas of learning than be told about their content by the instructor.

Suggested activities—College (Art Teacher Education)

Creative art activities are an important part of nearly every course included in curricula designed to prepare art education specialists. No longer are students of art education taught only *about* art history or *about* the art activities which children and adults of various interest and ability levels enjoy. Students are also given numerous opportunities to experiment with and develop proficiency in many art media, processes, and activities. Students studying art

154

Broad-scope studio and workshop courses in the first two years introduce art education students to a wide range of activities and processes, such as silk screen printing, from which they may choose one or two for specialization in junior and senior year elective courses.

history might decide to experiment with encaustic painting after having learned of its early use.

Creativeness is as essential in the teaching of children as it is in painting, graphic arts, and sculpture. Students of art education should be encouraged in their undergraduate years to practice the art of creative teaching, either in affiliated elementary and secondary schools or in community social agencies.

CREATIVE GUIDANCE—COLLEGE (ART TEACHER EDUCATION)

It is as important in college as it is in the first grade to encourage the individual to experiment with new media, to develop his own solutions to problems posed by various processes, and to make full use of original ideas and ways of working. Here, as in the elemen-

Figure painting is one of many studio courses in the art education curriculum which offers students an opportunity to develop personal styles of expression and a greater understanding of the ideas and working methods of others.

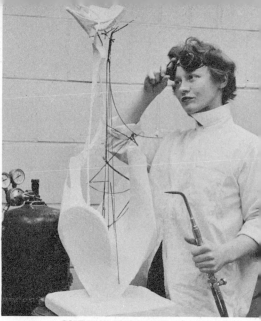

Etching and other studio courses cannot be taught entirely by class lectures, assigned readings, and discussions. Individual instruction and small classes are necessities. Artist-teacher George O'Connell watches a student prepare to make a print.

After an intensive four-year art education curriculum, students have often had as much studio work as they would receive in a three-year professional art school. Most art education students spend an additional year working toward a master's degree, during which they take many more, advanced studio courses.

tary school, technical instruction in art activities should include explanations and demonstrations of potentially dangerous processes, such as etching, wood block cutting, and sculpture. Demonstrations of how to draw, paint, or construct specific things, or even techniques (such as swirling brush strokes or special carving methods), can cause mass uniformity in students' art expressions. On the other hand, demonstrations of stretching canvas, laying the palette, operating a potter's wheel, and tool conditioning and care are necessary and valuable.

Art works of all periods, styles, and fields (architecture, industrial design, painting, etc.) should be frequently studied and discussed, and students should be encouraged to develop critical judgment which applies to their own as well as others' work. Many hours of creative experimentation under skillful guidance should be devoted to each art area, followed by visits to galleries, planned communities, interior design shops, craft studios, and well-designed stores or buildings. Also helpful are appropriate films, slides, traveling exhibitions, film strips, and recordings.

Students of art education need to develop considerable proficiency in a wide variety of art media and processes, yet they cannot be expected to excel in all of them. More desirable are highly developed imagination and skill in one medium, considerable imagination and skill in several media, and knowledge of the possibilities and limitations of many others. Such proficiency is developed through experimentation, instruction, and continued work in the graphic and craft media. Future art teachers should also experiment and receive instruction in all of the graphic and craft media and activities suggested for children.

Some students of art education as well as the children they will eventually teach, excel in painting-type activities. Others do better work in activities which require greater manipulative ability and memory for details of processes; and a few are able to develop proficiency in all types of art activities.

COLLEGE AGE: PROFESSIONAL ART STUDY

ART-EXPERIENCE NEEDS

It is essential to seek out youngsters with outstanding interest and ability in art who may, through advanced professional study and additional personal creative development, make a contribution to our culture as well as to their own happiness and satisfaction. Although professional art schools today enjoy larger enrollments than at any time in their history, it is important that we attempt to discover and encourage even more persons who show promise of continued creative development in the arts.

Most children have a deep interest and adequate ability in art, but this seems to lessen somewhat during the age range of eight or nine to eleven or twelve. This is often due to their inability to represent things on paper or in clay in a manner which is personally satisfying. If children were adequately encouraged to carry work out at an *achievable level* or to use media of their own choice, more of them would later elect art courses in secondary school. From this increased number of students, art teachers could further encourage those who would likely benefit from professional art instruction. Every one of the latter should be brought into contact

COURTESY COOPER UNION
ART SCHOOL, NEW YORK,
PHOTO BY IRVING SCHILD

Designer-teacher Warren Nardin, right, listens attentively as advanced student of advertising design explains his plan for a layout.

with representatives of college and university art departments and professional art schools. Many secondary school art teachers, guidance counselors, and principals fail to give adequate attention to this important phase of professional guidance. They are often unaware of the many scholarships and other benefits available to outstanding students, not to speak of the responsibility which all of us have to do everything possible to strengthen and enrich our culture.

Professional art school students need to see and study important, original art work of all kinds, just as the writer needs to read important books and the drama student needs to attend the legitimate theater. In addition to recognized masterpieces, they should study the *frontiers* of contemporary paintings and sculpture. Jack Madson's *Pursuit Number 3*, is an example of abstract expressionism by a younger member of the "New York School."

COURTESY COLLECTION WHITNEY MUSEUM OF AMERICAN ART, NEW YORK

A professional art school student employs certain techniques of armature building and clay modeling learned from her instructor, and willingly accepts his criticism. But the figure she designs is her personal responsibility.

COURTESY THE ART SCHOOL, PRATT INSTITUTE, BROOKLYN, N. Y.

SUGGESTED STIMULI—COLLEGE (PROFESSIONAL ART STUDY)

Some successful professional artists who lack art school training advocate inedependent, "self-taught" development for talented youngsters. But most professionals, many of whom teach in art schools, realize that a good art school background is an essential step in the young artist's development.

The young creative artist needs to *use his time wisely*. He can be stimulated and helped by professional artists who work in an orderly, diligent fashion. He will thus come to understand that a professional art career is as much work as it is pleasure; as much joy as it is dissatisfaction.

Also desirable is a pleasant, functional, and friendly environment. The artist needs a place to work where he can concentrate. This he usually finds in the college or special art school, although some prefer private studios.

Most professional art schools are located in metropolitan areas because of the proximity of cultural resources such as art museums and galleries. Since art exhibitions are for the student of professional art what libraries are to the university student, the necessity of their availability is obvious.

SUGGESTED ACTIVITIES—COLLEGE (PROFESSIONAL ART STUDY)

In addition to drawing, painting, and sculpture, professional art includes the following areas: advertising design, architecture, landscape design, interior design, ceramics, jewelry making, industrial design, silversmithing, fashion illustration, clothing design, weaving, fabric design, community planning, illustration, photography, type

159

face design, etching, lithography, silk screening, wood cutting, and engraving in metal and wood.

Most professional art school students spend a major portion of their freshman and sophomore years experimenting and becoming familiar with a wide variety of materials and tools in order to develop individual creative ability and an understanding of basic design structure. Following this broad study and experimentation, students are encouraged to select the area in which they are most interested and in which they have demonstrated the greatest degree of professional promise and personal satisfaction.

CREATIVE GUIDANCE—COLLEGE (PROFESSIONAL ART STUDY)

Demonstrations, explanations, lectures, discussions, movies, field trips, reading assignments, and suggestions for out-of-school creative work are among the instructional methods utilized in professional art schools. Careful attention is given to the development of original expression and the production of works of quality.

When the possibilities and limitations of a process such as silk screening are demonstrated, explained, and discussed, the student will want to use the techniques to express his own ideas. Therefore, instructors may demonstrate processes freely. Only a strong, dominating style or personality will lead a younger person into imitation. Such domination may also be exercised by another student, if not carefully checked.

These graphic workshop students in an extra-curricular publication planning session receive suggestions from a faculty advisor and printer, both of whom are professional designers.

COURTESY COOPER UNION ART SCHOOL, NEW YORK, PHOTO BY IRVING SCHILD

Through prolonged study of important historic and contemporary art works, such as Picasso's *Head of a Girl*, graduate students of art are able to penetrate more deeply into the process of creativity and the quality of excellence in art. Many major museums maintain collections of original prints, as well as paintings and sculpture, which are available for study. In addition, every college, university, and art school should own or develop its own art collection.

PRIVATE COLLECTION

THE NATURE OF ART WORK—COLLEGE (PROFESSIONAL ART STUDY)

The quality and breadth of a student's work is expected to improve continuously. Students entering professional study in a reputable art school soon learn that professional art is a way of life, not an eight hours per day type of work. Student work should be based upon a thorough knowledge of basic principles, yet it is also expected to be as richly varied as the individuals who produce it.

COLLEGE AGE: GRADUATE STUDY

ART-EXPERIENCE NEEDS

An urgent need for graduate study exists today, not only in the fields of education, science, medicine, engineering, and the liberal arts, but in all art areas as well. At the present time there is little opportunity for artists or art educators interested in working beyond the master's degree to engage in top level graduate study under outstanding artist-teacher instruction. The doctorate in art education or creative art, as such, is rarely offered. There are few organized programs of instruction on the doctoral level. Only a small number of graduate schools offer study leading to a doctorate in education or philosophy in which even part of one's time may be devoted to work in art education or art.

Most of this country's leading institutions of higher learning consider the doctorate a prerequisite for top professorial positions, although a few will accept "recognized, exhibiting artists" with professional reputations in lieu of this degree. It is unfortunate that many persons who are qualified for and interested in doctoral level graduate study cannot more easily find programs suited to their needs.

SUGGESTED STIMULI—COLLEGE (GRADUATE STUDY)

Many leading artists and educators have indicated an interest in additional professional study and would welcome opportunities to participate in doctoral level art programs. If, and when, such opportunities are offered in all parts of the country, graduate study by those already interested would serve as an adequate stimulus for subsequent participation by others.

On the master's degree level, where a wide variety of programs in art education and art are currently available, little additional stimulation seems necessary because of the large number of art educators and artists who are actively enrolled. Widespread college, university, and state education department requirements have encouraged many people to continue their professional preparation beyond the bachelor's degree level. Others have sought graduate study because of personal convictions relative to the importance of this work.

Additional stimulation in the arts is needed, however, for students engaged in programs of graduate study in fields such as medicine, engineering, law, and liberal arts. They, like art majors, should have courses in the humanities, science, and social studies included in their programs of graduate study. The Massachusetts Institute of Technology has recently enriched its curricula by adding courses in the arts. All too frequently graduate programs do not provide the breadth of learning that is demanded in contemporary life.

NEW YORK UNIVERSITY,
PHOTO BY IRWIN GOOEN

Graduate study should provide ample opportunity for the development of significant individual expression through competent and detailed professional criticism.

It thus becomes the responsibility of the student to include some study of the arts in his graduate work.

Most important as a stimulus for graduate students, whether they are art majors or not, are outstanding works by leading historic and contemporary artists. Whenever possible, they should be studied in original form, supplemented by extensive gallery and museum visiting, independent reading, slide lecture-discussions, and a study of reproductions.

SUGGESTED ACTIVITIES—COLLEGE (GRADUATE STUDY)

Among the art activities desirable for non-art graduate students are creative expression (drawing, painting, sculpture, etc.) art in everyday life (home planning, clothing design, industrial design, etc.); and art aspects of student's professional studies (medical illustration, structural planning, philosophy of art, etc.). Graduate students majoring in non-art areas should have at least one general art course designed to introduce them to a variety of personal creative expression activities and to acquaint them with the many ways in which art can serve them in everyday home and professional life. This should be followed by an opportunity to elect from a variety of art courses in which they could do additional work.

Among the courses for art majors working toward master's or doctor's degrees should be an amplification of the graphic and craft areas. There is a pressing need for further study and research in such areas as: the nature of children's creative expression; the determination of benefits children derive through art experiences; art education for adolescents; art activities in adult education programs; art education for exceptional children; the organization of community art centers; city planning and landscape design; the preparation of art teachers, and the production of aesthetically significant art works. Also needed, because of the lack of opportunity for doctoral study in the arts, is research on the types of programs which would be best suited for students interested in post-master's degree research, experimentation, and independent creative work in art.

CREATIVE GUIDANCE—COLLEGE (GRADUATE STUDY)

Non-art graduate students require competent, creative instruction from teachers who understand adult psychology and are aware of the needs of students who are not planning to make a career of the arts. Since some students may not have had previous art courses and others will have had a background of art instruction on every educational level, graduate art instructors should be able to meet students' needs on widely varying levels of interest and ability.

Considerable variation in art background will also be noted among art major students working toward master's or doctor's degrees. For the most part, however, they are capable of individual research and experimentation, and with the guidance of outstanding artist-teachers they can progress rapidly toward high-level competence in various art areas. Probably the best creative guidance on the graduate level is offered through cooperative program planning whereby each graduate student works closely with his adviser (or a faculty committee) in setting up desired goals and possible means of reaching them.

Outstanding professional artists often provide a depth of inspiration for graduate art students which has lasting beneficial effects. Many colleges and universities have secured recognized professional artists as teachers or artists in residence for this important purpose.

THE NATURE OF ART WORK—(GRADUATE STUDY)

The art work produced by non-art major graduate students will range from the childlike works of beginning adult amateurs to high-quality professional work, dependent upon the interests and abilities of individual students. The art activities in which many non-art graduate students can excel are those connected with interior and architectural design, clothing design, and furniture or industrial design. Following adequate instruction in the art qualities underlying good examples in these areas, students can often produce satisfying, high quality, creative work.

Graduate students working toward degrees in art are expected to produce high quality work. It is especially important for them to retain their individuality during this period of study, since many of the teachers with whom they work will be strong, influential artists and designers whose work might be unconsciously (or consciously) imitated.

Graduate students require time and means for perfecting techniques such as pottery making.

More than 10,000,000 adults are now enrolled in adult education art classes in the United States alone.

In the more progressive graduate schools, provisions are made for students to choose between a written thesis and a creative project, such as a series of paintings, a planned community, an architectural design, pieces of sculpture, or a mural.

ADULT EDUCATION

ART-EXPERIENCE NEEDS

Shorter working hours, earlier retirement, increasing longevity, and higher standards of living have brought many adults face to face with the problems of making more valuable use of their increased leisure time. Art is a constructive yet at the same time relaxing and enjoyable pastime. During the past decade it has become one of the most popular of all adult education activities.

Adults who have participated with some success in any one of the craft activities readily testify that it does more than occupy leisure time constructively. Most persons, *regardless of age or physical condition, can develop satisfactory proficiency in at least one art activity,* if appropriate guidance is offered by instructors. People who cannot seem to do personally satisfying work in painting, for example, should be introduced to other art activities, such as ceramics or jewelry making.

SUGGESTED STIMULI—ADULT EDUCATION

Most adults feel inadequate in art, yet they are eager to know more about it, particularly if in so doing they can improve the appearance of their homes, better their grooming and dress, and make more constructive use of leisure time.

Exhibitions of the work of other adults are helpful in stimulating the interest of potential students. These decorative ornaments were cut from tin cans and fashioned with simple metal working tools. Surface designs were added by means of ball-point paint tubes.

COURTESY BINNEY AND SMITH CO.

An increasing number of people are encouraged to participate in adult education programs by friends, by literature concerning these programs which is distributed in many school districts, and by books and articles which describe this type of education. Nearly all adult education literature indicates that beginners are welcome, that no previous experiences or special talents are necessary, and that course offerings are practical.

Because most adults have had little or no art in their previous schooling, they need to be offered beginning activities which are simple yet challenging, through which they can produce personally satisfying work.

SUGGESTED ACTIVITIES—ADULT EDUCATION

Many adult education students seek a pleasant, semi-social diversion in art activities. Some of them find it relaxing to dabble in paint or clay, even though they may not produce objects of lasting value. However, a larger proportion of adults, both men and women, seek something practical. They want to make ceramic objects for their homes, paintings for their walls, furniture for their game rooms, block-printed drapes for their windows, and many other specific things. This wide variation in individual needs requires extensive guidance and accurate catalog descriptions of available activities.

Mosaics being made by community art center participants.

COURTESY DELAWARE ART CENTER, WILMINGTON, DELAWARE

Initial experiences in making wheel-thrown pots.

One of the best ways to meet individual needs without sacrificing essential qualities of originality and sound craftsmanship is to offer an introductory course in which a variety of art activities are explored, ranging from interior design to crafts and painting. Here the basic design fundamentals which underlie all art activities can be taught through practical application, individual interests can be followed, and adults can better choose specific art activities in which they wish further instruction.

Creative guidance—adult education

Adult education students usually have a strong desire to produce finished work, whether it be a painting or a piece of furniture. Many of them are willing to sacrifice originality for finished appearance, and instructors are often asked to help out by drawing a tree which is too hard for them or by designing a table which they can reproduce and take home. It is difficult to make many adults realize that the most important thing about *any* art or craft activity is creative, personal expression. It may take months, even years, to convince them. The instructor needs to stimulate his students' interests deeply and then offer them as much technical instruction as possible without actually drawing, painting, designing, or building an object for them. To avoid copying, the teacher sometimes demonstrates a variety of ways of doing a specific thing rather than just one way, and removes his examples after the demonstration has been completed.

To maintain student interest, the experienced instructor suggests beginning projects which are relatively simple and which lend themselves to originality rather than conformity. He will do everything possible to help the beginner complete a first project that is his own, is personally satisfying, and is finished looking. He will try to help the beginner select a project which will help him to learn new techniques and skills.

More advanced students expect to learn new ways of working.

167

Although repeated attendance develops strong social ties, students expect more than a place in which to visit while they do their own work. They are interested in a forward-moving program of instruction as well.

THE NATURE OF ART WORK—ADULT EDUCATION

It is quite common for adult students to bring picture postcards, photographs, and illustrations with them for the first few class meetings. Even though their instructor may indicate at the outset that copywork can never be as good as that which is original, adults frequently desire "artistic crutches" upon which they may lean until they feel competent to develop an original project. This does not mean that they should be encouraged to copy or borrow ideas. Yet they should not be forbidden to copy, or ridiculed for such practice. Being adults, they have the privilege of discovering right and wrong attitudes their own way. Gradually they can be led into more creative self-expression.

Art objects made by adult students vary from the primitive type to sophisticated, finished works.

THE EXCEPTIONAL CHILD

These three children, suffering from the after-effects of polio (left), congenital heart trouble (center), and physical deformity (right), are absorbed in the enjoyment of mural making.

COURTESY GOODRICH SCHOOL, AKRON, OHIO

This nine-year-old rheumatic heart disease victim is receiving special art instruction sponsored by the New Mexico Heart Association and the Junior League of Albuquerque.

The term "exceptional" here applies to those who differ physically, mentally, emotionally, or socially from the average. The exceptional child or adult usually requires special services from both teachers and parents in order to develop to the fullest possible degree.

Exceptional children have basic concepts, goals, and ideals common to all children. In general, they develop as all children do. *Recognition must be given to their likenesses to normal children, their differences from normal children, and to their special individual needs.* The exceptional child can do virtually everything that the normal child can do. His mental and creative abilities are probably his most unique characteristic. In the past the trend was to isolate the exceptional person. Every effort is now being made to help him live as close to a normal life as he possibly can, since he will be living in a world of average people in adulthood. Only for those activities which require special tools, equipment, or instruction need he be with children of similar gifts or handicaps. Many school systems now bring the children together in common areas of learning. At all times the teacher of exceptional children should be alert to the vocational and avocational possibilities of school offerings, for society is just beginning to accept fully the exceptional person, particularly those who are handicapped, on an equal employment level. Except in rare cases, exceptional individuals should be treated normally. Terms or expressions which tend to emphasize their deviations should be avoided.

Very few children are in perfect health or happy at all times. Their physical ailments may vary from minor disturbances to complete physical disabilities. A child may be affected emotionally, mentally, or socially by a broken home. A temporary economic setback may cause mental conflicts or frustrations in the entire family.

170

Children in the 8-11 year age range frequently become interested in portraying details of objects. Sometimes this interest is coupled with a desire for increased security at home or school which is often revealed through unusual amounts of detail, or labels such as those shown in this crayon and pencil drawing by a 9-year-old girl. The art teacher should wisely use such pictorial clues to his pupils' personalities, and where necessary, make referrals to the school psychologist or administrator. Labeled pictures may, on the other hand, mean nothing more than a child's solution to the problem of "correct" representation, provided the subject matter is normal.

Classroom or playground arguments may upset the morale of a child. Regardless of the cause, these incidents may injure the child emotionally even though they may not seem to affect him physically. Unless the adult is alert, he will have no way of detecting early symptoms that may cause eventual deviations.

The U. S. Office of Education estimated that 12.4% of all school children may be classified as exceptional.* Included in this classification are those who are: blind, crippled, deaf, hard-of-hearing, mentally retarded, partially seeing, socially maladjusted, have special health problems, speech handicapped, and gifted.

In America we believe that every child is entitled to an education to the limit of his capacity. We are committed to the principle of education for all, regardless of race, creed, or ability. When we give each child, including the exceptional, ample educational, social, and professional opportunities, we are making an application of our belief in true democracy.

Before one begins providing exceptional children with educational or art services, a special effort should be made to find out as much as one can about them. Depending on the teacher's area of responsibility, the method of seeking this information must through necessity be handled tactfully, for certain elements of the outline can become very personal. On the other hand, if a maximum service is expected, close cooperation must develop between the child, his parents, the doctor, psychiatrist, therapist, specialist teachers in fields such as art and science, and the service agencies participating in the program.

Art for exceptional children. Art may serve as an emotional outlet for the child, and may also help his teacher decide how he

---

* "Some Problems in the Education of Handicapped Children," Office of Education, U.S. Government Printing Office, Washington, D. C., 1952.

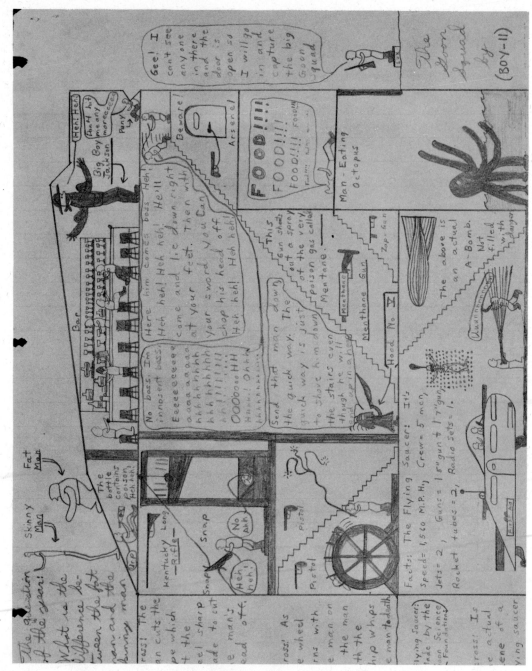

deviates from the average. The handicapped child frequently becomes emotionally disturbed by his inability to participate in normal physical or social activities or to achieve academic and personal successes. The gifted child may be disturbed by his uniqueness as well. The opportunity to resolve these conflicts and to decrease tensions resulting from frustrations is important in the

Eight to eleven-year-olds' interest in details sometimes causes them to pour out their feelings and clearly indicate their needs, as well as certain emotional and mental conditions. It is often the art teacher who first notices a child's deep preoccupation with unusual subject matter, such as the house of torture and death pictured and described in this pencil drawing by an 11-year-old boy. Although one might hope that the tiny "first aid" sign on the flying saucer at lower left means this youngster has some interest in human welfare, the remainder of the picture would seem to indicate an unusual degree of preoccupation with activities which are well beyond "cowboy and Indian" or "space ship" interests. Referral to the school psychologist would, in this case, be imperative.

educational development of the exceptional child. His aggressions and disappointments may be expressed in a harmless and socially accepted manner through self-expressive activities.

The educational program should be flexible and adaptable to the specific needs of children of all ages, grades, and capacities. Knowledge of children's abilities, needs, interests, superiorities, and limitations should be acquired by their teachers. *Children must not be expected to do more or less than they are capable of doing.* Whether or not they are gifted or handicapped, older children resent art projects which are beneath them, while young children become frustrated if confronted with activities they cannot accomplish.

To offset the diverse forces acting on a child, creative experiences should be made so pleasant that learning will naturally take place. To meet the varying interests and needs of each child, the curriculum should offer a wide range of art activities, including three-dimensional experiences with wood, clay, papier mâché, and other

By encouraging the child to discuss his finger painting, the therapist is better able to encourage mental and physical growth, personal expression of problems, and the development of better muscular coordination.

173

COURTESY AMO BERNARDIS,
PORTLAND, OREGON

Some of the most valuable and enjoyable hours in an exceptional child's life may be derived from participation in art activities which are carefully selected according to his interests and needs.

materials. The art program should stimulate interest in creative activities not only in school, but at home as well, especially in the case of pupils who are temporarily or permanently confined.

Great care should be exercised in studying the needs of exceptional children. Published studies, specialists, and constantly cumulative data should be consulted in gathering knowledge and information. Also important is the need to improve methods of reporting progress to parents and aiding them in offering effective out-of-school guidance.

Each child's needs must be considered in suggesting art materials, processes, and equipment to be used. Difficult learning problems thus can more easily be grasped. Children often improve their arithmetic by learning measurements involved in building an object in wood. The rhythmic sounds of music usually relieve tensions, organize thought, and induce security. Better and more relaxed self-expression can sometimes be fostered by asking children to compose and chant or sing simple poems while they work at finger painting, clay modeling, or woodworking.

Some art activities offer remarkable therapeutic values. Emotionally disturbed people tend to isolate themselves and live in a world of their own making. The arts can penetrate this isolation where words fail. A person afflicted with cerebral palsy often experiences tensions when he consciously tries to place his hands in a certain position, but when the same person has his attention focused on art activities, reading, singing, or manipulating an instrument, the spasms sometimes occur less frequently. Similarly, a person might be helped to recover from a muscular injury by working at a loom or potter's wheel. Every effort should be made to enrich exceptional children's everyday experiences. Art activities are ideally suited for this purpose.

Art activities for the blind. There is little that the blind child cannot do in a manipulative way. The current trend is not to isolate

174

the blind, but to help them adjust to the world of the seeing. In every activity they should be with seeing children except for Braille lessons and certain physical play activities.

Blind children should be taught a wide variety of crafts. These children need numerous and varied tactile experiences. They enjoy working with clay or plasticine, not only for the finished product involved, but for the pleasure and satisfaction they derive from the process as well.

Music is very important in the life of a blind person. Provided he has the necessary desire, encouragement, sense of hearing, and coordinative ability, there are virtually no instruments which he cannot learn to play. His satisfaction is great, for he can judge his music as well as anyone. Manual dexterities gained through continued participation in art activities help the child in acquiring subsequent musical skills.

Art activities for the partially seeing. The degree of vision possessed is the only limiting factor in activities for the partially seeing child. Art can be a very important element in broadening the abilities of children with impaired vision. Pictures, gestures, and pantomime are helpful in improving their understanding of a wide variety of subjects.

Depending on doctor's orders, the partially seeing should have many opportunities to engage in art activities such as clay modeling and finger painting, since these media are helpful in sight saving. The differing textures of various materials provide satisfying tactile experiences for everyone, yet they do not require visual scrutiny. By feeling textures they can learn the meaning of such words as smooth, rough, soft, stiff, fuzzy, and bumpy.

Through art media, a visually handicapped child can show what he thinks, sees, and feels. Thus the teacher will quickly learn things about the child's world which might otherwise not be as well understood.

Partially seeing children should be provided with construction activities that require the use of their fingers, hands, and arms. This is an aid to the further development of manual dexterity. Among the materials provided should be large sheets of paper, brightly colored paints, large brushes, moist clay, wood, tools, cardboard, and a variety of adhesives. Pieces of tape-edged glass, sponges, and paints for monoprinting should also be available.

Extended work periods and activities requiring close concentration are fatiguing to all children, but especially so to those who are partially sighted. Large-muscle activity is natural and healthy for them, both physically and psychologically. When people finger-paint to music, for example, their entire bodies seem to respond. Repeated experiences of this type help them to develop better muscular control. Much time can be profitably spent in writing, typing, dictating, illustrating, telling original stories, composing, and playing tunes.

Children in sight-saving classes usually respond well to the same stimuli, at the same times, and use the same materials as children with normal vision. Their appreciations are about the same and they usually attain the same ultimate goals of enjoyment and relaxation. In some ways, their sensitivity to art values is even greater, due to the compensatory increase of response through senses other than sight.

Art activities for the deaf. Art education for the deaf child differs little from that suggested for children with normal hearing. Since art is predominantly a visual subject, and since the education of the deaf is more visual than verbal, the art teacher has a natural basis for direct and effective communication.

One of the first objectives is to help the child develop a visual vocabulary and thus an additional means of expression. He should frequently draw, paint, and model subjects of interest to him, such as animals, people, games, automobiles, airplanes, and rockets, and identify them with words and sounds.

Since deaf children are taught to speak, read lips, or both, the presentation of the art lesson differs little from that which would be offered to the child with normal hearing, except for careful enunciation. Visual demonstrations prove most effective. Instead of verbally suggesting what the children might like to do, the art teacher can effectively utilize visual aids for this purpose, being careful to avoid those which would induce stereotyped expression. The handicapped child should not be further limited by having his creativity hampered.

All art media and tools, including paints, scissors, paper, paste, scrap materials, wood, plastics, crayons, metal, or modeling clay can be used successfully with these children. Originality often appears in unique forms in the work of the deaf child since he does not usually think with words.

As in the case of normal children, art activities for the deaf should not be looked upon as a means of developing professional art ability, but rather as a means of developing better-adjusted individuals. Art helps all children improve their daily living by discovering more and varied insights as well as richer and deeper feelings, understandings, and observation faculties. Art can become an unusually valuable means of communication for the deaf.

Art activities for the hard-of-hearing. Hard-of-hearing children participate in normal art activities. Hearing aids may virtually eliminate their handicap. It is essential, however, that they hear or otherwise understand directions concerning the safe and effective uses of tools and media they have chosen. As in the case of teaching art to the deaf, visual demonstrations are helpful, and much can be learned by careful watching.

Hard-of-hearing children usually like vibrations. Any material suitable for pounding can be enjoyed. They also enjoy vivid, gay colors. Encourage them to develop hobbies and meet others with similar interests. A creative activity hobby helps immeasurably in fostering social as well as individual adjustment and happiness.

Art Activities for Children with Speech Defects. Most adults know from personal experience that certain situations can affect us to such an extent that a speech difficulty may result. Conversely, children's speech defects can be improved by certain projective activities, such as playing with puppets, dolls, pets, play-radio, play-television, and play-stage acting. Beyond the important therapeutic values of projective techniques are the values inherent in the processes of making and manipulating objects such as puppets and marionettes. A number of art activities make direct contributions to the creative, dramatic, and physical needs of youngsters. Children with speech defects can, of course, enjoy every art activity suitable for the normal child.

Art activities for the mentally retarded. Experiences in the field of art have an important place in the educational program for retarded children. Interest and ability in some phase of art activity is one of the strongest assets which most retarded children possess. Art activities serve as emotional stabilizers, yet at the same time they broaden and enrich the lives of most of these pupils. Retarded children may not become exceedingly adept in their art performance, but they will secure emotional satisfaction and in some cases will make creditable progress, thus becoming socially more acceptable in a normal group. They will also become happier individuals once they have produced an art object in which they can take some justifiable personal pride.

The ability to understand and use art elements, such as shape, texture, and color in picture study, drawing, modeling, and various craft activities, gives to intellectually subnormal children the same opportunity for enjoyment and creative expression that it gives to normal children.

After a child has learned to manipulate the materials with which he will work, his performance usually improves. In his creative activities he should be given frequent opportunities to exercise his own judgment and to arrive at his own conclusions.

Some retarded children find it hard to differentiate subtly related colors and to recognize various shapes of a specific hue. For this reason it is necessary for them to have experiences in color discrimination. This does not mean that they are insensitive to color, texture, and other art elements, but that their observation is often less acute. With help, they can develop considerable perceptual acuity and aesthetic sensitivity.

Retarded children enjoy using paper, paints, crayons, clay, plasticine, wood, and cloth, and often give surprising attention to details. Common types of discarded materials have found their way into the art room for subsequent transformation into objects of beauty. Corn husks can be used for weaving mats, making napkin rings, and creating dolls. Scraps of wood can be fashioned into trays, jewelry boxes, bookends, and shelves. As the pupil reaches adolescence, special emphasis can be placed upon manual experiences that not only satisfy his creative desires but also have values for possible occupational activity. Since the mentally retarded child's areas of interest may be limited, every effort should be made to provide for his avocational and leisure time needs.

Art activities for the physically handicapped. Physically handicapped children can learn to do virtually everything that the normal children can do. The only limiting factor is a particular physical ailment.

Art, music, dramatics, and other creative activities are an important part of educational and recreational programs for physically handicapped children. Almost any type of art material used by normal children, such as finger paint, clay, textile and poster paint, crayons, and wood can be used to offset some of the feelings of in-

COURTESY ANNA HENRY

Physically handicapped children, like all others, should be encouraged to produce work which is unique and based upon personal interests.

adequacy occasioned by a child's inability to hike, play ball, dance, run, or jump.

Nearly every art activity must be adapted to the needs of individual handicapped children, as suggested by the doctor. Weaving and knitting are popular therapeutic activities which have artistic values as well. Wood or stone carving is enjoyed by many children with muscular problems, but can be hazardous for those with poor coordination. Aluminum wire sculpture is satisfactory for most youngsters since it is pliable, not dangerously springy, and easy for children to manipulate. Children who are able to sit up or stand enjoy working with papier mâché. Bedridden children need special help with this medium because of its messiness. As a rule it is advisable to use art media which are easily manipulated, and activities which assure satisfying results. Moist clay modeling is ideally suited to nearly every physical handicap.

No physically handicapped child should leave school without a knowledge of vocational rehabilitation services. He should be made aware of the many areas of vocational training in the arts and other areas which are available to him through public and private rehabilitation agencies.

Art activities for the socially maladjusted. Art teachers are often called upon to advise youth activity groups. Inasmuch as busy, hobby-minded youngsters are seldom delinquent, it is imperative that art teachers play an increasingly more important role in providing constructive, interesting, and time-consuming art activities for young people.

Participation in art activities can also be relaxing, especially for the emotionally disturbed child. He can derive satisfaction from finger painting, pounding and squeezing clay, or by painting or drawing "monsters" to show what he thinks of the "bullies" in the world and release his frustrations, perhaps in a laugh when he views his finished work.

For adults, many major companies provide noon hour and other recreational activities, including the arts. Studies indicate that there is a close correlation between happiness at work and off-duty activities. This applies to office workers as well as those who labor with their hands.

The armed forces have in recent years begun to employ group recreation leaders in art activities. These teachers provide much needed art experiences for military as well as for service-connected civilian personnel.

Art activities for the gifted. In the past, few provisions were

A six-year-old boy created this pencil drawing which shows unusual attention to detail, precocious representational ability, yet shows (in stereotyped tree symbols and house "standing" on steps) a clear need for specialized art instruction.

made for meeting the educational needs of the gifted child. As a result, potential leaders may have been lost to our society. *The gifted child needs an enriched program.* Not only are there great needs for people of genius in philosophy, education, politics, science, economics, and mathematics, but there are also pressing needs for people of genius in the broad field of the humanities, which includes the arts.

There are probably as many variations among the gifted as there are in the other areas of the exceptional. But because of the obvious urgency of matters affecting handicapped exceptional children, their needs have been given first attention. Now that we are beginning to meet at least some of their needs it is time to systematically study and meet the needs of exceptional children who are gifted.

If we are interested in discovering special talent in art it will be necessary to provide all children with frequent opportunities to express themselves in a variety of art media throughout their formal education. For those who show unusual interest or ability in art, there must be additional and more frequent opportunities of increasing magnitude and intensity.

An authoritative report of the National Education Association, Research Division, raises some important questions about the identification of gifted children:

The unreliability of teachers' judgments as a method for identifying gifted children was studied by Carroll. He found that only 15.7 percent of the children nominated by 6,000 teachers (each child as the most intelligent in his class) were found to be qualified for the gifted group. (Carroll, Herbert A. *Genius in the Making.* New York: McGraw-Hill Book Co., 1940. p. 9.) Likewise, the report issued in 1950 by the Educational Policies Commission on the education of the gifted indicated the unreliability of teachers' judgments in the selection of gifted children. (National Education Association and American Association of School Administrators, Educational Policies Commission. *Education of the Gifted.* Washington, D. C.: the Commission, June, 1950, p. 35-37.)

Identification by intelligence test is also questionable. If a promise of creativity is the characteristic of a gifted child, the most commonly used intelligence tests are poorly designed to identify such characteristics, for creativity implies originality, and originality implies successful management, control, and organization of new materials or experiences. The contents of most intelligence tests lack situations which disclose originality or creativity. (Witty, Paul. "Contributions to the IQ Controversy from the Study of Superior Deviates." *School and Society* 51:504; April 20, 1940.)[*]

---

[*]"The Education of Gifted Children." *"Research Bulletin* of the National Education Association, 35: 164; December, 1957.

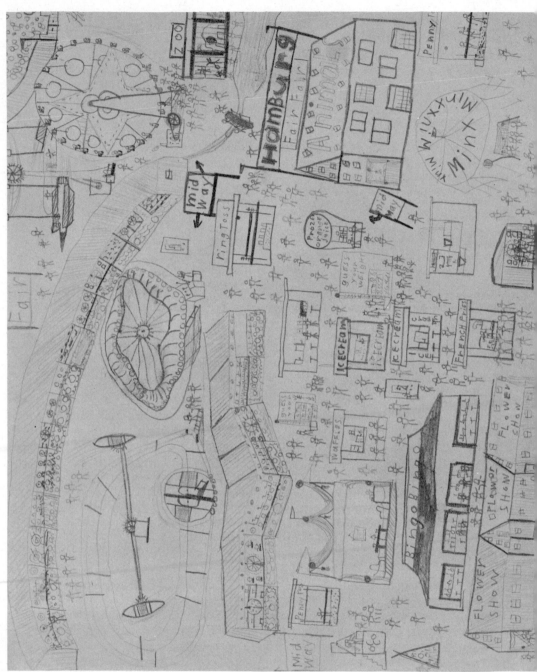

A nine-year-old boy did this picture along with several hundred other drawings, during the course of a few months. Preferring pencil to all other media, he worked with equal facility from memory or direct observation. His photographic mind, acute powers of visualization, and draftsmanship provide clear evidence of his artistic precocity.

Heightened visual acuity and interest in both idea and detail are characteristic of perceptively gifted children.

This design-conscious gifted child is better able to see the underlying artistic structure of realistic subject matter than a child with less visual perception.

The extreme variety of works and ways of working in the arts makes it difficult, if not impossible, to describe adequately the nature of individuals who are gifted or works which indicate brilliance. Making the matter even more complex is the fact that there is no proved correlation between brilliance in general and brilliance in art. Too often brilliance means precocity in verbal concepts and abilities. Such a gift is often determined, or classified, through the use of verbal intelligence tests, such as the Stanford-Binet, which do not measure ability or quality in art expression.

To a large extent, however, brilliance in art can be determined by the *interest of a young person,* by his persistence, and by the attention his work receives from others. It should be understood that talent may not necessarily lead to a professional art career, but may possibly be an indication of brilliance in other fields directly or indirectly related to art expression.

Parents, teachers, or other interested adults may help the gifted child, but they might inadvertently hinder him. Genuine, specific praise and advice are always helpful. Overzealous adulation or "di-

The children shown here and above are members of a special Saturday art class sponsored by a board of education.

COURTESY SCHOOL BOARD, VANCOUVER, B. C.

183

NEW YORK UNIVERSITY,
PHOTO BY MILTON MICHELSTEIN

Artist-teacher Hale Woodruff offers professional criticism to
scholarship students at university-sponsored class for gifted
high school pupils.

rection" of his work might stultify him. One of the finest ways of
showing genuine interest is to select works which one honestly feels
are outstanding, have them tastefully framed or mounted, or encourage the child to choose some of his works and frame or mount them
himself, and display them in the living room, classroom, or office.
Actual art instruction is usually helpful but should not be attempted
by the unskilled adult or by means of "how-to-do-it" books on art.
The gifted child who is properly guided might one day become an
outstanding painter, sculptor, craftsman, or commercial designer.

The question most commonly asked by parents of children gifted
in art is, "Should I provide my child with special instruction?" Dependent upon the nature of the instruction, the answer would probably be "Yes." Even if such instruction did no more than supply
the child with a constructive hobby interest, it would be valuable.
In order to be of value, specialized art instruction needs to be creative and stimulating.

Becoming familiar with artist-teachers and their work enables gifted students
to understand more clearly the relation of the artist's personality and beliefs
to what he attempts to express in his work. Illustrated here is *Hierarchy* by
Hale Woodruff.

COURTESY BERTHA SCHAEFER GALLERY, NEW YORK

The best type of specialized instruction in art is secured in public and private schools where art is related to the total development of the child. In some schools this is effected through special classes; in others, pupils are given individual instruction and projects to develop during free periods in school and at home. Also beneficial are art clubs which meet during or after school.

If specialized art instruction is not available in school, or in cases where additional specialized instruction is felt desirable, after school, Saturday, and summer classes in art may sometimes be found in the YM and YWCA's, YM and YWHA's, CYO's, recreation centers, playgrounds, 'teen centers, art museums, and educational programs for children and adolescents in colleges and universities.* In some communities, local artists and art teachers conduct private classes for small groups of children. *In all cases, the parent or teacher seeking additional art instruction for a gifted child should make certain that the artist, art teacher, or recreation program leader under whose guidance the child will work is an able, effective, and, most important, creative teacher.* Careful inquiries should be made in advance, both of the teacher concerned and of enrolled pupils and their parents. Prior to formal registration, a parent or interested teacher from school should visit a sample class with the child to observe the instructor and his pupils in action, ask him questions, and look at representative examples of pupil work. Evidence of stereotyped, directed teaching should probably disqualify the instructor under consideration. While some professional artists may win first prize at regional art shows, they do not always possess creative teaching ability; yet others are excellent, even though they have had no specialized preparation in teaching.

Art activities for children with special health problems. There are many children who are not orthopedically handicapped, but who have special health conditions. These childlren often look and act well, but may have a history of rheumatic fever or other heart conditions, asthma, diabetes, or allergies. They may be in regular schools. Others may be in hospitals, sanatoriums, residential schools, homes, private or public specialized schools, or convalescent homes. The educational program for these children is essentially the same as that for normal children except for disability allowances. In order to properly modify the educational program, parents and

---

* For example, New York University offers a tuition-free full year Scholarship Painting Workshop for gifted high school students; and the State University Teachers' College at New Paltz, N. Y. offers a two-week summer art workshop for high school students who pay only room and board.

teachers must be aware of their children's individual health conditions and the activities in which they can or cannot participate. Art activities as well as the rest of the educational program must often be built around the recommendations of the attending physician, with the teacher, parents, and physician working together.

THE TEACHER OF EXCEPTIONAL CHILDREN

Information and suggestions have been presented with the hope they will be implemented by teachers of exceptional children. The well being of the teacher himself is also important. He must deal effectively with his *own* emotional, social, physical, and teaching problem. His attitudes have a direct affect on the learning and health of the children with whom he works.

The effective teacher of exceptional children needs to have something of the quality of a good nurse or doctor, being able to overcome tendencies to become emotionally involved with the problems of exceptional children, yet remaining warm, human, even tender, and certainly concerned with the welfare of all children for whom he is responsible.

PARENTS OF EXCEPTIONAL CHILDREN

No program can be fully effective without the cooperation of parents. They should be helped to understand the importance of creative activities in the exceptional child's development. They should provide art materials for their children to use at home. Some schools now provide classes for the parents of exceptional children where needed information can be presented in a well organized and effective manner.

Parents are aware of their children's energy potential; of the frequency of their reactions to their physical disability; of social, emotional, and physical changes; and of improvements. They can make valuable suggestions to teachers, nurses, or doctors, concerning methods of achieving better cooperation and desirable behavior in working with their child. When programs in art are suggested, parents can help to promote their child's interest in creative activities.

ORGANIZATIONS FOR EXCEPTIONAL CHILDREN

Following is a list of organizations dealing with various types of exceptional children which may be called upon for advice and suggestions:

186

General Agencies for Exceptional Children (Publications italicized)

Children's Bureau, Dept. of Health, Education, and Welfare, Washington 25, D. C. *Children*

Community Chests and Councils of America, 155 E. 44th St., New York 17, N. Y.

Federation of the Handicapped, 241 W. 23rd St., New York 11, N. Y.

Goodwill Industries of America, 1222 New Hampshire Ave., N.W., Washington 6, D. C. *Goodwill Bulletin*

International Council for Exceptional Children, 1201 16th St., N.W., Washington 6, D. C. *Exceptional Children*

National Association for Mental Health, 1790 Broadway, New York 19, N. Y.

National Committee for Mental Hygiene, 1790 Broadway, New York 19, N. Y. *Mental Hygiene; Understanding the Child*

President's Committee on Employment of the Physically Handicapped, U. S. Bureau of Labor Standards, Washington 25, D. C. *Performance: The Story of the Handicapped*

U. S. Office of Education, Exceptional Children and Youth, Department of Health, Education and Welfare, Washington 25, D. C. *School Life*

U. S. Public Health Service, Washington 25, D. C. *U. S. Public Health Report*

World Health Organization, Palais des Nations, Geneva, Switzerland

Agencies for the Blind and Partially Seeing (Publications italicized)

American Association of Instructors of the Blind, c/o Neal Quimby, State School for the Blind, Alamogordo, New Mexico

American Association of Workers for the Blind, 15 W. 16th St., New York 11, N. Y.

American Foundation for the Blind, Inc., 15 W. 16th St., New York 11, N. Y. *New Outlook for the Blind; AFB Publications* (Pamphlets, monographs)

American Foundation for the Overseas Blind, Inc., 22 W. 17th St., New York 11, N. Y.

American Printing House for the Blind, Inc., 1839 Frankfort Ave., Louisville 6, Kentucky

Guide Dog Foundation for the Blind, Inc., 71-01 Austin St., Forest Hills 75, N. J.

Howe Braille Press of Perkins Institution, 175 N. Beacon St., Watertown 72, Mass.

International Guiding Eyes, Inc., 5501 Lankershim Blvd., N. Hollywood, Calif.

Library of Congress—Division for the Blind, Washington 25, D. C.

National Society for Prevention of Blindness, 1790 Broadway, New York 19, N. Y. *Sight Saving Review* (Quarterly); *Eye Health and Safety News* (Irreg.)

Pilot Guide Dog Foundation, 31 East Congress St., Chicago 5, Ill.

The Seeing Eye, Inc., Morristown, N. J.

U. S. Office of Vocational Rehabilitation Services for the Blind, Department of Health, Education and Welfare, Washington 25, D. C.

Agencies for the Deaf and Hard-of-Hearing (Publications italicized)

Alexander Graham Bell Association for the Deaf, 1537 35th St., N.W., Washington 7, D. C. *Volta Review* (monthly)
American Hearing Society, 817 Fourteenth St., N.W., Washington 5, D. C. *Hearing News*
American Speech and Hearing Society, Wayne University, Detroit 1, Michigan
Conference of American Instructors of the Deaf, Gallaudet College, Washington 2, D. C.
Conference of Executives of American School for the Deaf, Gallaudet College, Washington 2, D. C. *American Annals for the Deaf*
Volta Speech Association for the Deaf, Volta Bureau, 1537 35th St., N.W., Washington 7, D. C.

Agencies for Children with Speech Handicaps (Publications italicized)

American Speech and Hearing Association, Wayne University, Detroit, Michigan. *Journal of Speech and Hearing Disorders*
Speech Association of America, 12 E. Bloomington St., Iowa City, Iowa. *The Speech Teacher*
National Society for Crippled Children and Adults, Inc., 11 S. LaSalle St., Chicago, Illinois

Agencies for the Mentally Retarded (Publications italicized)

American Association of Mental Deficiency, Inc., Mansfield Depot, Conn. *American Journal of Mental Deficiency*
National Association for Retarded Children, Inc., 129 E. 52nd St., New York 22, N. Y. *Children Limited*
The Training School, Vineland, N. J. *Training School Bulletin*
National Association of Mental Health, Inc., 1790 Broadway, New York 19, N. Y.
Most states have Mental Health Associations.

Agencies for the Physically Handicapped Children (Publications italicized)

American Academy for Cerebral Palsy, Inc., 4743 N. Drake Ave., Chicago 25, Ill.
American Legion National Rehabilitation Commission, 1608 K Street, N.W., Washington 6, D. C.
American Congress of Physical Medicine, 30 N. Michigan Ave., Chicago 2, Ill.
American Occupational Therapy Association, 33 W. 42nd St., New York 18, N. Y. *Public American Journal of Occupational Therapy* (Bi-monthly)

188

American Orthopedic Association, 8 The Fenway, Boston 15, Mass. *Journal of Bone and Joint Surgery*

American Physical Therapy Association, 1790 Broadway, New York 19, N. Y. *Physical Therapy Review*

Association for the Aid of Crippled Children, 580 Fifth Ave., New York 19, N. Y.

Association of the Junior Leagues of America, Inc., The Waldorf Astoria, 305 Park Ave., New York 22, N. Y.

Children's Rehabilitation Institute for Cerebral Palsy, Corkeyville, Md.

Institute for the Crippled and Disabled, 400 1st Ave., New York 10, N. Y.

International Society for the Welfare of Cripples, 127-129 E. 52nd St., New York 22, N. Y. *Bulletin*

Kessler Institute for Rehabilitation, Pleasant Valley Way, West Orange, N. J.

Muscular Dystrophy Association of America, 39 Broadway, New York 6, N. Y. *Muscular Dystrophy News*

National Foundation for Infantile Paralysis, Inc., 120 Broadway, New York 5, N. Y.

National Epilepsy League, 130 N. Wells St., Chicago 6, Ill.

National Committee on Social Aspects of Epilepsy, c/o Muscatatuck School, Butlerville, Ind.

National Multiple Sclerosis Society, 270 Park Ave., New York 17, N. Y. *AARMS Forward*

National Organization for Public Health Nursing, 1790 Broadway, New York 19, N. Y. *Public Health Nursing*

National Rehabilitation Association, Arlington Bldg., 1025 Vermont Ave., N.W., Washington 5, D. C. *Journal of Rehabilitation*

National Society for Crippled Children and Adults, Inc., 11 S. LaSalle St., Chicago, Ill. *Crippled Child* (Bi-monthly); *Bulletin on Current Literature* (monthly bibliography)

Orthopedic Appliance and Limb Manufacturers Association, 336 Washington Bldg., Washington 5, D. C. *OALMA Journal*

Pope Foundation, Inc., 197 S. West Ave., Kankakee, Ill. *Braces Today*

Sister Elizabeth Kenny Foundation, Inc., 507 Fifth Ave., New York, N. Y.

Shut-In Society, Inc., 221 Lexington Ave., New York 16, N. Y.

United Cerebral Palsy Association, Inc., 369 Lexington Ave., (at 41st St.) New York 17, N. Y.

Agencies for the Gifted Children

American Association for Gifted Children, Inc., 15 Gramercy Park, New York 3, N. Y.

Agencies for the Socially Maladjusted Children (Publications italicized)

American Association of Social Workers, One Park Ave., New York 16, N. Y.

American Orthopsychiatric Association, 25 W. 54th St., New York 19, N. Y. *American Journal of Orthopsychiatry*
American Public Welfare Association, 1313 E. 60th St., Chicago 37, Ill.
American Recreation Association, 315 4th Ave., New York 10, N. Y. *Recreation*
American Vocational Association, 1010 Vermont Ave., N. W., Washington 5, D. C.
Child Care Publication, 30 W. 58th St., New York, N. Y. *Nervous Child*
American Association of Psychiatric Clinics for Children, 1790 Broadway, New York 19, N. Y.
American Group Psychotherapy Association, Inc., 228 E. 19th St., New York 3, N. Y.
American Psychiatric Association, Inc., 1270 Ave. of the Americas, New York 20, N. Y.
American Psychological Association, Inc., 1333 16th St., N.W., Washington 6, D. C.
Department of Social Affairs, Division of Social Welfare, Social Reference Centre, New York, N. Y.
Council of Social Work Education, 345 E. 46th St., New York 17, N. Y.
Family Service Association of America, 192 Lexington Ave., New York 16, N. Y. *Social Casework*
Midwestern Psychological Association, 1007 S. Wright St., Champaign, Ill.
National Committee for Mental Hygiene, 1790 Broadway, New York, N. Y. *Mental Hygiene* (Quarterly)
National Association of School Social Workers, One Park Ave., Room 810, New York 16, N. Y.
Western Psychological Association, Institute of Child Welfare, University of California, Berkeley 4, Calif.
Problem and Parole Association, 1790 Broadway, New York 19, N. Y.

Agencies for Children with Special Health Problems (Publications italicized)

American Cancer Society, Inc., 47 Beaver Street, New York 4, N. Y. and 800 Bay St., Toronto, Canada. *Cancer News*
American Congress of Physical Medicine, 30 N. Michigan Ave., Chicago, Ill. *Archives of Physical Medicine*
American Council on Rheumatic Fever of the American Heart Association, 44 E. 23rd St., New York, N. Y.
American Diabetes Association, 1 Nevis Street, Brooklyn 17, N. Y. *A D A Forecast*
American Heart Association, 1790 Broadway, New York 19, N. Y. *The American Heart*
American Medical Association, Bureau of Health Education, 535 N. Dearborn St., Chicago 10, Ill. *Today's Health; American Journal of Diseases of Children*

American Public Health Association, 1790 Broadway, New York 19, N. Y. *American Journal of Public Health*

American Rehabilitation Committee, Inc., 28 E. 21st St., New York 10, N. Y.

American Rheumatism Association, Inc., 620 W. 168th St., New York 32, N. Y.

Arthritis and Rheumatism Foundation, 23 W. 45th St., New York 36, N. Y.

Association for Physical-Mental Rehabilitation, V.A. Hospital, Canadiagua, N. Y. *Journal*

Association of the Junior Leagues of America, Inc., The Waldorf Astoria, 305 Park Avenue, New York 22, N. Y.

Canadian Arthritis and Rheumatism Society, Inc., 270 MacLaren St., Ottawa, Canada

Canadian Tuberculosis Association, 265 Elgin St., Ottawa, Canada

Commission on Chronic Illness, 525 N. Dearborn St., Chicago 10, Ill. *Chronic Illness Newsletter*

Helen Hay Whitney Foundation, 525 E. 68th St., New York 21, N. Y.

National Conference of Tuberculosis Workers, 1790 Broadway, New York 19, N. Y.

National Organization for Public Health Nursing, 1790 Broadway, New York 19, N. Y. *Public Health Nursing*

National Rehabilitation Association, Arlington Bldg., 1025 Vermont Ave., N.W., Washington 5, D. C. *Journal of Rehabilitation*

National Tuberculosis Association, Inc., 1790 Broadway, New York 19, N. Y. *NTBA Bulletin*

One of the best ways for parents to endorse their children's creative activities is to place an occasional example on the wall. A small investment in a frame adds much, and convinces them more fully of the seriousness of parental interest.

6: Evaluation

*The **area of evaluation** in art education has gained in importance in recent years. Methods as well as the aims of evaluation have changed. Numerical ratings were once given to pieces of art work, whether they were produced by children, adolescents, or college students. During the 1940's and 1950's, many art teachers gave up numerical grading in favor of letter grades, but they managed to maintain a number of calibrations by making lavish use of plusses and minusses. During this same period, students often had difficulty in determining the difference between C and B.*

Letter grades are little more than disguised numerical ratings, but they continue to be used by some teachers "because the administration requires it," "because parents want it that way," "because a college will accept only a letter grade," or for some other seem-

Although a child's total performance and evidence of growth might be reported to parents as "progressing satisfactorily," "needs help," or "excellent," a separate work, such as this oil painting by a seven-year-old girl, simply cannot be given a particular letter or number grade. The child painted creatively on top of a numbered painting canvas.

COURTESY SCHOOL ARTS

192

ingly imperative, but actually inadequate reason. It should also be noted that there are still a few art teachers who even continue to grade art works on a numerical basis, awarding an 83 to one child, an 82 to another, etc.

Many teachers today clearly understand that letter and numerical grading of art work is undesirable not merely because it attempts to pin-point and classify something which can neither be pin-pointed nor classified, but because *the most important element to be evaluated is not exclusively the work of art, but the growth which the individual experienced during the process of producing and subsequently self-evaluating a piece of creative work.*

Statements by two art educators, concerning the importance of the child and his process of working, may help clarify the foregoing statement. Ernest Ziegfeld states:

As art teachers, we must evaluate the growth of the pupils with whom we work, not paintings or sculpture, or art notebooks, or house plans. These, it is true, provide some of our most valuable evidence, but it is as evidence that we must view them, not as ends in themselves. Although for the pupil the product may often be of great importance, as far as the teacher is concerned this interest in the product should be seen as another manifestation of the experience which the pupil is undergoing. A second grade child may complete a painting which to us has real merit as an artistic statement and, as soon as he has finished, may destroy it because in terms of his values it is unsatisfactory. Or a high-school student may be extremely pleased with what we consider to be a second-rate design for an automobile. In both cases, only as we consider the work and its creator together can we arrive at a true evaluation of the growth of the pupil.*

Concerning the highly individual nature of creativity, Lowenfeld has said:

. . . . the more we penetrate into the nature and complexity of personality growth the more we know that there are no accurate measurements for it. We cannot measure mental growth with a yardstick nor can we put creativity on a scale. . . . Since creative activity is intensely personal, we can only expect general guides in evaluation of creative works.**

*Ernest Ziegfeld, "Art in General Education," *This is Art Education,* 1951 Yearbook of the National Art Education Association, Kutztown, Pennsylvania, pp. 65-66.

* * Viktor Lowenfeld, "The Purpose of Evaluation of Creative Products," *Research Bulletin,* Eastern Arts Association, Vol 2, No. 1, March, 1951, p. 5.

Encouraging signs of progress are noted in an in-service study of evaluation in art education.

The teachers were agreed that evaluation is concerned with the measurement of growth as evidenced by behavior change. In gathering evidence of such growth, attention is focused upon the behavior of a particular child in a particular situation as compared with his past behavior in other similar situations, rather than with the comparison of the performance or behavior of one child with that of another. Evaluation is an integral part of the complete learning situation and is, therefore, a continuous process. It is essential that both teachers and pupils participate in it together.

. . . However, since children vary in their potentialities, develop at different rates, and differ in so many aspects of their experience, the teachers were agreed that there could be no fixed standards of achievement for all children at any one grade level.[*]

Fortunately, an increasing number of teachers on every level of education understand contemporary educational philosophy, and have put newer methods of evaluation into practice. Thus they have taken the first step toward the elimination of letter or numerical rating requirements in art. Once they have helped fellow teachers, school administrators, and boards of education to understand the workability and effectiveness of evaluation of individual growth through art, the problem will near a solution.

The attitudes of some alert secondary school students toward letter grade evaluation in art are revealed in an interview-study. John E. Courtney states that he:

. . . interviewed twenty groups of secondary school adolescents (70 girls and 57 boys) from thirteen different schools and agencies . . . whose backgrounds and art interests showed wide variance. The groups discussed at length various aspects of their art experiences and, generally speaking, their comments were enlightening and challenging; at times they were deeply stirring.

Interrogator. How do you feel about marks on the work that you do? . . .

Lee. Well, I think that all works you couldn't mark by grades—eighty-five or ninety, because they're so different from each other; you could just say they were fairly good or they were excellent. I don't think you can mark all of them exactly as to grades.

---

*Edith M. Henry, "Evaluation of Children's Growth Through Art Experiences," *Art Education*, Vol. 6, No. 4, May, 1953, p. 5.

Norma. I feel that marks are important. You want to know how you are doing, and if you can improve, but it's hard to give a mark in art. The really important thing is what you've gotten out of it yourself, and actually how does the teacher know?

Miriam. I think that your art work, or whatever you do, is finished when you get the same feeling from looking at it, or from holding it, that you do from your original idea. And that's why you really can't be marked on what you do, because it's what was in your mind that you're trying to recapture, and not how the teacher feels about it. I also feel that if by any chance you do change your work, it is more or less out of respect for someone—to show them that you think enough of what they say to do something about it.

Interrogator. You didn't tell me what you thought about getting a grade on your art work. Does that bother you? . . .

Barbara. (8th grade) . . . when a teacher looks at a painting, I don't think he should say, 'That's a good picture, I'll give that person a one.' I think he should, in a way find out who the person is. The teacher should learn to know what ability each person has.

Felix. (7th grade) I think that the work should be graded on your progress, how you progressed from the lesson before.

Carol K. (9th grade) Well, in evaluating work, I've seen teachers sort of mark like on the curve it's called. It was done in our own art class. The first group gets up, and they do what they have to do, and she says, 'Well, that's good, but I can't mark it till I see someone else's.' Now if the second group shouldn't be as good, they'll probably get a ninety, and the second group could be worth about eighty, because she's marking according to somebody else, and not exactly on what is done.*

The secondary school students whose opinions are quoted above show a remarkable degree of perception regarding the nature of art experiences and the means by which these experiences may stimulate growth. Yet, as anyone who has chosen to draw forth sustained and sincere opinions from students will testify, the opinions cited here are more common than rare.

WHO SHOULD EVALUATE

Self-Evaluation. Perhaps the most effective form of growth measurement is self-evaluation. Even in the early years of childhood this ability can be effectively encouraged and developed, sup-

---

*John E. Courtney, "Grading and Marking in Art," *Art Education*, Vol. 7, No. 1, Jan., 1954, pp. 5-7.

Though she would probably be unable to understand the art qualities which underly Georges Rouault's *Maria Lani,* the five-year-old girl who painted this black outlined pumpkin-like head and neck might enjoy seeing the similarities between her work and his *after* having completed her own. Classroom teachers and parents might profit in another way by making this comparison. Young children frequently achieve a quality of artistic significance in their work which should to the fullest possible extent be carried over into later life.

Georges Rouault's *Maria Lani* is child-like in its strength and simplicity, yet it is not childish. The fact that features of young children's paintings often compare with outstanding professional works does not mean that their art work should receive unusual acclaim. Paintings by Rouault, as well as Matisse, Leger, and Miro, are ideally suited for display in elementary school classrooms and corridors.

COURTESY OF THE ART INSTITUTE OF CHICAGO. GIFT OF THE ARTS CLUB

196

plemented, of course, by friendly, sincere, and timely evaluation by teachers and parents. As the child grows older and becomes more critical, he expects more detailed and constructively critical evaluation, yet even here the emphasis should be on the further development of self-understanding. For example, it is pointless, at times harmful, to tell a child a work he is producing or a way he works is "good," "nice," or "I don't like it." Even in their pre-school years and increasingly so as they grow older, children need and want to know the reasons why something they have done, or the way they have done it, is good, mediocre or less than satisfactory. The parent or teacher who says, "Those colors are very nice together," or "You enjoy using red and gray together, don't you?" instead of merely saying "Nice," helps a young child to form value judgments.

Children, as well as adolescents and adults, can do a lot more self-evaluating than they believe themselves able to do. For example, a skillful art teacher in conversation with an individual engaged in a creative activity can draw forth comments about the process and product which were not previously realized on a conscious level. Sometimes a statement such as, "Now, tell me just what you are trying to do," will start the flow of perceiving, reacting, and thinking which results in self-evaluation. In other cases a more pointed remark may be effective: "That shade of green you have mixed is very effective against the light blue. Do the other colors please you as well?" A question such as "How did you get that rough textured appearance?" might make the creator consciously aware for the first time that there is a rough texture and that he developed it.

Concerning the importance of self-evaluation in the critical adolescent period Lally and LaBrant have said:

Art educators and psychologists have indicated that interest in art tends to diminish at each level as children proceed through the inter-

At times children become aware of movement qualities in their art work and enjoy physical expression of some of the feelings thus suggested.

PHOTO BY DEWEY EKDAHL

197

Students usually possess a keen interest in their·work and can learn to evaluate their own products.

mediate and upper grades and on to secondary schools. This is certainly true in schools of the old type, but observation of children at work in progressive schools and classes over the past fifteen years leads one to believe that *motivation and stimulation of a dynamic sort, together with standards of evaluation devised by the children themselves, have succeeded in retaining the interest of large numbers of young people in creative art production.* It is only in schools and classes where child art is not appreciated that a tremendous decline in creativity occurs. . . .*

Effective learning takes place within the individual. Effective evaluation, therefore, is based upon the individual's understanding of his work. Improved and intensified self-study should be the aim of all evaluation, whether it originates with the creator, the teacher, or the parent. Methods of evaluation which do not induce self-appraisal are usually superficial and meaningless.

The criteria suggested in the section "What to Evaluate," pp. 20A-206 are not intended as a direct "check list" for self-evaluation. For example, the art teacher should not ask a child, "Are you identifying yourself in your art work?" although the response to such a question might in some cases be amusing. The various criteria presented here may be translated by a skillful teacher or parent into terms which would have real meaning for the child. For example, the important criterion, "ability to think for oneself, to use initiative," can be translated into, "I'm glad to see you like to do your own work instead of copying someone else's," or, "Why do you think it is better to do your own work than to copy someone else's?" Initiative can be further encouraged by tactfully discouraging (but not condemning tracing or filling in drawings made by others.

---

*Ann Lally and Lou La Brant, in *The Gifted Child,* Boston; D. C. Heath & Co., 1951, p. 250. (Italics not in original quotation.)

The art teacher. The person best suited to evaluate individual growth through art is the art teacher. Although in a great number of cases the classroom teacher understands the total personality needs and strengths of a child better than the art teacher, it is usually the art teacher who most fully understands the characteristics of children's creative and aesthetic growth in art. The art teacher spends a greater portion of his time working with many children every day who are engaged in creative activities. This daily experience, based upon four or more years of specialized college education usually permits him to be better able to form generalizations concerning the characteristics of children's art work and processes on various interest and ability levels. When supplemental information concerning an individual child is desired, it can be secured from the classroom teacher, parents, or school records.

Actually, the best evaluation of growth through art takes place when the child, the art teacher, the classroom teacher, the parents, and the school administrator are working as a team. With such an arrangement, opportunities for the use of evaluation as a stimulus for increased growth through art are limitless.

The classroom teacher. The classroom teacher plays an impor-

Classroom teachers often supplement the art specialist's teaching by encouraging children to create interpretations such as this three-dimensional farm, which aids them in understanding and remembering study units.

COURTESY APPLIED ARTS DEPARTMENT, TEXAS TECHNOLOGICAL COLLEGE, LUBBOCK, TEXAS

tant role in the teaching of art. Among her responsibilities is the evaluation of pupils' growth through art. Working closely with the art teacher, she should take advantage of every opportunity to learn more about the characteristics of children's interest and ability levels in art. Since art is an important part of everything children do in and out of the classroom, it is obviously to the teacher's advantage, as well as advantageous to the children, to find out as much as possible about evaluating their growth in art.

Children who are permitted to have a rich background of creative experiences in school and home life will usually retain their creativeness much longer than those who are less fortunate and have their creative imaginations dulled by adult-drawn and designed coloring books, numbered painting kits, pre-designed craft kits, and teacher-illustrated worksheets.

The following example of a comparison between creative worksheet drawings and workbook illustrations is enlightening. The illustrations on pages 202-203 are from "A Study of the Effect of

nine green trees   five red houses

Many teachers have developed their own worksheets, providing an opportunity for the child to draw his own objects instead of filling in adult-drawn subjects. The above portion of a first grade worksheet illustrates how art activities can be used to foster abilities in counting, reading, understanding content, determining size, and following directions, without sacrificing creativeness. Classroom teachers who use such worksheets report that the children's own drawings intensify rather than lessen the skills which they intend to develop.

The fireman
I live in a Red house.
I live on the left side.
I am a fireman.
I get Gas for my truck at
Joe's Gas Station.
DaVid Jones

COURTESY MRS. HELEN SHANK, ELMA, NEW YORK

On the second grade level pupils were encouraged to write and illustrate stories. Note the interesting concept of the modern fire truck, presumably emerging from the firehouse. It indicates a high degree of perceptivity on the part of seven-year-old David, and is a good example of a child relating an illustration to his story.

Workbook Copy Experiences on the Creative Concepts of Children" made by an elementary education director and an art supervisor.* Their captions tell the story.

---

* Irene Russell and Blanche Waugaman, in *Research Bulletin,* Eastern Arts Association, Vol. 3, No. 1, April, 1952, pp. 8-9.

FIGURE ONE

1. *No change*—drawings were identical to the ones made by the child before.
2. *Slight change*—minor aspects of drawings resemble workbook copy.

1. Before exposure.

Workbook copy.

2. After exposure. Notice change "head" according to workbook tern. "Profile" has not been un stood, but rigidly applied. See gre stiffness also in "legs."

3. After exposure. Notice the "chimney" and "roof" as "greater changes." While two sides of the house were drawn "before exposure" only one side appears in the changed view.

Workbook copy.

Before exposure.

FIGURE TWO

3. *Greater change*—major aspect of drawing resemble workbook copy.

4. *Whole concept resembles copy.* The drawing made by the child after work-book exposure was completely changed from his original drawing and identical to workbook copy.

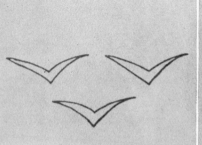

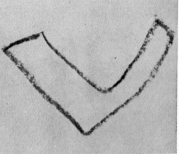

ore exposure. Notice richness
oncept.

Workbook copy.

After exposure. Notice the com-plete dependency to workbook copy. Also notice that workbook symbol has been entirely misun-derstood.

FIGURE FOUR

5. *Concept changed but no resemblance to copy.* The drawing after exposure is different from first but there is no resemblance to workbook copy. It is possible that this student did not respond to direct influence that caused slavish copy work in the other cases. Yet he doubts his own concepts of certain features.

After exposure. Notice particularly symbols for "hands" and "feet." The symbol for "foot" resem-bles slightly the work-book copy.

ore exposure. Notice richness of
bols for "hands" and "feet."

Workbook copy.

boy

Parents and relatives. With the cooperation of parents and relatives, the educational program can be greatly improved. On the other hand, parents and relatives who encourage copying, tracing, or the use of coloring books can actually nullify many of the potential values of creative art education.

One way of achieving parents' cooperation in the evaluation of creative growth through art is the "letter to parents" idea, described on pp. 219-222. Also helpful is an occasional article on children's creative activities found in popular magazines.

School adminstrators. Essential to the success of any aspect of the educational program are school principals, superintendents, curriculum coordinators, elementary and secondary supervisors, guidance counselors, and other administrative personnel. Their support lends the seemingly necessary stamp of approval to newer trends in educational theory and practice. One of these newer trends is the evaluation of the individual through creative art activities in place of grading pupils' art work on the basis of their ability to copy or imitate. Many school administrators have assumed leadership in setting up educational programs based on newer educational theories. Most administrators are familiar with the basic nature of creative activity and its importance in nearly every area of the curriculum.* The art teacher has a good professional friend in the school administrator; a friend who should be called on for advice as well as support of developments in the art education program. Every administrator prefers to be called in "to look at some work our children are doing" or to "give me some suggestions for better organizing the art room," instead of feeling obliged now and then to drop in to see what's going on. Similarly, the administrator is often pleased as well as qualified to be consulted about the improvement of evaluation techniques. It is one of the important responsibilities of the art teacher to work with the administration in the improvement of the art program, and to implement any suggestions for curriculum revision or extension which are bonafide, meritorious, and within the scope of available time, facilities, and materials.

WHAT TO EVALUATE

The chart which follows lists criteria intended for use in measuring growth through art. Most of these criteria can be applied at

---

*The 1956 conference of the Association for Supervision and Curriculum Development, was centered on creativity. The 1959 conference of the American Association of School Administrators was focused on the arts.

all educational levels. These criteria are not intended for use in arriving at a letter or numerical grade. As they now stand, the various items vary in relative importance; they will vary even more when they are used to evaluate the growth of individuals.

The key to successful evaluation is a concept of growth measurement, as contrasted with the determination of status. The touchstone of growth is the individual himself—*what he was, what he is,* and *what he gives promise of becoming.*

Criteria Suggested for Evaluating Individual Growth Through Art

EVIDENCE OF INDIVIDUAL GROWTH IN:

Total personality development
Individual uniqueness
Ability to think for oneself, to use initiative
Ability to identify or put something of oneself into one's work
Ability to concentrate upon creative art expression to a point where the individual is not easily distracted.
Ability to express moods and sincere feelings through art expression
Ability to work to the capacity of one's ability
Ability to evaluate oneself
Ability to receive and profit by deserved praise and constructive criticism
Ability to derive personal satisfaction and justifiable pride from accomplishments in art

Social competence
Ability to enjoy others' uniqueness
Ability to work cooperatively with others
Ability to evaluate growth in others

Creativity
Willingness to experiment with ideas, materials, and tools
Interest in art activities which involve personal value judgments and unique working methods
Enjoyment of the learning process as well as the end product
Ability to express ideas in two- or three-dimensional form as well as in words
Ability to express oneself through abstract as well as realistic symbols
Ability to work creatively, with steadily decreasing interest in the use of non-creative devices

Aesthetic understanding and art ability
Ability to produce art works which possess increasingly significant form. This comes about intuitively, in children, as a result of deepened interest and sincere expression in art activities. On this level, the quality of *form* in the art work is merely an indication of deepened interest and sincerity, and is not something to be evaluated in itself. On the adolescent and adult

levels, however, the ability to produce art works which possess increasingly significant form becomes more important to both student and teacher.

Ability to observe design in everyday environment

Willingness to attempt and ability to solve increasingly more complex problems

Ability to make use of increasingly more complex processes and tools

Ability to choose and correctly use best-suited tools and equipment

Use of art knowledge in selection of personal clothing and grooming styles, living quarters, manufactured items, and art objects

How to evaluate

In order to evaluate individual growth through art, it is first necessary to develop a personal philosophy of art education. Throughout this book an attempt has been made to set forth the elements of contemporary educational philosophy from which a personal set of principles might be derived. It may be necessary, in some cases, for the reader to list the elements of educational philosophy in which he believes before a satisfactory approach to evaluation may be determined.

One of the important elements in contemporary art educational philosophy is the relation of means and ends. Evaluation should not be an end in itself. It should be a means of encouraging growth in the individual being evaluated. It is also used as a means of reporting pupil progress to parents, other teachers, school administrators, and members of the board of education. When evaluation is used as an end, as indeed it has been in too much of the history of education, whatever growth may have taken place usually stops when the mark is received.

Questionable means can hardly be justified by seemingly desirable ends. Some teachers of art honestly feel that the letter or numerical grade they give their students is not a stopping point but a means of encouraging continued interest and development in art. Others feel that grades *should be* stopping points, and they are generous with "D's" and "E's" or "50's" and "60's." These teachers often save good grades or high numerical ratings for their gifted pupils. Both of these points of view would seem to have been outdated long ago. Most educators prefer individual evaluation designed to encourage, rather than tabulate, growth.

Understanding the nature of children and their art work. There is no question that "experience is the best teacher." It is one of the best ways to understand the nature of children, the ways in which they work, and the nature of the work they produce. For this reason art teacher education programs are including more and more actual teaching experiences in their curricula, supplemented with films, texts, and lecture discussions. Art educators have found that first-hand observation, participation, and actual teaching experiences can profitably be offered students as early as their freshman year in college, and that students' summer camp work with children is further helpful. Lectures, texts, and vicarious experiences will not, in themselves, enable the art teacher properly to evaluate growth through art. These aids to learning can never be used as substitutes for direct life experiences.

The answer, then, is comparatively simple: to be able to evaluate individual growth through art it is necessary to observe and work closely with groups of people in a variety of educational situations (i.e., classroom, playground, recreation center, Sunday school) over an extended period of time. It is necessary to observe the ways in which different types of individuals work, as well as the products they produce. It is helpful to compare what is learned in this way with what has been written or filmed about the age level in question, to validate or extend these findings in light of personal experience. A variety of actual teaching experiences coupled with the best available lectures, films, discussions, and readings is the best way to develop the abilities necessary to evaluate growth through art.

WHEN TO EVALUATE

There is no one time when it is best to evaluate an individual's growth through art. Current methods of evaluation suggest a *continuous process* in which many persons need to participate. Pupils of any age, their parents, teachers, school administrators, and school board members should be concerned with evaluation. When a youngster is making progress in his educational development, everyone should rejoice. Each person should ask, "How am I contributing to his growth?" The pupil should be encouraged to ask himself "What has caused me to do better work?" Following this assessment, all parties concerned should inquire "How can we make further contributions to this person's growth?" When a youngster is failing to progress in any area of his educational development, he should be encouraged to ask himself, "Why did I fail?" Each person connected with the child should ask himself, "How did I contribute to his failure?" and ask him, "How might I have helped you more than I did?"

Providing conditions which encourage growth. One can hardly decide when to evaluate growth until conditions have been provided which foster it. An art supervisor and a group of classroom teachers in Denver, Colorado, prepared an excellent statement of some conditions which promote growth. A portion of their report, based on years of practical experience in daily classroom activity with boys and girls, follows.

. . . if children are to become cooperative, self-directing, creative individuals, they need:

Opportunities for creative art experiences

Experiences that are firsthand, continuous, and varied, and that involve the senses, memory, imagination, and observation.

Experiences that provide opportunities to select those things that are important to them and to organize them to their satisfaction.

Interesting, challenging learning situations

Situations in which expectancies are in harmony with their maturity level and experimental background.

Situations in which they share in determining purposes, setting goals, and planning the means for achieving them.

Situations in which there is freedom to investigate, to try out ideals, to make mistakes, and to assume responsibility for results.

Situations in which they are encouraged to want to learn and to develop their varied resources.

Situations in which they are helped to know and understand the world in which they live and to cope with change.

Situations in which they have some opportunity to work both as individuals and as members of a group, respecting the rights of others and accepting responsibilities.

Situations in which they have the opportunity to share ideas and feelings with others.

Situations in which they can make selections and choices with maturing judgment.

Stimulating materials

Materials that are ample enough to permit wide exploration and necessary mistakes.

Materials that arouse curiosity and encourage investigation.

Materials that are suitable for a particular stage of maturity.

Materials that present a variety of possibilities and choices.

Ample time

Time to experiment with materials.
Time to make and carry out plans.
Time to· work at their own rate.

Adequate space

Space that permits them to work alone or in a number of small groups.
Space that enables them to work on large projects.
Space that allows them to arrange and care for equipment and materials easily.

Friendly, sincere, understanding teachers

Teachers who have experienced the thrill of creating something themselves.
Teachers who appreciate the creative work of others.
Teachers who possess skills needed to work with a variety of materials.
Teachers who see the possibilities for creative experiences in day-by-day classroom living.
Teachers who know the community and the demands it makes upon children.
Teachers who understand the stages of child growth and development and know what to expect at each maturity level.
Teachers who have wide personal interests.
Teachers who participate in community activities and have kept alive the "urge to learn" within themselves.
Teachers who can provide a stimulating environment organized to encourage children to work creatively.

Informed and growing parents

Parents who understand their form of expression.
Parents who are interested in their development and encourage them to continue their efforts in leisure time.
Parents who help them widen their experiences in looking, feeling, and understanding.

An atmosphere conducive to growth

An atmosphere that is friendly and warm.
An atmosphere in which you can make mistakes and be helped by others if "you get stuck."
An atmosphere that encourages different ways of doing things.
An atmosphere in which praise is offered sincerely.
An atmosphere that fosters self-respect, self-reliance, respect for others, and a cooperative attitude.*

*Edith M. Henry, "Evaluation of Children's Growth Through Art Experiences," *Art Education*, Vol. 6, No. 4, May, 1953, pp. 22-23.

On the pages which follow, several techniques for evaluating progress are suggested. To become effective, these techniques should be utilized frequently, not just at the end of a school term. Even the best evaluation techniques can be rendered ineffective through infrequent use. Yet such techniques as teacher-parent conferences can hardly be continuous. At best, two, perhaps three, teacher-parent conferences per semester would be possible. Practical considerations will probably cause the most frequently used techniques of evaluation to be: the observation of pupil work habits, teacher-pupil discussions of work in progress; class criticisms of completed works; written comments about each pupil, and careful examination of chronological files of works produced. Techniques such as teacher-pupil discussions of art work in progress might occur several times per week. If these discussions, however brief, are constructively critical, and not merely polite expressions, they comprise one of the strongest elements of continuous, cooperative evaluation.

RECORDING EVIDENCE OF GROWTH

In addition to the mental notes an art teacher makes about each of his pupils, other methods of describing and recording significant elements of growth through art are necessary. The recording system chosen by the art teacher will depend upon factors such as number of classes, interest in modern evaluation methods, and depth of interest in the individuals with whom he works. Briefly described on the pages which follow are several evaluation systems, some of which are widely used today and a few which are still largely in the philosophic stage.

The teacher's classbook. Probably the most widely used form for recording evaluation is the teacher's classbook. Its effectiveness, however, is limited by its format, a division of pages into small rectangles intended for letter or numerical ratings. An important factor in the continued use of classbooks is the philosophy of education underlying their use. As long as teachers are expected to give letter or numerical ratings, and as long as administrators and boards of education insist that they do, it is likely that classbooks will be popular in educational evaluation. Certainly the overcrowded, numerous classes which many teachers face each day will not likely encourage them to adopt more descriptive and time-consuming evaluation systems. Nor will the poor salaries paid by some communities inspire teachers to render greater educational services than they are doing at present.

Since numerical and alphabetical rating systems leave too much to the imagination of students and parents and since they do not provide any suggestions for improvement, a student is usually at a loss to know what methods he may employ to improve his grade. In light of these practical circumstances, some "emergency" criteria are suggested (pp. 212-213) for arriving at letter grades which may possess a greater degree of validity than those most often used for this purpose. Letter grades should continue in use only until a better annotated type of evaluation system can be instituted. *It should be clearly understood that in suggesting these criteria for arriving at letter grades for evaluative purposes no approval of the letter grading system is implied or conceded.*

Teacher-pupil conferences. One of the most effective means of reporting growth to pupils, and thus indirectly to their parents, is the teacher-pupil conference. With some children it may be necessary to hold a "formal conference" where pertinent evaluation factors may be discussed. With others, casual comments as the child is actively working on a project may be sufficient to bring about the desired results. It may be something as simple as "That's coming nicely, Mary," or "You're getting a little messy, aren't you John?" On the other hand, with older children, it might be more complex, but always within the understanding of the pupil: "Let's talk about the model house you are building. Your construction methods are excellent. You have securely fastened the model to the base. The colors you have chosen look very well together, and you have put the bright ones in the best places. However, you might have mixed your tempera paint more thoroughly, and brushed it on more carefully. It would give you a better looking job than you are now getting. You certainly don't want your fine construction work to be ruined by a poor paint job, do you?"

A few minutes spent in this type of conference is valuable to the pupil as well as the teacher, *whether or not* he is given a grade on the work. This type of conference is one of the best means of evaluation available to the pupil, encourages him to think more about his own work, and is helpful to the teacher as well.

Teacher-parent conferences. Probably the best means of reporting to parents is the teacher-parent conference. These should be scheduled at least once a year by the classroom or homeroom teacher, and should, when possible, include the art teacher as well as others (such as guidance, music, health education, industrial

Suggested Criteria for Improving Evaluation in Art Education in School Systems Where Letter Grades Are Required

Note: An "improved" system for letter grading in art has been suggested here — done to pupils who are given letter grades based on less valid criteria. only as a temporary measure to alleviate the harm which might other wise be

EXCEPTIONS	LETTER GRADE	USUAL VERBAL EQUIVALENTS	GROWTH IN DESIRABLE ATTITUDES	DEVELOPMENT OF CRAFTSMANSHIP	IMPROVEMENT IN EXPRESSIVE AND AESTHETIC QUALITIES OF WORK
For psychological or other reasons felt to be valid, A's and B's are sometimes given to individuals whose attitudes, work habits, and work quality are not outstanding, but need encouragement, security or group status; or who occasionally produce an excellent work, show excellent craftsmanship, or demonstrate the beginnings of desirable attitudes.	A =	Outstanding Superior Excellent Highly significant	Highly cooperative, deeply interested in welfare of students and teachers, enjoys receiving and profits by constructive criticism. Highly imaginative, very sincere, honest. Outstanding initiative. Able to make sound, independently formed value judgments.	Continuous improvement in already desirable work habits, safe and skillful use of tools, clean and artistic final presentation of work, careful attention to functional use of tools and media, and thorough preplanning of projects which necessitate this approach.	Increasingly original and more highly significant utilization of art knowledge in producing imaginative, and superior art works. Able to express self clearly in work, utilizing various techniques and material to interpret different moods, opinions and subjects.
	B =	Good Above average Better than average Commendable Significant	Cooperative, interested in welfare of others as well as self. Sincere, honest, imaginative, dependable. Shows initiative in art work. Treats others' work with respect. Able to concentrate despite minor distractions.	General improvement in functional and safe use of tools and materials. Shows increased interest in care and cleaning of room, issuing and collecting materials. Usually chooses tools and materials best suited to subject chosen or technique to be used.	Creative works hold increasingly well together (well composed, proportioned, and balanced; possess interesting and well-related colors, textures, lines, shapes, spaces) and show clear evidence of personal expression.

212

EXCEPTIONS	LETTER GRADE	USUAL VERBAL EQUIVALENTS	GROWTH IN DESIRABLE ATTITUDES	DEVELOPMENT OF CRAFTSMANSHIP	IMPROVEMENT IN EXPRESSIVE AND AESTHETIC QUALITIES OF WORK
For psychological or other reasons felt to be valid, C's and D's are sometimes given to individuals whose attitudes, work habits, and work quality are usually above average but who occasionally reveal weaknesses or do not continue to show growth.	C =	Average Medium Acceptable Satisfactory	Usually cooperative, often interested in the welfare of others as well as self. Sometimes volunteers for routine responsibilities. Shows slight improvement over previous attitudes.	Moderate attention to proper use of tools and materials, some attempt to clean up finished products before final evaluation, occasional awareness of others' safety and welfare while working.	Usually undistinguished, yet somewhat well organized and usually original work, showing acceptable, though not exciting, use of art elements and moderate understanding of art principles.
	D =	Below average Unsatisfactory Poor	Uncooperative and undependable. Rarely volunteers for art room duties. Resents constructive criticism from teacher or students.	Casual and occasionally careless treatment of tools and materials. Work habits disorderly.	Occasionally stereotyped, copied and poorly designed work, revealing neither representational nor design ability. Inartistic uses of color, texture, line and space. Intentionally not working to capacity of ability.
Considerable evidence points to the possibility that pupils do not fail, as such, but that teachers, educational systems, and parents fail to meet their needs and thus induce attitudes, work habits, and work qualities which are then called unacceptable or failing.	F =	Extremely poor Completely unacceptable	Hostile toward students and teacher; extremely uncooperative; insincere, dishonest; refuses to work or study. (Probably requires specialized psychological and/or psychiatric services.)	Intentional destruction of art materials, tools and products of self and others. Inability to implement principles of sound craftsmanship.	Quality of work lacks any trace of artistic significance or individual expressiveness. Copies work of other pupils.

The annotated record. A more desirable form for recording elements of individual growth through art is the annotated record. Some sample forms are presented below.

Chronological Annotated Record Forms

Suggested materials: 3"x5" cards, in file box
4"x6" cards, in file box
sheets of paper, in file folder
notebooks, looseleaf
notebooks, bound

For Daily Annotation:

SEPTEMBER, 19........   4th GRADE   JOHN JONES

9/11   Showed immediate enthusiasm for creative art activities. Uses bright colors, works fast.

9/12   Prefers to work alone, somewhat uncooperative. Uses scrap materials freely to supplement "flat work." Very well groomed and dressed.

9/13   Shared his materials with Paul Williams. Produced three clay objects to everyone else's one. Craftsmanship good.

For Weekly Annotation:

SEPTEMBER, 19........   KINDERGARTEN   RICHARD O'HARA

9/15   Reserved, quiet. Spent entire week in comparative isolation. Manipulates blocks freely, but extremely reticent about paint, clay. Uses hands rather freely to describe "news".

9/22   Still somewhat shy, but emerging. Tried paint and seemed to enjoy it, although said he didn't. Likes to arrange colored paper scraps on large sheet. Prefers not to use paste; likes mucilage dispenser better.

9/29   Invited Sharon Metz into his "private corner" to make "paste-up" pictures". Saw her using paste and tried it himself. Nice sense of color.

For Bi-Weekly Annotation:

SEPTEMBER, 19........   8th GRADE   JANICE BLACK

9/15   Very cooperative, friendly. Tends to be bit careless in cleanup. Works freely, without usual adolescent inhibitions. Draws realistically.

10/1   Attempted first design-type work, enjoyed it. Improving in cleanup, following suggestion. Willing to help others in construction-type activities, even if it means delay in her own work.

For Monthly Annotation:

DRAWING AND PAINTING   11TH GRADE   JEANETTE OWENS

SEPT., 19—.   Came with good background in creative expression. Works diligently and freely. Very attentive to cleanup responsibilities. Prefers street scenes, with sharp perspective, at which she excels. Color use somewhat restricted to grays, browns. Composition has improved continuously. Very happy and relaxed during art periods, despite great attention to detail in her work.

OCT., 19—.   Work of classmates has apparently influenced her use of brighter colors. Took kidding about "dismal" colors in good spirit from her chum. Joined art club, seems interested in carrying on art activities out-of-school. Has decided ability in composition, needs no help in this area. Sought information on art schools as possible place for further study.

NOV., 19—.   Outside sketching with charcoal has loosened her approach to composition considerably. Enjoys quick results afforded by charcoal sketching. Enlarged and painted two sketches at home, brought them to school. Excellent! Ability to include numerous details without sacrificing unity of work is amazing. Nice, humble attitude about her art ability. Gets along splendidly with all classmates.

214

For Irregular Annotations:

9/16   Overly reliant on parent and teacher directions. Cannot think well for himself. Very careless in use of art materials. Somewhat uncooperative.

9/29   Has developed some confidence in his own ideas. Still careless in use of paint and brushes. Prefers 3-D work in clay and wood. Enjoys working with others in 3-D work.

10/2   Brought in carved wood sculpture made at home. Very proud of it. Has responded well to suggestions for improved work habits ever since he began on his 3-D work. Becoming more cooperative.

For Checklist Annotations, Irregular:

19........, ... 3rd GRADE					
SALLY MENKE	9/16	9/30	10/5	10/25	11/3
Originality	fair		better		good
Concentration	good	good	good	good	exc.
Takes criticism	poor	fair		good	good
Self-evaluation	no	no	some	yes	yes
Cooperativeness	fair	fair		good	exc.
Works to capacity of ability	no	some	yes	yes	yes
OTHER CHARACTERISTICS					
Tempera	free, bright colors				
Clay		small, tight			
Linoleum printing			good in detail		
OTHER MEDIA					

For Annotated Summary Records:

HARRY PARKS   His behavior has improved during the year. Harry's deep interest in model building culminated with construction of detailed rocket model. Its exhibition in corridor brought him much needed status in his group, and he has subsequently taken art as a hobby. Needs guidance in use of harmonious colors—has little sense of color intensity or value.

SUSAN DAVIS   Progressed slowly at first, then developed sincere interest in art activities as result of textile painting project. Made skirts, neckerchiefs, etc. for all friends and family members. Nice sense of design, uses appropriate textures, color combinations. Good craftsman. Well adjusted, few personal or social problems. Should be given special attention in eighth grade, opportunity for further work in textile designing, printing, and sewing techniques.

arts, and home economics teachers) who contribute to the child's educational development. If the number of pupils served by the art teacher is small enough, art teacher-parent conferences are desirable.

The portfolio. A collection of each pupil's art work, arranged chronologically over a period of time, provides an excellent source of study for the teacher interested in assessing individual progress according to such criteria as identification of self with subject matter, use of color and texture, and ability to organize subject matter elements in compositions.

The use of the portfolio alone, however, without reference to evidence of growth in personality and other factors mentioned under "What to Evaluate," could be as limiting as letter grade or numerical rating. The portfolio should be used in conjunction with a recording of general progress.

At least two problems are inherent in maintaining portfolios. (1) Pupils like to take home examples of their work shortly after they have been completed. Therefore, only representative examples of art work should be saved for later study by the teacher. (2) It is difficult to store three-dimensional works for subsequent comparative evaluation. In most situations, where storage space is limited, but where necessary money is available, 2" x 2" color slide photographs of pupils' art work may be made and easily stored. Color slides have additional uses for class discussions, P.T.A. meetings, or community talks. Considered for these additional uses, their expense is justified.

Although excellent portfolios are available commercially, and might well be used for storing representative examples of pupils' art works during the year, pupils can easily make their own. Large sheets of bookbinders' cardboard (a sheet of pressed multi-layer cardboard about $\frac{3}{16}$" thick) can be purchased inexpensively in quantity, and should be included in the art department supply budget. The boards can be hinged with buckram or sturdy cloth and covered with materials of individual preference. The design and construction of a portfolio is, in itself, an excellent art activity which lends itself to further evaluation of such abilities as craftsmanship and design. Ideally, the portfolio would be constructed early in the year in order that works might be safely stored in a place where they can later be found. The portfolios themselves may be stored in pull-out bins or deep shelves. Pupils' names should be lettered or taped on the portfolios in a place where they may be identified at a glance.

An important duty of every teacher is reporting the progress of his pupils, both as an aid to the child and as information for his parents. As indicated by the complexity of the section "What to Evaluate," this is a challenging task for the art teacher.

Report cards. The most frequently used form of reporting is the report card. This instrument is usually limited to a series of letter grades or numerical ratings.

The idea of reporting to pupils and their parents is basically good, and it is our intention to encourage it. We will, however, suggest changes in the report card format. Not all parents will be able to attend the teacher-parent conferences which are suggested here; but even if they were, written reporting would retain certain values.

Ideally, the report card would summarize all evidence of growth suggested in the "What to Evaluate" section, pages 204-206. Such a card would provide for teachers' comments rather than bare grades or numerical ratings. It would also summarize teacher-parent conférences, and provide space for parents' comments.

Evaluation of Growth Through Art From _____ to _____

PUPIL.............Theodore Martin.................   ART TEACHER...............Mellquist................
GRADE...........4...........   ROOM...........108...........   (1st semester)

ART TEACHER'S SUMMARY:*

(Date) Ted began the year by relying heavily on the teacher. His hand would go up for assistance the minute I would say, "All right, let's begin." He indicated he was getting a lot of help in various activities at home, and wanted me to help him draw cars, faces, trees, etc. I would have to tell him "how he was doing" every five or ten minutes. Early in the year he was careless with materials. He was somewhat uncooperative, and preferred to work alone.

By the end of September, however, he had begun to develop more confidence in his own ideas, thanks to the cooperation of his parents following the conference noted below. His work habits as well as his interest in art improved greatly as a result of his interest in three-dimensional work. He should be given ample opportunity at home, as well as in school, to develop his interest in sculpture to an even greater extent.

TEACHER-PARENT CONFERENCE SUMMARY:

(Date) Requested by art teacher. Both parents attended, and showed great concern over Ted's over-reliance upon them as well as the art teacher. Discussion did not indicate insecurity at home or other factors which might cause this tendency to continue. I felt that next area of work in three-dimensional materials would help Ted. Follow-up conference planned for next semester.

PARENTS' COMMENT:

(Date) We are both pleased by the individual treatment our family has received as part of the school art program. We're looking forward to our next conference. Do you have any art courses for grown-ups?

*Derived from annotated record illustrated on page 215.

A description of the evolution of teacher-parent conference programs in two communities may prove helpful in providing suggestions for the development of conference programs in other areas.

Aberdeen, South Dakota:

Unlike many other school systems, we were actively encouraged by
parents to shift from the standard send-home report cards.

After parents expressed dissatisfaction with the status quo, parent-teacher
conferences were given a trial run in one elementary school. . . . At
the end of the year, the parents voted overwhelmingly for continuance
of the plan.

Parents of children attending other schools began to bombard the school
board with requests that the conference method be used throughout the
city, and . . . this was finally done in all elementary schools.

Our parent-teacher conferences take place three times a year. For each
conference the teacher assembles samples of the child's daily work;
achievement-test results and other pertinent materials that reflect the
child's progress; and a report card, retained by the teacher, which covers
work habits and social behavior as well as scholastic achievement.

A survey of parent reactions made in 1950 showed that 80% preferred
conferences to send-home reports. A similar survey sent to all teachers
revealed them to be almost unanimously in favor of the change, despite
its time-consuming nature.*

Highland Park, Illinois

At the Ravinia School the faculty intermittently studied the kinds of
parent reports they were using and the kind which were being used
in other suburban communities. Constant revisions were made so that
as much unfair competition as possible was eliminated. The conclusion
was finally reached that no report card could possibly do the job to be
done. Teachers in the middle grades asked the administration if they
could carry on an experimental program, using conferences as a substitute for the report cards. They agreed that all parents should be invited
to have two conferences a year with the homeroom teacher. A conference
form was then formulated to serve as a guide for the discussion at the
conference. It included the areas of social and emotional, physical and
academic growth. This blank was to be prepared by the teacher before
the conference. Samples of work were to be available for reference so
that parents could see actual examples of the children's academic achievement. It was also agreed that all conferences should be held at the
school during the course of the school day, at times when teachers were

*Edna J. Durland, in "Making the Grade with Parents," NEA Journal,
April, 1953, p. 214.

free. Thus a pattern was set that has been followed ever since. Conferences have now been substituted for report cards in all grades at the Ravinia School, kindergarten through eighth.

. . . . . Parents new to the school said they felt the conference helped most in giving them an idea of the philosophy of the school. They knew what the school was striving to do for their children. Also, they felt much more a part of the school and community through this personal contact.

Other significant advantages as expressed by the people interviewed were as follows:

1. Children work harder because of greater parent interest.

2. Areas which cannot be graded can be discussed.

3. Decreases possibility of misunderstanding between home and school.

4. Curriculum is explained.

5. Makes for closer direction of the total child's personality development.*

Letter to parents. Descriptions of various art media and processes, field trips, class discussions, and comments on subjects such as creativity and coloring books can well be summarized and circularized to parents. Not only do letters to parents provide them with more knowledge of the art program in the school, they are also an

---

*Raymond J. Naegele, "Achieving a Pupil-Progress Report," *Phi Delta Kappan,* Vol. XXX, No. 8, April, 1949, pp. 309-310.

Clarence, N. Y., public schools offer regular bulletins to parents based on class experiences such as this.

PHOTO
COURTESY
JAMES
BATTISONI

excellent means of bettering general public relations. Also desirable are printed brochures describing broad aspects of the total school program. The latter is actually the only means of reaching the majority of parents in a school district, since some do not attend P.T.A. or other school meetings.

Teacher-parent-pupil conferences. A combination of the two reporting methods suggested above has several advantages. Used exclusively, it would have certain disadvantages.

Primarily, the teacher-parent-pupil conference is advantageous because it indicates to the pupil that his teacher and parents are working cooperatively in his behalf. In turn, it precludes the possibility that the outcomes of teacher-pupil conferences will be erroneously reported to parents by their children. It also removes evaluation from its traditionally "secret" position and helps it to become a frank, sincere, everyday happening to be looked forward to instead of being dreaded by all parties concerned.

Used exclusively, the teacher-parent-pupil conference would make difficult the occasional necessity for confidential teacher-parent conferences dealing with such characteristics as shyness, extreme extrovert tendencies, and various other emotional, mental, and physical problems. In every community there are a certain number of parents who will not participate in their children's educational program, even if there are special problems. Thus it is occasionally necessary to visit homes to confer with parents.

Class discussions. Another effective means of evaluation which lends itself well to better self-understanding, as well as to the understanding of others, is class discussion. This might be held prior to, during, or following art activities. With proper teacher guidance, the class discussion can provide stimuli for better work habits, social attitudes, and products of art experiences than are otherwise attainable. Particularly with regard to discussions of works in progress or already completed, this means of evaluation can bring forth ideas which otherwise might remain dormant. Children are often notably candid in discussing their own and others' work before a group. A classmate's comment on the colors used or subjects portrayed in an art work may have more pronounced effect on a pupil's further growth than anything a teacher might say. But it is important for the teacher to guide such discussions in a manner which minimizes severe pupil comments.

On the following two pages is reproduced a booklet issued to parents by the Seattle public schools.

HOW WE TEACH ART

● OUR CURRICULUM STAFF has prepared this short statement in answer to usual questions which come to it about how art is taught in the Seattle schools. If you have further questions, will you please consult your local school faculty.

Samuel E. Fleming

Superintendent

Why We Teach Art

We teach art because we believe children should receive as complete and as balanced an education as we can give them. Art contributes to your child's education by encouraging creative growth and developing aesthetic understanding.

What Do We Mean by "Creative Growth"?

Creative growth is growth in becoming more inventive and resourceful. As your child develops in this direction he becomes more confident of his own abilities and more able to express his ideas and feelings.

There are many ways ideas and feelings can be expressed. They may be expressed by writing, singing, dancing, speaking, acting. In art we help your child express himself through painting, drawing, constructing, modeling, and designing.

What Do We Mean by "Aesthetic Understanding"?

Aesthetic understanding gives people the ability to judge whether or not a piece of furniture is well designed, whether a particular color is pleasing in a room, or whether the proportions of a lamp are good. With a young child, aesthetic understanding may begin with the recognition that colors are different, or with the discovery that the blobs of paint he smeared

on his paper yesterday can be arranged into a simple design today.

At first whatever understanding occurs is almost intuitive. A child may recognize, without being told or knowing why, that the figure he has painted is too small to look right in his picture.

As your child progresses from grade to grade he has many opportunities to talk over both what he made and how he made it. Through this evaluation he becomes better able to interpret the meaning of his own and his friends' work. He becomes more aware of color, texture, space, shape, form, and line.

What Are Other Values in Art?

In art we emphasize originality, simplicity, and tolerance.

Originality

Your child learns more, and gains more self-confidence, if he paints or draws his own ideas than if he copies. It is better for him to do his own work in his own way than to copy the work of even the very best artist. When your child studies about Mexico in the third grade, he may want to help other children paint a large mural as part of their study. He will read about the life of Mexican people and look at many photographs or films which describe clothing, homes, work, geography, agriculture, and industries of Mexico. With preparation of this kind your child acquires many ideas about Mexico to put into the mural. He also has had previous opportunity to use the colored chalks or paints with which the mural will be made. He learns more about Mexico and gains more confidence in his ability to learn and express himself through this procedure than if the teacher gave him a picture of a Mexican village and asked him to copy it.

Simplicity

Whatever your child does in art he is encouraged to do as simply as possible. Simplicity is natural for a primary grade child, but an intermediate child, who knows more about art and has had many more experiences, must be helped to become more selective.

A first-grade child may put in his picture such objects as himself, his house, a sun, a tree . . . but a fifth-grade child will want many more things in his picture. He may try to put in all of them and find his picture too full. He must learn to choose which things are important. We stress simplicity because is requires children to be selective and analytical.

Tolerance

Your child learns to become tolerant by seeking the good in other children's work. He is quick to recognize and give credit to those who show creative ability. The teacher sets the example by seeking to approve the best efforts of all children. She follows their growth carefully and comments on improvement. She tells one child that he has been able to get more "action" into his clay figure. She remarks to another that he has shown that he has looked carefully at the milk truck he included in his picture. Her comments are positive and encouraging, rather than negative or discouraging.

How Does Your Child Progress In Understanding Art?

Your child's understanding of art starts with his simple, intuitive efforts to express ideas. It finally becomes a thoughtfully directed use of art knowledges and skills to satisfy the requirements of everyday living.

If he is in the primary grades he first finds what he can do with his tools and materials, then tries to put down his feelings and ideas.

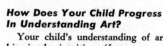

He does not try to paint a picture to hang on the wall or model a figure to decorate the mantel. His ideas are very personal and usually have to do with things he has experienced at home or at school.

If he is in the fourth, fifth, or sixth grade he also uses art to record his everyday experiences. However, he may try to use his knowledge of design for specific decorative purposes. He may stencil a pattern on a cloth to be used for a table mat, or arrange a school bulletin board.

What Materials Does Your Child Use?

He may use many materials. In the primary grades he paints with powder, finger, and water-color paint, draws with crayon, cuts paper, models with clay, and weaves with heavy yarn. From the fourth grade on, the variety of materials may increase to include even thin sheets of aluminum foil, soft wire, scraps of wood or cloth. Scrap materials or native materials are often used in craft work. Fourth-grade children may make figures with cork, pipe cleaners, wire, or cloth, or any other scrap materials they bring to school. By learning to substitute one material for another, by working out their own ways to put materials together, they become more resourceful.

Should Your Child be Given Special Help in Art at Home?

All elementary grade children have many interests and needs. The regular art program is usually sufficient even for those with obvious special ability and interest. However, there are children whose vitality and interest in art can be satisfied only if their extra hours are occupied creatively. Parents may provide special equipment, opportunity, and encouragement at home for creative activities. Special training should not keep children from exploring and enjoying many varied activities.

Does Your Child Learn about Modern Art?

Children's art is simple, direct, uninhibited, colorful, spontaneous. These qualities are admired by modern art. If your child's art appears abstract, it is because he has yet had enough experience to represent his ideas realistic. Conscious painting or modeling of abstractions is usually d by trained adult artists, not by small children.

Large reproductions of the best of all periods of pain are displayed regularly in the schools. This is done to acqu the children with the work of recognized painters whether t paint abstractly or realistically. We want children to main open-minded curiosity about all periods of painting.

How Can Parents Help?

- By looking with favor upon the efforts of their children to exp themselves artistically.
- By making available inexpensive art materials and an access place to keep and use them.
- By placing high value on originality and inventiveness.
- By encouraging their children to try continually to set for th selves standards of achievement high enough to call for extra eff but not so high as to discourage interest.
- By working creatively with their children and encouraging t to help in planning for decoration or improvements in the ho
- By giving importance to design, color, and texture of their dren's clothing.
- By providing opportunities for their children to see exhibits furniture, textiles, housing, painting, sculpture, or craft.
- By providing opportunities for their children to take part in c tive activities provided by community agencies other than sch

PUBLISHED BY THE BOARD OF SCHOOL DIRECTO
JAMES A. DUNCAN, President • L. KENNETH SCHOENFELD, Vice Pres
MRS. HENRY B. OWEN • JOHN H. REID • DIETRICH SCH

Drawings in this folder are reproductions of primary children's art w
MAY 1953

In addition to its use for evaluation the class discussion lends itself well to the maintenance of regular class hours in situations where time is an important factor. It is often difficult for an art teacher to remain aware of the passage of time when a class is engaged in an art activity. Sometimes the bell rings before some-one has noticed that it is time to clean up; and either the room is left in a mess or the students are late to their next class. This seldom happens if class discussions are regular features of the last five or ten minutes of the class period, since these discussions follow (and hasten) cleanup, and can be conveniently terminated in a matter of seconds. This suggestion is not made with the intention of under-writing rigid scheduling of periods for art, but merely to improve upon situations where time scheduling is presently required.

Appearance of art room. Although easier to maintain than a studio, academic classrooms set the standard by which we are often judged. For this reason, the clean-up period is as important as the proper storage of supplies.

Striking photographs such as these are a great influence in developing an appreciation of children's art in the community.

. . . no educational system is possible unless every question directly asked of a pupil at any examination is either framed or modified by the actual teacher of that pupil in that subject.*

Standardized art tests. A number of attempts have been made to devise tests intended to measure or determine art ability, art aptitude, art judgment, art vocabulary, and design judgment. More recently, an attempt has been made to measure creativity.** To date, none of these tests has proved valid on a wide scale. Standardized art tests are less popular today among teachers of art than they were a decade ago. There is a noticeable trend to evaluate each individual's total personality instead of attempting to measure isolated art ability or aptitude. This is indicated in reviews of art tests*** and a statement by Lally and LaBrant:

. . . it is obvious that as yet we are unable from tests to identify the child gifted in the arts.****

Harmfulness of school art tests. Because of the pressure sometimes exerted by school principals and superintendents, or possibly through personal preference, some art teachers still administer tests designed to evaluate pupils' status or growth in art. Some of these tests are devised by local art teachers, some by city or regional art supervisors or directors, some by standardized test authors, and others by state art supervisors or directors. Although they are undoubtedly designed and administered with good intentions, these tests usually fail to measure growth through art.

The potential harmfulness of school art tests is indicated by the following factors:

1. Individual art expression is extremely varied. No two individuals react in the same way to the same experience, and no two

---

*Alfred North Whitehead, *The Aims of Education*, New York; The Macmillan Co., 1929.

**Lambert Brittain of the Department of Child Growth and Development at Cornell University reports that an experimental study he conducted "indicates that it is possible to describe certain aspects of creativity and that it is possible to gather together material which is of such a nature as to make these aspects testable." Eastern Arts Association, Research Bulletin, Vol. 5, No. 1, March, 1954, pp. 12-14.

***Williams B. Micheels; Harold A. Schultz; and Edwin Ziegfeld, in *The Fourth Mental Measurements Yearbook*, Oscar K. Buros, Ed., Highland Park, N. J.: 1953, Gryphon Press, pp. 220-225.

****Ann Lally and Lou La Brant, *The Gifted Child*, Boston: D. C. Heath & Co., 1951, p. 248.

Children must work at their own rate of speed in a friendly, permissive atmosphere. This child may spend ten minutes deciding just where to glue the strip of balsa wood she holds tentatively in one position.

COURTESY MAPLE GROVE SCHOOL, VANCOUVER, B. C.

art products can be exactly the same. Even verbal discussions of similar experiences are varied if sincere individual reactions are sought. Tests which are designed to draw forth identical "correct" responses, by the teacher's or test author's standards, either visual or verbal, do not measure creative art ability but instead are more apt to indicate a pupil's ability to conform.

2. The time limitations imposed by art tests makes response in terms of *art* expression virtually impossible. This is because the most sincere and significant art expression takes place in an informal, permissive atmosphere where pupils have an opportunity to "warm up" to the medium used and to crystallize their ideas in periods of time varying according to their individual needs.

3. The very word "test," the unnatural quietness and atmosphere of authoritarianism prevalent in rooms where tests are being administered, and the pressures of "doing your best here and now" cause psychological blocks to develop in many individuals, even adults.

4. The continuous and unified nature of art expression does not lend itself to the selection of isolated development levels. Just as any one element in a painting is not representative of the total quality of the painting but can be judged only in its relationship to other elements in the work, no one aspect of art expression is representative of the total growth of any pupil. One cannot isolate a child's ability to use color, for example, by asking him to "make

a simple design using two colors which go well together," since the colors a child would choose under normal, non-testing conditions would vary, depending upon the mood of the child, his reaction to the subject he chooses to depict, and endless other considerations.

5. Some tests, such as those prepared by art supervisors or art directors who have not actually taught the children who are to take the tests, are even less effective and are more harmful than tests which might be prepared by local art teachers.* Such tests disregard entirely pupils' normal interests which would, during the course of a semester or year, lead to widely varied degrees of art interest and ability. As a result, in school systems where administrators permit regional or state art supervisors to administer standardized art tests, art teachers feel forced to prepare their pupils for the type of test they believe will be administered. Even those teachers who understand the ineffectiveness of standardized art tests sometimes cooperate under the subtle pressures of local administrators and state art supervisors. They may rationalize their intentions of contemporary educational aims by telling themselves this procedure will "please the administration" and "probably won't really hurt the children." However, it is encouraging to learn that some progressive state art supervisors have managed to eliminate state-wide standardized art tests and are encouraging local schools to adopt more contemporary evaluative procedures.

Art competitions. Competitions are in direct contradiction to the aims of art education. The reasons for this have been clearly and courageously stated by the Council of the National Committee on Art Education.

The National Committee on Art Education believes that it has become the professional responsibility of teachers of art to express their disapproval of sponsored contests and competitions in the general art program of the elementary, junior high and high school. Where the art program forms a part of the general education of children the introduction of contests and competitions promoted by commercial or community agencies is educationally unsound because it usually has a discouraging effect on those who are "ungifted" but need creative expression most urgently.

Three major arguments have been advanced *on behalf* of such contests:

1. That competition in the classroom helps students to prepare for life in a competitive society.

---

*See statement by Alfred North Whitehead on p. 224.

2. That competitions are a defensible way of providing school assistance to altruistic and useful community groups.

3. That school and community interest in such competitions strengthens the art education program.

None of these arguments appears convincing to the Council.

1. We are all agreed that the school must prepare its students for careers which will include competitive activities. But such competition is of a professional or vocational character and has little or no reference to the general educational significance of art to foster creative expression, to enhance cultural life, and to serve personality growth. Further, the arts, like the pure sciences, do not derive their power from competitive impulse. "To covet excellence in art or science," writes John Stuart Mill, "does not imply that one shall outstrip or deprive others, but that *one shall judge oneself.*" It is the inner demand which is most critically important in the arts and in art education. We best prepare children for life by sound educational practices and through the fostering of a healthy personality.

2. We are all agreed that good causes deserve support; we can and do best contribute to them both as teachers and as citizens by sound educational practices. We want our children to know about health problems, about humanitarian ideas and programs. But it has been shown that the sponsored competition is not only time consuming but most often miscomprehended and therefore does not assist good causes or the teaching of children. In the case of our students, educational principle is the first cause.

3. We are obviously all concerned to further our programs and policies in the schools. But to gain temporary school or public interest at the expense of our own real objectives, and at the expense of our students, appears to the Council very seriously mistaken. Creative expression must neither be regimented nor become the means of the few who can compete with others. The serious harm which competitions have already caused is greatly felt especially by those who are by nature or otherwise not adequately equipped in expressing themselves freely. We have avenues to interest and support more in keeping with what we believe.

Two other points appear of major importance to the Council:

1. The use of any classroom for purposes of *commercial advertising* is as indefensible as the use of the classroom for political propaganda. Not only does it violate educational principle and economic fair play, but the advertising contest—like some non-commercial contests—forces the child to activities often remote from his own interests and needs. Such imposed activity is without meaning.

227

2. The role of the teacher in connection with the sponsored contest is also of concern. Situations inevitably arise in which the teacher must either act against his own principles and judgment or run the risk of being compared unfavorably to the teacher whose students carry off the prizes.

The Committee on Art Education urges administrators, teachers, parent groups, and community agencies to declare themselves opposed, on educational grounds, to the introduction of sponsored contests in the general art program of the elementary, junior high and high school.

(*Note:* This statement does not deal with the art school, college, vocational high school, or with special art programs at those levels; we feel that the problems here are sufficiently difficult to warrant separate consideration.)*

*Mimeographed statement issued by the Council of the National Committee on Art Education in connection with its 11th Annual Conference held at the Museum of Modern Art, New York, March, 1953.

These fortunate students are working in a fully-equipped, modern art room.

7: Art Facilities and Materials

SCHOOL BUILDINGS *must be suitably located, properly equipped, and adequately maintained. There are many important and interesting factors to be considered in planning art facilities in the total educational program. Some of these are: contemplated changes in school population; revisions in the educational program; changes in the needs of the community; school plant modification; and proposed new buildings.*

To obtain a flexible, functional environment, well-designed furnishings must be utilized. A carefully planned, fully stocked, and well-equipped art room contributes far more effectively to significant educational development in art than does an inadequate, cluttered, converted classroom or a program forced to operate almost exclusively on scrap materials and tools brought from home.

In planning the design of art rooms, whether they are in forthcoming new buildings or existing buildings being modernized, the architect and interior designer should consult and work closely with the art teacher and possibly a representative from a nearby college or university art education department. The art room should be designed primarily to meet the needs of the age group which will most often use the room. If older or younger groups are to use the room on an occasional basis, tables and stools of adaptable height might be purchased or constructed.

Handmade t o o l s and inexpensive metal may be used in making etchings. This boy is using a phonograph needle set in wood, and the material is tin instead of expensive copper.

229

Despite the obvious handicaps of working with inadequate facilities, these upper grade youngsters are doing their best to create cleaning bag costumes and paper-bag masks.

LOCATION OF THE ART ROOM

If possible, the art room should be located on the ground floor, where pupils, teachers, and visitors can easily observe the interesting art activities going on within it as well as the finished products which are displayed on its shelves and adjacent display boards and cases. Part of the corridor wall of an art room might be constructed of glass in order that passers-by might easily observe the visual activities which are carried on, without having to enter the room and disturb the pupils.

A ground floor location for an art room is further necessitated by the materials, equipment, and exhibits which are frequently received. A direct-access location also provides for outdoor activities on a painting-sketching-sculpture patio (see suggested art room floor plan enclosure).

When possible, the art room should have a northern exposure in order to provide non-glare daylight. Since costume and stage design are part of the art program, it is desirable to have the art room located near or adjacent to the rooms used for scenery and

230

prop construction and storage, costume making and storage, and the theater-auditorium. Proximity to homemaking and industrial arts facilities is also desirable. In some schools, these curriculum areas have been grouped into a single department or area of the arts.

THE GENERAL-PURPOSE ART STUDIO-WORKSHOP

A specially prepared art teacher and a modern art studio-workshop can make outstanding contributions to the school and community educational program. A room of the type discussed here is flexible and functional, and can accommodate a number of art activity groups simultaneously and/or sequentially. This all-purpose art studio-workshop is designed for a space approximately 27′ x 80′, although nearly any proportion utilizing this much or more space would be satisfactory. Part of this room, or if possible, an adjacent office-studio, should be made available for the art teacher's personal creative use. The university artist-in-residence idea can be duplicated on a small scale in every school, with proportionate educational rewards. The art teacher might make use of such space during free periods, after school, and on week-ends. Advanced students should also have use of the art room at certain out-of-class hours.

Contained here are facilities for teaching art to as many as 35

This view of one end of an art room, although smaller in size, differently arranged, and less fully equipped than an all-purpose art-studio-workshop, is similar in general layout and helpful in visualizing its appearance.

students, although 20 to 25 should be considered maximum class size for greatest educational benefits.

ACTIVITY CORNER IN AN ELEMENTARY CLASSROOM

The modern elementary classroom contains space for group and individual work, where learners can effectively and sometimes simultaneously carry on a variety of activities. The illustration on this page suggests a plan which would enable elementary classroom teachers and children to engage freely in supplemental art activities. It is not proposed as a substitute for the elementary school art room, but merely as a unit of classroom space which should be used as regularly as chalkboards.

Elementary classrooms should contain adequate storage space for art materials, equipment, and projects. Each room should have a sink, work table with vise, and basic tools. It should also contain a table for clay work and craft activities, several easels or painting tables, and a large table for general activities in which small groups might simultaneously engage. The walls should provide adequate display space for two- and three-dimensional student projects as well as original art works and reproductions of work by famous artists.

ART SERVICE ROOM FOR AN ELEMENTARY SCHOOL

Elementary schools which do not as yet have the services of a full-time art teacher should include an art service room, containing general resource facilities for all pupils and teachers to use. It provides a place for experimental work with art materials in addition to facilities for temporarily storing unfinished art work. It serves as a place for preparing scenery, costumes, and properties for school dramatic productions; preparing art materials for distribution to the classrooms; and for such special equipment as a printing press and kiln.

Woodworking and other art experiences may be offered in the activity corners of elementary classrooms. The ease of operation and safety of certain pieces of light power equipment make it possible for classroom teachers to become competent in supervising their use.

COURTESY SCHOOL ARTS
AND HELEN PATTON,
RACINE, WISCONSIN

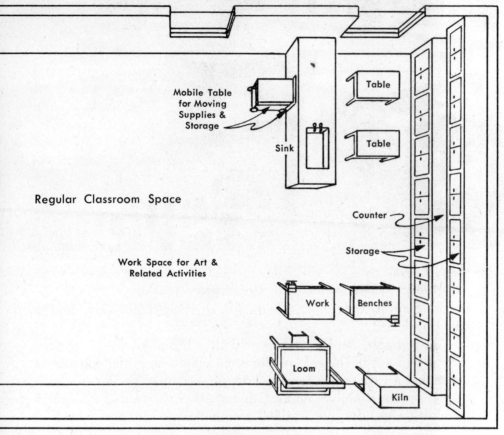

Regular Classroom Space

Mobile Table
for Moving
Supplies &
Storage

Sink

Table

Table

Counter

Storage

Work Space for Art &
Related Activities

Work | Benches

Loom

Kiln

Corridor

ACTIVITY CORNER IN AN ELEMENTARY CLASSROOM

The art service room should be about twice the size of a regular classroom in order that groups might be brought there for activities which require a large space and elaborate materials, tools, and equipment. It should include clearly labeled drawers for tools, papers, cloth, and wood scraps; cupboards for costumes, drums of clay, marionettes, murals, and small tools; cabinets for various supplies and equipment; a sink with drain boards; work space on counter tops; open shelving for the storage of books and materials; bulletin boards for work on scenery and murals; and kiln equipment.

Furniture and equipment might include: work benches with vises; stools or chairs; several large work tables with adjustable height legs; a mobile art wagon or cart, a printing press; a kiln; a large paper cutter; an adjustable-opening pencil sharpener; two 25 gallon clay crocks; a dispenser for 36" (or wider) wrapping

This art service room was locally designed and constructed at little cost by an interested school principal and a group of classroom teachers.

paper; trays with compartments for carrying paint jars; and a wedging board.

Cut-through display windows with adjustable height shelves should be built in the side of the room which faces the corridor in order that a variety of completed art projects may be shown. Such displays often stimulate interest among other children and teachers in addition to affording justified recognition to children who produce the objects.

The art service room as well as the idea underlying its use should be looked upon as a temporary arrangement designed to improve an otherwise restricted art activity program. As soon as budgetary conditions permit, part-time (services shared with a nearby school) or one or more full-time (one for each 350-600 pupils) art teachers should be secured.

ART ROOM REQUIREMENTS

There is no specific school building design that is universally acceptable, since no plan fits the needs of all communities, all groups of pupils, or all philosophies of teaching. Schools must, therefore, be designed to meet the needs of specific groups of children and community residents.

The size of art rooms is sometimes determined by the *expected* size of the school plant or population. For groups using this planning technique, it is recommended that art studio-workshop sizes provide at least the following square footage, with ceilings about 11 feet high:

Large plants—27 feet wide by 80 feet long, inside dimensions.

Medium plants—24 feet wide by 60 feet long, inside dimensions.

Small plants—24 feet wide by 40 feet long, inside dimensions.
Under more ideal conditions, the art room size would be determined by *expected* average class size. Thus the most workable solution would be the choice of the largest art studio-workshop size listed above.

Acoustics. To be able to hear well without interference from extraneous noises is essential to good school work. Sound can now be controlled in all parts of a building through the use of insulating and noise absorbing materials.

Teachers and students making oral presentations to the group should be heard distinctly in any part of the room when speaking in a slightly louder than conversational voice. Ceilings and parts of walls should be covered with sound absorbing materials. Noises can also be reduced by installing floor covering such as rubber tile, by using tackboards in place of some chalkboards, and by hanging drapes. Since many acoustic materials possess aesthetic as well as purely functional qualities, their color and pattern should be considered carefully in making a selection. Drapes, tiles, and all other colored or patterned material should be selected cooperatively by the art teacher and a competent, modern interior designer.

Because of the continual changes being made in materials and acoustical engineering, a careful study should be made of all the materials that are available before installations are made.

Electrical outlets. Outlets for 110 and 208 or 220 volt electrical services should be located on the basis of preferences for various types of work. They should require a minimum amount of connecting cord. In some cases, this will necessitate floor outlets, flush mounted for pedestrian safety—although this calls for special care when the floor is washed. Some electrical engineers also advocate ceiling outlets extending down to within reach of adults, where electrical equipment is needed in the center of the room.

Provision should be made for the use of: portable and permanently installed power tools, some of which require special voltage outlets; slide, filmstrip, and motion picture projectors; hot plates, ceramic and enameling kilns, most of which require special voltage outlets; and other electrical equipment necessitated by the special interests and abilities of individual art teachers and groups of students.

Permanently installed power equipment, especially kilns, should be wired on separate lines controlled by individually locked switches or from a central warning unit equipped with a door which can be locked.

Gas outlets. Gas burners for jewelry and other three-dimensional design in metal are needed in every art room, except in cases where the department is large enough to permit a specially equipped studio for this purpose. Gas outlets should be spaced about 30 inches apart along the top rear of a long, asbestos-covered crafts bench. A special gas outlet should be provided in an enclosed work area for larger soldering and annealing work with compressed air torches. All gas outlets should be controlled by a master valve which can be locked. A separate connection and valve lock should be provided in rooms which have a gas-fired kiln, since it might otherwise be shut off accidentally with unfortunate results to pieces being fired. Where bottled gas is used, local regulations governing its use should be adhered to.

Compressed air or oxygen. Those art departments which use the air brush and do forge and metal work should have permanent installations for air compressors or oxygen bottles. The practicability of permanent or portable equipment should be considered carefully with the assistance of experts.

Floors. The floor of an art room should be attractive, easy to service, and durable. Light colored rubber or asphalt tile is light-reflecting, easily maintained, and less fatiguing than stone or wood for those who must walk on it all day. Speckled or geometrically patterned tile designs show less soil than solid colors and are available in a wide range of hues which can be chosen to harmonize with wall, drapes, and furniture colors. Much of the furniture and equipment in the room can be moved or rearranged to provide for varying needs.

Lighting, ventilating, and heating. Scientifically planned lighting, ventilating, and heating facilities not only protect the health of pupils and teachers but also contribute to a stimulating environment in which learning may more effectively take place.

A temperature of 68-70° Fahrenheit is recommended for school rooms in which pupils are engaged in quiet activities such as reading. Warmer temperatures will induce sleepiness and lethargy. Art rooms, laboratories, and other activity rooms should be maintained at 65-68° Fahrenheit, with a recommended relative humidity of 45%. Most modern schools have a combined heating and ventilating system which regulates temperatures and humidity and provides an even, draft-free distribution of air. However, in cases where these are not functioning properly, the art teacher should open windows, adjust the thermostatic regulator and notify the custodian, or principal, depending on local procedures.

After consulting with lighting engineers and art teachers who will use the rooms, architects should select the best lighting system available which will provide a uniform distribution of shadow-free and glare-free illumination. To supplement this, especially for demonstration areas and displays, movable spotlights can be placed in the ceiling or on light poles and can be adjusted for special lighting. In one-story structures, skylights and translucent, light-diffusing plastic domes may be used for additional lighting.

Opaque shades, drapes, Venetian blinds, or skylight louvers should be provided at all openings which admit daylight. If the room is used frequently for projection purposes, built-in slat runners along the sides of windows and skylights provide channels through which shades may be drawn to eliminate annoying light reflections.

Art room interior colors

School architects, paint experts, and local art teachers should cooperatively select the colors for art room interiors. Wherever possible the art teacher should make final decisions on matters of interior color selection. Yet his choice should be tempered by the advice of the architect, who should be concerned with the harmonious relationship of interior colors to the achitectural plan as a whole, and the paint expert, who understands the scientific data concerning reflective qualities of certain hues, values, and intensities. Paint can be tested for reasonably accurate judgment as to their visual appeal by painting sample areas about one foot square, allowing them to dry, and viewing them under natural and artificial lighting conditions. The Munsell Color Company of 10 E. Franklin St., Baltimore, Maryland, has available a 22 x 28 inch chart illustrating the colors sometimes recomended for the walls of art rooms with windows facing in various directions. It also indicates the percentages of reflection afforded by various dilutions of pure color with other hues and white. Controlled studies have been made on the influence of color on the learning climate within the classroom. Proper color selection can now be made scientifically as well as artistically.

Equipment—sinks and drains

An acid-resistant, all-purpose double sink projecting into the art room to give access on three sides is essential. It should be lo-

237

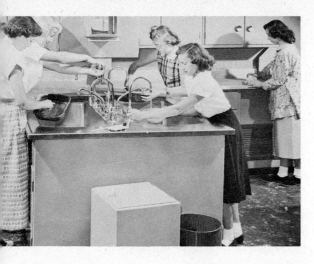

A peninsula-type, multi-spigot, double sink is essential for every art studio-workshop. As many as six students may be simultaneously accommodated, eliminating the loss of valuable class time and encouraging good cleanup habits.

COURTESY E. H. SHELDON AND CO.,
PHOTO BY DALE ROOKS

cated reasonably near all working areas in the room, but not close to power tools or electrical outlets.

Art room sinks should be: large in size; located against a ceramic tile wall and/or on a tile or other waterproof floor; equipped with four or more swivel spigots, each with hot and cold water controls; should have drainboards or built-in drying racks; and should contain a special trap to prevent clay, plaster, and other materials from clogging the drainpipes. Whenever possible, a smaller, separate sink with clay trap should be installed in the ceramics area. All sinks should be deep enough to permit washing items about 15 inches tall, as well as to reduce splashing.

Stainless steel, monel metal, and soapstone sinks have been found satisfactory for art room use. They do not stain and are easy to clean.

EQUIPMENT—STORAGE

The storage of art materials, tools, and certain pieces of equipment is a problem which must be carefully solved in terms of available space and facilities. Some schools have a central storage space for bulk art materials. In other schools, each art teacher stores all of his own materials, tools, and equipment within the art room proper. Whatever the arrangement may be, controlled conditions should be established and maintained:

•Paints, acids, and cleaners should be stored in closed metal cabinets. Paint cans should be kept closed. Solvents, thinners, and cleaners should be stored in safety cans. All such materials should be carefully and accurately labeled. In addition, they should be appropriately marked "caution," "poison," or "flammable," depending on their contents.

•*Promptly after use,* oily rags and papers should be placed in metal waste cans with hinged metal covers.

•If possible, everything should be stored within reaching height, without having to use potentially dangerous step ladders.

•Items should not be stored on the floor because someone may inadvertently trip over them. If they happened to be carrying a sharp tool or a jar of acid, the results could be disastrous.

•Use storage trays and racks for small tools and materials.

•Narrow width vertical and low height horizontal shelving is desirable for various types of paper storage.

Tool and material storage. It is usually advisable to have tools located on wall panels adjoining the space in which they are to be used. Perforated pressed board and hanging devices are useful. Portable panels are recommended where it is desirable to use sets of tools in different parts of the room or to transport them to other rooms. Such panels might be made of ½ or ¾ inch thick plywood approximately 18 x 24 inches in size. A hook or other hanging device and a painted silhouette should indicate where each tool belongs on the board. Similar colors on both tools and board can identify parts of a set. Special cabinets, built on the order of drawing board racks, may be constructed to store tool boards when they are not in use.

Large, easily manipulated drawers for large water color paper and poster board provide easy access to these materials and afford greater protection against damage to costly paper.

Project storage. Adequate space should be provided for the storage of partially completed art projects. It may be within the art room and/or in a room immediately adjacent. Since products made with clay, finger paint, block print ink, oil paint, or papier mâché will be wet when they are completed, the storage area must have many shelves and must be well ventilated for quick drying to prevent mold or warping. Works containing turpentine or drying oils should be properly ventilated to eliminate the possibilities of spontaneous combustion. It is always advisable to consult the fire department for advice on meeting regulations.

Large sheets of poster board, mats, and water color paper are stored in slide-out drawer cabinets to prevent damage to these expensive materials.

COURTESY E. H. SHELDON AND CO.,
PHOTO BY DALE ROOKS

COURTESY EDMUND BACH,
HAMBURG, N. Y. HIGH SCHOOL
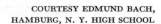

This highly functional arrangement of paper storage shelves was designed by a secondary school art teacher and built by the school carpenter. Vertical storage for small sheets of paper permits students to choose a sheet without pulling out an entire pile. Colors of paper lend themselves well to interior design and may, if organized as well as this, be left visible at all times.

Aluminum or plastic trays which slide into grooved racks are excellent for storing wet work. A portable, waterproof tray is easy to transport, to work on, and to store with a minimum amount of effort and infrequent damage to work in progress. A grooved rack makes it possible to arrange space adjustments to accommodate varying heights of objects without wasting space between shelves. Vertical racks on the tops of shelves or cabinets permit the storage and drying of such items as oil paintings or mounted water colors.

Drawers or compartments which can be individually locked provide protection and space needed for the storage of jewelry, leather projects, and other expensive or extremely delicate materials and tools. These drawers should be designed so that they can be used as tote trays. Vertical racks should be available for drawing boards. Mechanical, architectural, and other drawings might be removed from the boards and stored in blueprint-type storage drawers, unless there are sufficient boards to permit each student to keep his work mounted upon one during an entire project. In such cases provisions may be made so that drawing board racks can be locked.

Bulk storage of art supplies. Provision needs to be made for storing reasonably large quantities of art supplies. A room which can be locked, adjacent to the art room, serves this purpose most advantageously since it prevents needless space consumption in the art room. Smaller quantities of materials may be taken from the storage room to the art room every few days.

The store room should be equipped with deep, adjustable height shelves of varying dimensions. These shelves can be mounted on casters for easy handling of large bulky materials. The removal of materials from bulk to current storage should be carefully supervised by the art teacher, since pupils often damage items such as Bristol boards by removing them carelessly from shelves or by dropping part of a load which could better have been transported in several trips or on an art cart.

Display cases. Several display cases should be built through the walls which separate each classroom from the corridor. In them may be shown the work of pupils as well as exhibitions of professional art work, both of which tend to broaden the art knowledge of pupils, teachers, and visitors in the school.

About half of the display cases need to be planned for showing objects within the classrooms. The remainder can face the corridor. All cases should be fronted with flush-wall plate glass, and should contain adjustable height shelves for three-dimensional objects. The backs of the cases might be fitted with laminated wood doors covered with corkboard on both sides. Back-entry doors will permit easy installation of displays without finger marking the cover glass. The corkboard covering permits the display of flat work on both sides of the doors. All cases should be equipped with built-in locks since many exhibits are expensive and all are irreplaceable. All cases should be properly illuminated. There are many ways of providing light depending on individual preferences and the types of materials to be displayed. Manufacturers or distributors of lighting and display materials can usually give the latest and best information on this subject.

Furniture. The uses to which an art room is subjected neces-

Flush-wall, glass front, adjustable shelf display cases should be strategically located throughout the school at a height where the center shelf is at the average eye level of pupils.

COURTESY ARTS AND ACTIVITIES
AND JOHN WESLE, ILLINOIS
STATE NORMAL UNIVERSITY

241

This tilt-top individual work table may be used also as a flat top table and moved.

A tilt-top individual work table with adjustable height.

Work bench for ar studio-workshop equipped with tw woodworking vises.

sitate a careful study of the furniture requirements. There will be painting, sawing, welding, printing, and many other types of art activities. Each requires a different type of furniture and surface. It is important that people responsible for furnishing the art room consult several manufacturers of art room equipment. The U. S. Office of Education and the National Art Education Association can furnish information and addresses to those who are planning art rooms.

Art room furniture and equipment should be planned for comfort, health, safety, and the educational and artistic needs of the students and teachers who will use it. With these purposes in mind, W. Edgar Martin of the U. S. Office of Education, Washington, D. C., prepared a reference handbook, *Basic Body Measurements of School Age Children*. It contains information on the variability of 53 different body measurements for boys and girls from age 4 to 17 years. This handbook should be studied by architects, school officials, design engineers, and art teachers prior to the purchase, design, or construction of art room furniture.

Bin-type clay storage unit for built-in installation.

Three-station craft bench and storage unit with asbestos-impregnated working surface.

Movable clay stora cart designed to fit ir wall storage area wh not in current use.

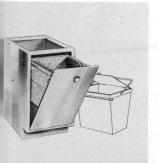

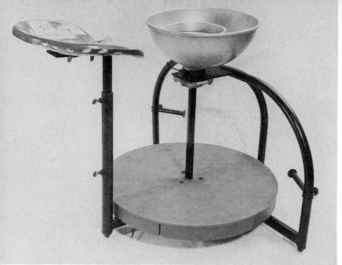

Craftsman-designed potter's kick wheel; and studio-workshop chairs featuring strong construction, portability, and "stackability" for compact storage.

In addition to the specialized equipment and storage facilities described above, many of which are often classified as "furniture," art studio-workshops should contain at least the following:

4 to 6 tables, about 3 x 6 feet; height dependent upon age of students
25 chairs, stools, or benches, sizes dependent upon age of students
1 desk-worktable, about 3 x 5 feet, for the art teacher
3 arm-type modern side chairs, for visitors
6 craft work stools, approximately 18" in height
2 worktables, about 2 x 4 feet
1 work bench, with 2 vises, about 3 x 6 feet
1 kiln, at least 12 x 15 x 18 inches
1 built-in asbestos top jewelry and metal work bench, about 18 x 96 inches
2 four-drawer, 16 inch width filing cabinets
4 counter-top storage units, four drawer, about 30 inches high
1 potter's wheel
1 graphics press

Certain smaller furniture and equipment items are listed under Art Materials and Tools pp. 245-251.

Art materials, tools, and supplies. Nearly every person can be creatively guided toward significant art expression in at least one art medium or process. To foster this important opportunity, the very least the school can do is provide the art teacher and pupils with ample supplies of art materials and tools.

Even the most elaborate art programs cost only three or four dollars per pupil per year. In terms of the rewards gained in personal

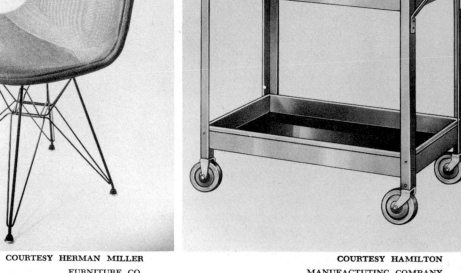

Modern, upholstered side chair for art teacher's desk, guests, or art studio-workshop library corner. Designed by Charles Eames.

Mobile art cart for distributing supplies, facilitating cleanup, and moving materials and art from one room to another.

satisfaction through the production of various art objects, as well as the improved art knowledge and overall personality growth which such production fosters, a generous art materials budget is more than justified.

The list which follows includes nearly every type of manufactured art material. The unit description represents the quantity in which the item is usually sold. For example, one orders a gross (144 sticks) of white chalk rather than a stated number of dozens or sticks. Similarly, one usually orders a ream (500 sheets) of paper rather than a stated number of dozens or sheets, except for unusually expensive papers such as imported watercolor sheets. Quantity orders in less than the usual gross or ream amount, dependent upon the material being purchased, are usually not economical.

No attempt has been made here to prescribe certain materials for certain age levels, since practice has shown this to be undesirable, even educationally unsound. The art teacher who does not wish to offer oil painting experiences to children, or crayons to adults, will merely by-pass these categories. It is noted, however, that successful uses of these media on the age levels cited have been experienced by a number of respected art educators.

Art Materials and Tools

ITEM	DESCRIPTION	SUGGESTED QUANTITY
Drawing Pencils		(per year, except for permanent items, "per room" means "for a one-teacher art room, with moderate enrollments, for one school year")
Carbon and wax	soft lead	1 per pupil
Varied hardness	6B, 4B, 2B, HB, 2H, 4H	12 each per room
Assorted colors	set of twelve	12 per room
Sketching, soft	each	1 per pupil
Erasers	soft rubber	1 per pupil
	art gum	1 per pupil
	kneaded	1 per pupil
	ink	6 per room
Crayons		
Wax, large, unwrapped	box of 16 ass't colors	24 per room
Wax, large, wrapped	box of 16 ass't colors	24 per room
Pressed, small, wrapped	box of 8 ass't colors	12 per room
Conte crayon	box of 24 sticks, black, terra cotta	12 each per room
(NOTE: most frequently used colors may be ordered in bulk if desired)		
Charcoal		
Compressed	box of 12 sticks	12 per room
Vine	box of 50 sticks	6 per room
Charcoal pencils	box of 12	6 per room
Chamois pieces	each	24 per room
Stumps, rolled	box of 24	2 per room
Chalks		
Colored	12-stick box, ass't colors	24 per room
Pastels	24-stick box, ass't colors	6 per room
White, blackboard type	gross	2 per room
Lecturers chalk, large, round or square sticks	box of 12	2 per room
Inks, Pens, etc.		
Penholders	each	1 per pupil
Pen points		
straight	set of 12 ass't sizes	2 per room
ball	set of 12 ass't sizes	2 per room
chisel	set of 12 ass't sizes	2 per room
Felt tip pens, fountain type	each	12 per room
Felt tip pen nibs	each, ¼" and ½"	24 per room
Felt tip pen ink	pint, black	4 per room
Felt tip pen solvent	pint	2 per room
India ink	¾-oz. bottle, black	12 per room
	quart bottle, black	2 per room
Colored inks	2-oz. bottles, ass't colors	12 per room
Pen cleaner	2-oz. bottle	6 per room
Drawing Tools and Equipment		
Compass	each, inexpensive type	12 per room
Drafting sets, case	each	6 per room
T-Squares	24", celluloid edges	12 per room
Triangles	8" celluloid 45-45-90°, 30-60-90°	6 each per room
Drawing boards	18"x24"	24 per room
Rulers	12", 18"	12 each per room
Fixatif	12-oz. compressed, cans with spraying device attached	12 per room
Yardsticks	each	12 per room

ITEM	DESCRIPTION	SUGGESTED QUANTITY
		(per year, except for permanent items, "per room" means "for a one-teacher art room, with moderate enrollments, for one school year")
Painting		
Tempera, liquid, blue, green, yellow, purple, orange, brown, black, magenta, turquoise.	quarts	4 each per room
White	quarts	8 per room
Brushes	ass't sizes, ¼"-1" width, bristle, "flat" style	24 each per room
Containers for water	cans or jars (from home)	1 per pupil
Palettes, metal, white enamelled, 4"x8"	each	1 per pupil
Water Color		
8-pan box (full pans)	each	1 per pupil
16-pan box (½ pans)	each	12 per room
Tubes, ½"x3"	ass't colors	12 sets per room
Brushes	ass't sizes, 0-12, sable or camel hair	6 of each size
Palettes (see above)		
Containers for water (see above)		
Cellulose sponges	1"x4"x6", each	1 per pupil
Wiping cloths	each, clean, absorbent, (from home)	2 per pupil
Finger Paint	ass't colors, quarts	4 each color per room
Oil and Casein Paints		
Tubes of color, 1"x4"	ass't colors	3 tubes each color per medium per room
Tubes of color, white, 2"x6"	each	12 per medium per room
Palettes	tape-edged glass, wood, tin, enamelled tray, or peel-off	1 per pupil
Brushes	sable, bristle, ass't sizes from 3-12, "flat" style	6 each size per room
Painting knives	each	6 per room
Palette knives	each	1 per pupil
Textile Colors		
Ass't colors, with extendor, brushes, solvent	sets	4 per room
Enamel and House-type		
Oil Paints		
Ass't colors	pints	1 each color per room
Sculpture		
Clay		
Moist	pounds	5 per pupil
Oil base (Plasticene)	pounds	1 per pupil
Plaster of Paris	pounds	1 per pupil
Modeling tools	sets, assorted, wood and wood with wire	12 per room
Modeling turntables	each	1 per pupil
Armatures	lead wire on wood base, each, (pupils make own)	1 per pupil
Stone, limestone, etc.	piece, from local quarries, pupils bring in	1 per pupil
Wood, cherry, oak, etc.	piece, from local area, pupils bring in	1 per pupil
Stone carving tools	sets	6 per room
Wood carving tools	sets	6 per room
Sharpening stones	each	6 per room
Rasps, Chisels, Gouges, Knives	ass't sizes	4 each per room
Mallets, hammers	ass't sizes and materials	4 each per room
Vises	swivel, wood type	6 per room

ITEM	DESCRIPTION	SUGGESTED QUANTITY
		(per year, except for permanent items, "per room" means "for a one-teacher art room, with moderate enrollments, for one school year")

Sculpture (continued)

ITEM	DESCRIPTION	SUGGESTED QUANTITY
Metal, lead, copper, brass, steel, aluminum	sheets, approx. 2'x2' or as available	1 per pupil
Wire, lead, aluminum, steel, etc.	50' rolls	5 each per room
Tin snips and heavier metal shears	each	4 per room
Brazing and welding tools and equipment	sets or units	1 per room
Soldering irons	each, large and small	4 per room
Solder, ass't types	rolls, boxes	4 per room
Portable electric drill with polishing attachments	(metal drilling bits) set, each	1 per room
Vise, metal, swivel mount, 4" jaw	each	2 per room
Files, ass't sizes	each	6 per room
Hack saws, 16"	each	4 per room
Rivets, copper, soft metal alloy	box	2 per room
Punches, metal	ass't sizes, each	1 per room
Wire cutters	ass't sizes, each	4 per room
Pliers	ass't sizes, each	4 per room
Coping saws	each	4 per room
Coping saw blades, for metal cutting	pkg. of 12	12 per room
Sculpture stand, heavy duty	each	3 per room

Graphic Arts

Etching

ITEM	DESCRIPTION	SUGGESTED QUANTITY
Copper, zinc, steel	plates, ass't sizes	1 per pupil
Enamelled trays approx. 12"x18"	each	3 per room
Celluloid	pieces, ass't sizes	2 per pupil
Etching needles	each (used dental tools may be sharpened for this use)	1 per pupil
Burnishers, scrapers	each	4 per room
Etching ground	container	2 per room
Nitric acid or Dutch mordant	16-oz. bottle	1 per room
Kerosene	gallon can	1 per room
Etching press	each	1 per room
Felt pads	each, for press	4 per room
Ink	cans, black, 6 oz.	5 per room
Inking slab, marble or heavy glass	each	2 per room
Wiping cloths	each, about 2' square	2 per pupil
Blotting and backing papers	approx. 18"x24", each	100 per room
Daubers, leather or cloth covered	each (students make own)	1 per pupil

Linoleum Block Printing

ITEM	DESCRIPTION	SUGGESTED QUANTITY
Battleship linoleum	sheets, ¼" thick, ass't sizes	1 per pupil
Linoleum blocks, wood mounted	4"x6" to 10"x15", (optional)	1 per pupil
Linoleum cutting tools	sets	12 per room
Brayers, geltatine or soft rubber	6"-8" width	6 per room
Ink slabs, marble or glass	12"x18" to 18"x24"	2 per room
Ink, black, dark red, green, blue, etc.	Cans or tubes, 2-4 oz.	12 per room

247

ITEM	DESCRIPTION	SUGGESTED QUANTITY
		(per year, except for permanent items, "per room" means "for a one-teacher art room, with moderate enrollments, for one school year")
Presses, hand type, Letter and Franklin	each	1 per room
Kerosene	gallon	2 per room
Wiping cloths	each, 2'x2', from home	2 per pupil
Lithography		
Lithography stones	12"x18", or larger, each	6 per room
Lithographic crayons	box of 12	3 per room
Cellulose sponges	each	6 per room
Mullers, glass	3" width base, each	2 per room
Pumice	container, pound	1 per room
Lithographic press	each	1 per room
Lithographic ink	can, 6 oz.	4 per room
Wood Engraving		
Wood engraving blocks, end grain	4"x6"-10"x16"	1 per pupil
Wood engraving tools	sets	6 per room
Whiting	pound	2 per room
Printers ink, black	can, 6 oz.	2 per room
Sharpening stone	each	2 per room
Wood Block Cutting		
Plank grain wood blocks	4"x6"-1'x3', each	1 per pupil
Wood cutting tools	sets	6 per room
Printers ink, black	can, 6 oz.	2 per room
Brayers	See linoleum block printing	
Ink slabs	See linoleum block printing	
Wiping rags	See linoleum block printing	
Crafts		
Jewelry and Metal Work		
Sheets, discs, strips, wire rolls of such metals as silver, copper, brass, nickel, pewter, aluminum.	pieces, rolls, etc.	Order in amounts needed for preferred projects
Borax slate, borax stick, flux brush, flux, Bunsen burner, blowpipe, chasing hammer, half-round file, metal snips, asbestos block, charcoal block, rawhide mallet, steel block, bench vise, ring gauge, bench pin, needle file set, ring clamp, saw frame and blades, binding wire, twist drill, hand drill, draw tongs, draw plate, flat and round nose pliers, wire cutting pliers, chain pliers, ball pein hammer, soldering tweezers, tweezers, scriber, ring mandrel, scraper, curved burnisher, pusher, wire gauge, dapping tool, etc.		1 each per room, minimum, more of certain items if possible
Enamels, ground, ass't colors	jar, each	1 each per room
Enameling kiln, electric	each	1 per room
Sand-filled hammering bags	each	6 per room
Wooden bowl and plate raising forms	each	3 per room

ITEM	DESCRIPTION	SUGGESTED QUANTITY
		(per year, except for permanent items, "per room" means "for a one-teacher art room, with moderate enrollments, for one school year")
Ceramics		
Moist ceramic clays, 25, 50, or 100 pound containers	each	200 lbs. per room
Wedging table and wire	each	1 per room
Plaster bats, 8" or larger	each	15 per room
Knives, paring or Sloyd type	each	15 per room
Metal pallets	each	15 per room
Rubber pallets	each	15 per room
Pointed tool (stick with sharp nail inserted)	each	2 per room
Elephant ear sponge	each	5 per room
Brushes, sable or camel hair	each	15 per room
Syringe, small	each	2 per room
Modeling tools	ass't	2 each per room
Kiln, 12"x12"x12" minimum	each	1 per room, or more
Kick wheel (or electric)	each	1 per room, or more
Covered containers for slip	each	6 per room
Glaze, ass't colors	each, jars, 2 oz.	1 each per room
Leather work		
Ass't leathers, cowhide, calfskin, etc.	pieces, skins	amt. for project
Scissors	8" pointed, each, pr.	4 per room
Leather carving, modeling, cutting and punching tools	sets	1 each per room
Findings: buckles, snaps, pins, etc.	dozen	1 each per room
Lacing, leather and plastic	roll	1 each per room
Lacing needles	each	6 per room
Plastic		
Sheets, scraps, etc. of various types of plastic	sheets, bags	amt. for project
Coping saws and blades	each	6 per room
Sanding blocks and paper	each	6 per room
Cloth		
Cotton broadcloth, denim, wool, felt, linen, bookbinders	pieces, rolls	amt. for project
Pinking shears	pair	4 per room
Scissors, 10" pointed	pair	4 per room
Thread, ass't sizes	spools	1 each per room
Needles, ass't sizes	packages	4 per room
Thimbles	each	4 per room
Sewing machine	each	1 per room
Weaving		
Looms, floor	each	1 per room, or more
Looms, table	each	4 per room
Weaving tools, shuttles, etc.	each	5 per room
Yarns, ass't colors, weights	skeins	6 each per room
Threads, carpet, linen, etc.	spools	2 each per room
Woodworking		
Wood, pieces, planks, sheets, pine, oak, plywood, masonite, etc.		amt. for project
Braces and ass't bits	each	2 per room
Brads, ass't sizes	boxes	1 each per room
Coping saws and blades	each; dozen	4 per room
Countersinks	each	2 per room

ITEM	DESCRIPTION	SUGGESTED QUANTITY
		(per year, except for permanent items, "per room" means "for a one-teacher art room, with moderate enrollments, for one school year")

Crafts (continued)

ITEM	DESCRIPTION	SUGGESTED QUANTITY
Cross-cut saws	each	2 per room
Glue, powdered or sheet	pound	3 per room
Glue pot, electric	each	1 per room
Hand drill and bits	set	2 per room
Mitre vise machine	each	1 per room
Nails, ass't sizes	pound	2 each per room
Planes, 7", 12", 16"	each	2 per room
Punches, nail	each	2 per room
Rip saws	each	2 per room
Screws, ass't sizes	box	1 each per room
Screw drivers, ass't sizes	each	1 each per room
Tacks, ass't sizes	box	1 each per room
Vice, wood	each	4 per room

Paper

ITEM	DESCRIPTION	SUGGESTED QUANTITY
Bogus, gray, 9"x12"	ream	2 per room
Bogus, gray, 12"x18"	ream	2 per room
Bookbinder's board, 20"x30"	sheets	50 per room
Bristol board, 22½"x35"	sheets	50 per room
Colored construction, 80#, 12"x18" red, brown, black, red-orange, orange, yellow orange, blue, gray, gray-blue, gray green, green, white, yellow, yellow green, blue-green, blue-violet, violet, red-violet.	package of 100 sheets	2 each color per room
Colored construction, 80#, 18"-24" (colors listed above)	package of 100 sheets	1 each color per room
Colored poster, 40#, 12"x18"	package of 100 sheets	1 each color per room
Colored poster, 40#, 18"x24" (colors listed above)	package of 100 sheets	1 each color per room
Charcoal paper, 19"x25"	quire (2 doz.)	4 per room
Finger paint paper, 16"x22"	package of 100	2 per room
Graph, 9"x12"	ream	1 per room
Illustration board, 20"x30"	package of 100	1 per room
Manila: cream, gray, white, 9"x12", 12"x18", 18"x24"	ream	1 of each color and size per room
Newsprint, 9"x12", 12"x18", 18"x24"	ream	1 of each size per room
Oak Tag, 9"x12", 12"x18", 18"x24"	ream	1 of each size per room
Project paper, 24"x150 yds., 36"x150 yds.,	roll	1 of each width per room
Scratchboard, 22"x30"	sheets	50 per room
Stencil paper, 9"x12"	quire	4 per room
Japanese rice paper, 22"x30"	sheets	50 per room
Blotting paper, 22"x30"	sheets	50 per room

Miscellaneous

ITEM	DESCRIPTION	SUGGESTED QUANTITY
Alcohol, denatured	gallon	2 per room
Cellophane tape, ½", 1" widths	roll	6 each size per room
Cellophane tape dispenser, ½", 1" widths	each	1 each per room
Easels, wood or metal, adjustable, floor type	each	4 or more per room
Eyelets, box of 100 pairs	box	2 per room
Eyelet punch	each	2 per room
File dividers, metal tab, insert	dozen	6 per room
File folders, manila or brown	box of 100	4 per room

250

ITEM	DESCRIPTION	SUGGESTED QUANTITY
		(per year, except for permanent items, "per room" means "for a one-teacher art room, with moderate enrollments, for one school year")
Glue, fish or animal, powdered	pound	3 per room
Linseed oil, artists' quality	quart	4 per room
Masking tape, 1", 2"	roll	6 each per room
Paper clips	box	6 per room
Paper cutter, 18"	each	1 per room
Paper cutter, 36", table type	each	1 per room
Paper punch	small, medium, large	3 each per room
Pencil sharpener, adjustable opening	each	1 per room
Paste, library type	quart	10 per room
Portfolio, cloth hinged, 22"x28"	each	24 per room
Raffia, plain and colored	pound package	1 each color per room
Revolving punch, 6 point	each	1 per room
Right angle, steel, 18"x24"	each	1 per room
Rule, steel, 36"	each	1 per room
Rubber cement, 4 oz. can, 16 oz. can	each	4 of each per room
Rubber cement solvent, can	gallon	1 per room
Rubber bands, ass't	pound box	1 per room
Scissors, 6", 10", pointed	dozen pairs	2 each per room
Shellac, white, orange	pint	4 each per room
Stapler, gun, table types	each	1 each per room
Staples, box of 1000	box	4 per room
Stencil knives	each	24 per room
Thumbtacks, solid head	box	4 per room
Tongue depressors, box of 500	box	1 per room
Turpentine, rectified	gallon	3 per room
Varnish, marine type	quart	2 per room
Varnish, damar, artists' type	quart	3 per room
Wheat paste	pound	36 per room
Wrapping tape, brown, 1", 2" widths	roll	3 each per room
Wrapping tape dispensers, 1", 2"	each	1 each per room
Equipment (additional to that listed in areas above)		
Graphic arts presses	each	1 each per room
Jig saw, table model, power	each	1 per room
Band saw, table model, power	each	1 per room
Lathes, wood and metal	each	1 each per room
Pebble mill, jewelry	each	1 per room
Power drill	each	1 per room
Power grinding tool	each	1 per room
Routing machine	each	1 per room
Sanding machine	each	1 per room
Art cart or wagon, mobile	each	as needed

FREE AND INEXPENSIVE ART MATERIALS*

The following materials can be found or inexpensively secured in most communities. They should be considered as important supplements, *but not alternatives*, to commercially manufactured art materials. Actually, nearly any material can be an art material if it is used creatively.

*Derived in part from a list in "Art for the Elementary Schools of Missouri," prepared by State Department of Education, Jefferson City, Mo., 1952, pp. 56-60.

The art teacher conducts a small group discussion at a large, well-designed art studio-workshop table. It is intended for use of 4 to 6 students, or smaller numbers of individuals working on over-size projects.

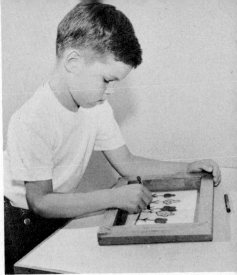

The frame upon which an inexpensive piece of organdy has been stretched for this boy's experience in silk screening costs little more than a box of crayons, and can be used over and over again.

CLOTH	SUGGESTED USES
Cheesecloth	Curtains; costumes
Burlap bags	Hooked rug base, costumes, stage scenery; weaving; embroidery
Cloth, cotton, etc.	Aprons; rag dolls; costumes; puppet clothes; strips for weaving
Cotton batting	Stuffing for dolls, toys, puppets, upholstery
Embroidery thread	Decorative stitching; bookbinding
Felt	Felt toys, protective pads on wood, clay, metal pieces; jewelry; printing pad
Fruit bags, mesh	Base for weaving with string, twine, yarn; materials for decorations and costumes
Men's shirts, used	For: painting smocks; tearing into strips for weaving and rug braiding; wiping cloths
Oilcloth	Table covers for painting, clay modeling; book covers; cushions; aprons; toys
Printed cloth	Strips for weaving and rug braiding; curtains; costumes
Rags, clean	For: painting smocks; tearing into strips for weaving and rug braiding; wiping cloths
Sacks, flour, feed, sugar	Curtains; rugs; wall hangings; craft work
Stockings	Hand puppets; rag dolls; weaving; hooked rugs; unravel for puppet hair
String	Bookbinding; puppet hair; kites
Twine	Mats; rugs; purses
Unbleached muslin	Luncheon sets; curtains; tie-dying; puppet bodies; crayon drawing projects
Window shades, cloth	Murals; scenery; bookbinding cloth
Yarn (scraps from partially used skeins; unraveled sweaters)	Embroidery; weaving; puppet hair; Christmas ornaments; knitting; rug hooking

FOODS	SUGGESTED USES
Beans, dried	Beads; pins; buttons; toy stuffing, collage pictures
Cocoanut shells	Musical instruments; jewelry; containers
Corn, dried kernels	Jewelry; fabric decoration; buttons; collages
Corn cobs	Dolls; pipes; buttons; painting or printing tool
Corn, popped	Christmas decoration strings
Cornstarch	Finger paint base
Macaroni	Dye and string for necklace; weaving
Potatoes, carrots, turnips	Printing tool, cut design in flat surface

GLASS	SUGGESTED USES
Bottles	Musical instruments; containers; mosaic pieces
Colored glass scraps	Mosaic pieces; study of color and light
Glass, clear sheets	Palettes; inking slabs; monoprint base
Jars, mayonnaise, cold cream, fruit, etc.	For paint, water, brushes, and paste; containers for nails, tacks, screws, and other small objects; for decoration as vases, pencil holders, etc.
Light bulbs	Marionette head base; Christmas tree decorations
Mirrors	To represent water in sand table or other models of countries, communities, etc; mobiles; playhouses; model rooms; collages; mosaics

LEATHER	SUGGESTED USES
Chamois skin, used, scraps	Purses; drumheads; musical instruments
Kid gloves, used	Puppet shoes; dolls
Purses, used	Billfolds; toys; hinges for puppets, etc.; bookbinding
Scraps of leather	For general crafts; jewelry

METAL	SUGGESTED USES
Bottle caps	Wheels, Christmas tree decorations; nail rows on board for shoe scraper
Coat hangers	Armatures for papier mâché figures, clay sculpture; mobiles and other three-dimensional constructions
Coffee cans and lids	Storage of individual clay projects; containers for mixing plaster of Paris
Nails	Construction work
Oil drum lids	Trays for distributing art supplies
Pins, straight, safety, hat, corsage	Thumb tack substitutes; collages; fastening puppet clothes; costumes
Pipe cleaners, new	Small figure armatures; painting tools; collages
Razor blades, single edge	Cutting stencils, thin wood, cardboard
Razor blades, injector type, new or used	(May be inserted in special mat-knife made for them, now available at art supply stores)
Paper clips	Ornament hangers; collages; small armatures
Tacks	Construction work; applying canvas to stretchers
Tin cans	Jewelry and other metalwork; ornaments; containers for pencils, brushes
Tinfoil (silver, gold, and colors)	Collages; decorations; ornaments; jewelry
Umbrella ribs	Clay modeling tools; stick puppets; shadow puppet controls
Wire, chicken	Three-dimensional map armature; sculpture
Wire scraps, plain or wrapped	Three-dimensional constructions; jewelry; puppets
Wire screen	Spatter printing; collages; constructions; sculpture; model house windows, terraces

NATURE MATERIALS	SUGGESTED USES
Acorns	Jewelry; buttons; ornaments; table decorations; scrap material printing
Bamboo	Musical instruments; place mats; drapes; frames; lettering pens; printing instruments; armatures
Bark of trees	Collages; three-dimensional constructions; quill pens; costumes;
Bone and ivory	Jewelry; carved figures; inlay work; tool handles; sections of salt and pepper shakers, etc.; three-dimensional construction
Branches of trees	Buttons; candle holders; center pieces; lapel pins; whistles; toys; musical instruments; furniture; seasonal decorations
Clay, moist, local deposits	Sculpture; ceramic pieces
Cornhusks; grass; straw; pine needles; raffia; rushes; reeds; cat tail straw; honeysuckle vine	Baskets; figures; brooms; brushes; braiding; weaving
Driftwood	Interior designs; carving; flower arrangements; mobiles and other types of sculpture
Feathers	Collages; three-dimensional constructions; quill pens; costumes; headdresses
Ferns; flowers; leaves	Photograms; spatter prints; table decorations
Fur	Toy animals; costumes; model house rugs; puppet clothes; hair for marionettes
Gourds	Musical instruments; ornaments; containers
Nuts	Scrap material sculpture; lapel pins; seasonal ornaments; jewelry; curtain pulls
Pine cones and burrs	Seasonal ornaments and package decorations; lapel pins; scrap material sculpture
Sand	Colored for sand painting; three-dimensional displays; sandbags for metal hammering
Sawdust	Mix with wallpaper paste for modeling figures, three-dimensional displays, puppet heads
Seeds, seed pods	Animals; dolls; jewelry; decorations; collages
Shells	Jewelry; mobiles; collages
Sponges	Painting tools; collage; miniature tree foliage; clean up (especially cellulose sponges)
Stones	Jewelry; large pieces for sculpture; paper weights; door stops
Twigs	Miniature cabins, wigwams; toys; sand table and model village Construction work; furniture; sculpture
Yellow pine; cedar; walnut	trees; dip in paint for seasonal decoration

NATURE MATERIALS—DYE SOURCES

Beets	Red-violet dye
Blackberries	Blue dye
Black walnut husks	Dark brown stain
Butternut bark	Brown dye
Citron	Yellow dye
Elderberry	Purple dye
Goldenrod	Yellow dye
Mountain ash	Orange dye
Polkberry	Purple dye
Raspberries	Dark red dye
Rhubarb	Light green dye
Sassafras root	Pink dye
Strawberries	Red dye
Tanglewood stem	Yellow dye

Berries and stems should be boiled in very little water about 2 hours, then strained through cloth 4 or 5 times. Mix three parts juice and one part wood alcohol, to retard spoilage. Note: Wood alcohol is POISONOUS.

Bark and roots should be boiled about 4 hours in very little water, then strained through cloth 4 or 5 times. Add tablespoon of salt to pint of juice to make dye more permanent. Dyes should be applied while hot on materials which are dry.

WOOD	SUGGESTED USES
Barrels, apple, etc.	Furniture; boiler for play locomotive; archery bows
Baseball bats, bowling pins (broken)	Hardwood for carving, construction
Berry boxes and baskets	Sewing frames; May and Easter baskets; paste sticks; delicate modeling tools; figure armatures
Broom handles	Tool handles; dowels; movie box rollers; armatures for life-size pasted paper constructions
Bushel baskets	Scrap wood containers
Chalk boxes	Birdhouses; containers; constructions
Cheese boxes	Miniature furniture; toys; looms; library card containers; storage of rulers, paint tubes; mobiles
Cigar boxes	Looms; letter container; toys; sculpture constructions
Clothespins, used or broken	Puppet armatures; modeling tools; clip items together; fasten drawing to easel
Coat hangers, wooden	Mobiles and constructions; papier mâché armature; display case racks
Ice cream spoons, washed	Paint mixers; paste sticks
Lath	Construction work
Orange sticks	Toys; constructions; modeling tools
Paddles from mustard jars, sucker sticks, ice cream bars, washed	Paint mixers; paste sticks; toys; model furniture
Small kegs	Drums; locomotive boilers; chairs; containers
Soft wood molding	Jewelry; sculpture; construction
Spools, all sizes	Toys; tool handles; wheels; printing tool; furniture construction; puppets
Tongue depressors	Modeling tools; constructions; mobiles; paint mixers; paste sticks; small loom shuttle
Wall board, building board	Bulletin boards; construction work; protective pads; picture frames; play houses
Wooden crates and boxes	Construction work; filing cases; storage; display cases; furniture; dioramas

MISCELLANEOUS	SUGGESTED USES
Beads	Jewelry; weaving; stringing; mobiles
Bricks	Sculpture; book ends; door stops
Collar buttons	Furniture handles (model houses)
Crayons, broken	Melted wax painting; crayon etching
Enamels and other paints	Construction work; easel painting
Inner tubes	Cut designs and mount on wood for printing; drum heads
Mica, powdered	Sand table snow; seasonal decorations
Nail polish, left over	Paint for mobiles, constructions
Paint brushes, worn, broken	Stencil brushes
Paraffin, used or broken candles	Batik; modeling figures, etc.
Plaster of Paris	Carving; molding; modeling
Plastic scraps	Jewelry; toys; mobiles; constructions
Shellac	Silk screening; waterproofing wood, paper, etc.
Toothbrushes, used, washed	Stencilling; spattering; painting; printing tool
Sponges, torn, used	Trees and shrubbery in model constructions; toys; figures; printing tools
Vaseline and grease	Prevent papier mâché from sticking to mold
Wallpaper paste, wheat paste	Add tempera paint and water for finger paint; paper mâché; pasted paper strip modeling

COURTESY APPLIED ARTS
DEPARTMENT, TEXAS
TECHNOLOGICAL COLLEGE,
LUBBOCK, TEXAS

Free or inexpensive materials may be u s e d creatively in many ways. This colorful collage picture was made from: seeds, flax, kidney beans, navy beans, and corn, mounted on emery cloth.

PAPER	SUGGESTED USES
Cardboard boxes	Construction work; storage files; stage sets; storage
Cardboard from shirts; tablet backs	Posters; paper sculpture; mobiles; simple looms
Catalogs and magazines	Cut and pasted paper pictures; color study; general reference illustrations (not for copying)
Cellophane	Windows in model house rooms; slides; collages; transparent pictorial designs
Cellophane straws, colored	Party favors; constructions; mobiles; collages; package decorations; weaving
Colored and construction paper scraps	Craft projects; cut and pasted paper pictures
Corrugated cardboard	Bulletin boards; posters; constructions; mobiles; stage scenery; collages
Crepe paper	Costumes; decorations; favors
Cups, paper	Paint containers; place cards; candy cups; favors
Doilies	Greeting card trimming; bouquet backgrounds; collages
Dry cleaning bags	Easel and mural painting; paper costumes; wrapping paper; finger paint paper
Ice cream cartons, round, all sizes to 10 gallon	Waste baskets; purses; string holders; button boxes; knitting cartons; scrap material containers
Mailing tubes	Pasted paper construction armatures; monoprinting tools
Newspapers	Protection for floors, clothes, tables; papier mâché; pasted paper; for watercolor or tempera painting surface
Paper bags, sacks	Paper bag masks; puppet heads
Paper tissues, napkins, towels (new)	Paper mache; pasted paper; blending charcoal and colored chalk; wiping up spilled paint, etc.; scrap material printing (crumpled)
Posters	Paint on backs; constructions; mobiles
Pulp paper trays, egg cartons	Collages, masks
Round oatmeal boxes	Drum bases; knitting boxes; totem poles (stack several)
Sandpaper, emery cloth	Collages; wood working
Seasonal cards	Use unprinted portions for graphics printing; greeting card designs
Shelf paper	Finger painting
Suit boxes	Collages; light construction work; mobiles
Tags, seals, spots, reinforcements, gummed	Collages, silk screen prints
Wallpaper	Paint on back
Wax paper	Use under wet clay and freshly painted objects to prevent sticking
Waxed cardboard milk containers	Molds for plaster carving blocks; for mosaic plaques
Wrapping paper	Murals; stage scenery; tempera painting and printing

256

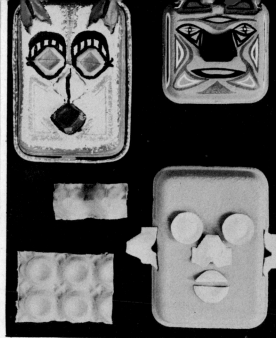

Mailing tubes were used as armatures for these pasted paper banks. Application of small strips of paper towel, sanding, tempera paint, and varnish completed the figures.

Interesting geometric shapes may be cut from egg cartons, paper plates, and pulp paper trays such as those used in supermarkets. They may be glued in place, adhered with pasted paper strips, or used as armatures for further construction in papier mâché.

THE PURCHASE OF ART MATERIALS, TOOLS, AND EQUIPMENT

To achieve the objectives of a modern art education program and to utilize properly the materials and tools listed in the foregoing sections, only the finest quality items should be purchased. The best tools are the safest and most economical tools, when properly used and maintained. The best tools and materials usually lend themselves to the most significant artistic expression. Although the purchase of the finest quality art materials and tools entails a considerable expenditure of money which must usually be spread

Gummed seals, reinforcements, and tags, as well as spots, free form shapes, and scraps of paper may be used as elements for silk screen designs. The demonstration model shown here illustrates possible effects without creating an actual design pattern.

257

over a period of several years, it is actually the most economical, safest, and most conducive to quality work.

When a limited budget governs the supply of art materials, tools, and equipment, art teachers in the same—or nearby—buildings might combine orders to secure lower, quantity purchase rates. They might also make more frequent use of free and inexpensive art materials. This procedure may make it possible to order certain high-priced items in areas where they are most urgently needed. A good quality, table-type jig saw, for example, could, if necessary be shared by several teachers. A cheap saw would deteriorate in a fraction of the lifetime of an excellent one, yet the cost is only a few dollars less.

Before placing an order, the art teacher should secure catalogs and art material samples from several firms which manufacture the desired products. One should purchase only items which have been personally tested or examined. Special care needs to be taken, especially on the elementary school level, to order materials which are non-toxic, since younger pupils put crayons, paint, and paste into their mouths. Manufacturers provide samples to teachers who request them on school letterhead stationery and will, if requested, often send a company representative to discuss materials and demonstrate their uses.

Art material order forms vary from one school to another. To find the most desirable form, sample copies of forms may be requested from surrounding schools or from art supply companies.

Careful and regular inventories of all items on hand will eliminate costly duplication and lengthy storage of excess materials.

ART ROOM SAFETY PRINCIPLES FOR TEACHERS

Safety education is an important part of the art teacher's responsibility. The art teacher, or responsible students carefully trained for this purpose, should demonstrate the safe as well as the unsafe ways of using various materials, tools, and equipment. In every instance where new materials, tools, or equipment are introduced, proper instructions regarding their use should be secured from the respective company and school or municipal safety officers. *The art teacher should frequently remind students of proper and safe working habits and dangers, since it is easy for people of any age to forget safety principles in the excitement of producing art objects.* If he fails to point out the dangers of materials, tools, or pieces of equipment· which subsequently cause injury to students under his direct supervision, *the art teacher could be judged negli-*

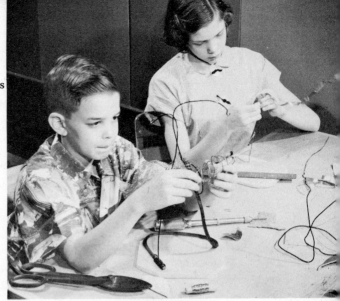

Small pieces of masking or cellophane tape folded over wire ends, and the use of soft aluminum wire, help eliminate hazards of mobile and stabile construction.

gent and in some cases might be held liable for injuries sustained in his classes. Each art teacher should thoroughly investigate both his personal and school insurance coverages to be certain that he is adequately covered.

The safety principles suggested below are probably not complete. Each teacher will wish to carefully examine this list in light of local conditions. It is suggested that missing items be added to this list and re-read every few months.

ART ROOM SAFETY PRINCIPLES FOR STUDENTS

Note: The art teacher may wish to place an abbreviated version of these principles on display in the art room.

• Follow teacher's advice on material, tool, and equipment use and study instructions carefully, understanding clearly that most accidents occur through either the incorrect use of the proper tools or the use of improper tools for certain types of work.

• Keep work area neat and free of extraneous materials at all times, realizing that cluttered work tables are dangerous.

• Report any injury, however slight, immediately; get first aid, and have all injuries checked by school nurse (or doctor, if necessary).

• Know where first aid equipment is located, how it is used, who to call for assistance in the event of injury, and to know what to do in the case of fire, escaping gas, broken water faucets, spilled acids.

• Report damage, however slight, of any tool or piece of equipment. Emphasis must be placed upon fact that the school pays cost of equipment repairs and replacement, that tools do wear out and eventually break through normal use over extended periods of time, and that they must be immediately repaired or taken out of use to prevent serious injury to other students. (Continued on page 262.)

259

Hand Tools and Materials	Frequently point out dangers of improper use and movement not only of tools, but of materials such as wire, stone, glass, acid, etc.
	Help students keep tools sharp and/or in good working condition.
	Repair or replace worn or defective tools.
	Paint tools with identifying colors to permit rapid return to proper shelf or rack of identical colors.
	Post signs containing safety instructions near most frequently misused tool.
	Keep enrollments to level where adequate supervision is possible.
Power Tools	Frequently point out great dangers of improper use. Install proper guards and other safety devices on all exposed moving parts of power tools.
	Repair or replace worn or defective power tools. Disconnect until repair or replacement has been made.
	Install master lock on switch box to prevent use of power tools in teacher's absence.
	Require wearing of goggles and hair nets (where applicable).
	Post signs containing safety instructions and power tool procedures near each machine.
	Consult experts on the proper type and placement of electrical outlets, extension cords, lighting, and all electrical equipment.
	Industrial color codes should be used to identify the various parts of equipment for safety of operation. Consult municipal industrial codes.
	Guard rails or "off limit" lines around power equipment will minimize injury to the user as well as the observer.
	Require that power tools be shut off when left for even short periods.
	Limit enrollment to number which can be carefully supervised.
	Require school officials to provide adequate space around base of each power tool.
Floor Surfaces	Keep floors clean, uncluttered, and use skidproof wax and polish.
	Place insulating, non-skid floor mats around power tool bases.

Fire Equipment	Proper fire extinguishers and/or water-filled red pails should be kept within easy reach.
	Inform all students of procedure in case of fire.
	Use correct wiring and voltage for power and other electrical equipment.
	Carefully instruct and caution students in use of gas jets, torches, soldering irons, kilns.
First Aid	Keep completely stocked, well-marked first-aid kit within easy reach. Staff and students should be instructed in its proper use.
	Have school nurse (or doctor if necessary) check *all* cuts, bruises, and other seemingly minor injuries even if proper first aid treatment has been administered.
	Require students to report all injuries immediately, no matter how slight.
Poisons	Clearly label all poisonous liquids and materials.
	Instruct students specifically about poisonous characteristics of certain art materials such as oil paints, dyes, acids.
	All poisons should be stored in metal-lined cabinets which can be locked.
	Glass containers or objects which break easily should not be used for storing poisonous material.
Cleanup	Instruct students on cleanliness for the sake of safety. Dirty, cluttered desks are dangerous.
	Highly flammable fluids should never be used for cleaning. Any flammable materials should be used only under the most careful supervision.
	Require students to wash and dry hands after completing work with toxic materials.
Lifting and Storage (See also special section on storage, pp. 238-241)	Instruct students on proper way to lift materials, tools, and portable equipment to avoid strain, dropping, slipping.
	Avoid placing heavy or otherwise dangerous materials on overhead shelves.
Miscellaneous	Sharp corners, protruding objects, precariously balanced objects, glass containers, poor arrangement of equipment are all safety hazards. Most city school systems and municipal governments will be able to furnish assistance in properly organizing the school plant to minimize dangers.

(Continued from page 259)

• Return materials, tools, and equipment to proper rack or storage area as soon as proper use has been made of them.

• Keep safety guards in place while using power equipment. Wear goggles and/or hairnets when necessary.

• Such items as neckties, ribbons, sashes, apron strings should be tied or removed so they will not get caught in power equipment. Long sleeves should be rolled up.

• Be constantly on the alert when working with hand or power tools, never pushing, running, turning around suddenly, or moving without looking. Only serious work should be carried on in the art workshop. "Roughhousing" cannot be tolerated here.

• Learn the proper color codes of dangerous parts of power tools.

• Be extremely cautious in use of gas jets, torches, soldering irons, the kiln, and other tools and equipment which are unusually hazardous.

• Wash and dry hands after completing work with toxic materials. Beware of accidental placement of poison-contaminated tools (such as oil paint brushes or nitric acid tongs) in mouth, eyes, or ears.

• Under no circumstances should students ever use gasoline or highly flammable cleaning materials.

• Learn to lift heavy materials, tools, and portable equipment correctly to avoid strain, dropping, or slipping. Do not place heavy or sharp materials or tools on high shelves.

• Place all oily or solvent soaked rags in covered metal container, not in waste basket.

• When in doubt about the proper use of any equipment, tools, or materials, secure instruction from instructor or authorized person in charge.

COURTESY E. H. SHELDON AND COMPANY

Adjustable-height storage shelves for paper permit better organization of various sizes, types, and colors, and prevent the pulling of an entire pile onto the floor while removing a sheet.

From the first day of each class, make students feel that the room is theirs in which to live and work during certain periods of the school day. They should be helped to understand that time spent in organizing and caring for materials and tools will pay high dividends in time saved, money (which their parents have spent in taxes or tuition), increased safety, higher quality products, and more enjoyable personal experiences.

• Newspapers, paper towels, and wiping rags for use with paint, chalk, and other media must be located conveniently on shelves, racks, or in bins and drawers.

• Wash *tempera* and *water color* brushes with mild soap and water, rinse, point with clean, damp hands, and place bristles-up in plastic or metal containers, or suspend from racks or hooks with bristles down but not touching anything.

• Clean *shellac* brushes in alcohol. Clean *oil paint* and *enamel* brushes in turpentine, kerosene, or other brush cleaning solutions. Remember that strong cleaners burn hands if exposed for long.

• Jar racks prevent tipping of tempera paint, enamels, and lacquers. Wooden dowels about ½ x 12 inches, or long-handled spoons, may effectively be used to dip out small quantities of paint instead of attempting to pour small amounts into mixing trays or palletes. Squeeze-type plastic catsup and mustard dispensers have been used with great satisfaction in dispensing tempera paints.

• Small glass jars with twist top lids are well suited for small amounts of left-over mixed colors.

• Store scissors in portable racks.

• Properly cover jars of paste to prevent drying.

• Empty chalk boxes can be used for broken crayons and stencil brushes. Label neatly with felt tip pens (or brushes and India ink) and store in cabinets.

Audile and visual materials in art education

The terms audile and visual ("audio-visual") are often thought of in connection with motion pictures, but they include many means of communication, including television, films, slides, film strips, recordings, radio, photographs, reproductions, maps, globes, graphs, specimens, models—and books. In fact, illustrated books are virtually a "filing cabinet" of visual materials.

Audio-visual materials are not substitutes for teaching or direct experience but offer a means of enlarging upon all direct educational experiences.

263

While the term "audio-visual" is of comparatively recent origin, the idea is very old. Primitive man's thoughts were conveyed by signs, pictorial symbols, gestures, facial expressions, and incoherent noises long before he could effectively communicate with verbal symbols. We have had printed material—cards, newspapers, magazines, books—for centuries.

Books. Among the finer picture books in the art field are those published by the Skira and Abrams houses, the New York Graphic Society, and the Museum of Modern Art in New York. Their products, as well as those of other publishers, should be included in the art library of every school and community. Those communities which are in the service area of a museum are fortunate in being able to secure the exhibits, reproductions-on-loan, and publications of the museum.

Newspapers. Newspapers such as the *New York Times* and *Christian Science Monitor* contain excellent art exhibition review sections, occasional art book reviews, reports of art conferences, examples of high quality advertising design, and other current information of value and interest to art teachers and advanced students. Secondary schools, colleges, universities, and professional art schools will want to subscribe regularly to such newspapers.

Periodicals. The following list of selected art periodicals are valuable to the art programs of schools on all educational levels, but especially for secondary schools, colleges, universities, and art schools. In addition, an increasing number of non-art magazines devote part of their contents to art subjects. The latter may usually be secured, second-hand, from students whose parents subscribe to them. Subscriptions to art periodicals are considered a standard element in the art department's annual budget.

ART PERIODICALS

Publishers' addresses and current subscription prices may be secured through most public and large institutional libraries. Virtually every major museum publishes a periodical of information pertinent to their collections and shows. These are usually available free or at a minimum cost of patrons of the museums. The art teacher will want to examine copies of each publication to determine those which are most desirable within his budget limitations.

American Fabrics
Architectural Forum
Architectural Record
Art a'Aujourd Hui (French)

Art Education (National Art Education Association)
Art Education Bulletin (Eastern Arts Association)

Art in America
Art in Industry
Art News
Arts
Arts and Activities
Arts and Architecture
Athene (British)
Bulletins of Art Museums
Burlington Magazine (British)
Camera (Swiss)
Cimaise (French)
College Art Bulletin
College Art Journal
Connoisseur
Craft Horizons
Domus (Italian)
Du (Swiss)
Eastern Arts Association Research Bulletin
Education Through Art
Everyday Art

Graphis (Swiss)
House and Home
Impression
Interiors
Journal of Aesthetics and Art Criticism
L'Oeil (French)
Newsletter, National Committee on
   Art Education
Pacific Arts Association Bulletin
Perspectives (British)
Pictures on Exhibit
Print
Progressive Architecture
Realities (French)
School Arts
Southeastern Arts Association Bulletin
Studio (British)
Theatre Arts
U. S. Camera
Western Arts Association Bulletin

NON-ART PERIODICALS

The following magazines frequently carry reproductions or articles of interest to art teachers and students. Publishers' addresses and current subscription prices may be secured from libraries.

American Home
Arizona Highways
Atlantic
Better Homes and Gardens
Consumer's Report
Consumer's Research Bulletin
Fortune
Harper's
Harper's Bazaar
House and Garden

House Beautiful
Life
Mademoiselle
National Geographic
Newsweek
Parents
Seventeen
Sunset (West Coast only)
Time
Vogue

TELEVISION

Television has proved itself an aid to education, both in school and out, for all age levels. Nearly every home in the United States is equipped with a television set, and many have more than one. The situation is becoming similar in other parts of the world. An increasing number of schools have television sets which are used for viewing educational programs and special events.

To improve the quality of television programs, individuals and groups are active in communicating with broadcasters, sponsors, and individual performers. Among the more effective communicators are P.T.A.'s, church organizations, and such national groups as the Joint Council on Educational Television with headquarters in Washington, D.C. The Federal Communications Commission, Washington, D.C., has set aside channels for educational purposes. These stations are absorbed by city school systems or institutions of higher learning. Many educationally-minded communities are securing options for these educational channels until service may be available. At this writing there are over thirty-three educational television stations plus over eighty affiliated commercial stations in the National Educational Television Network.

The power of the individual relative to television program modification should not be underestimated, for each letter of encouragement or complaint, particularly the latter, is carefully read by performers, broadcasters, and sponsors, and suggestions for improvement are often considered with care.

Television broadcasters themselves have done much to better the quality of their programs. In many communities, they sustain educational telecasts without commercial sponsorship, in the public interest. One of the pioneers in this type of service was station WBEN-TV of Buffalo, New York. An educational program of creative art activities for children, moderated by one of the authors of this book, was sustained for four years at a weekly cost to the station of nearly $400. This amount is more than some schools spend on art materials during an entire year! The WBEN-TV program was only one of about fifteen weekly educational programs sustained by this station alone, due largely to the human welfare interests of its manager and program director. In addition, there are other stations, both commercial and educational, which have rendered valuable public services in art education.

One of the newer uses of television is in teacher education. By means of closed circuit televising, art education students can observe a class being taught by an experienced teacher and still be free to discuss problems among themselves. Teachers who are already in the professional field can supplement their college education by watching programs where up-to-date teaching aids, subjects, and methods are demonstrated. This is particularly valuable for teachers who happen to live and teach in areas where opportunities for Saturday or evening class attendance are infrequent.

Television will never be a substitute for actual classroom experiences, because, as with movies and other visual aids, direct relationships between students and the performers are impossible. Yet, in cases of homebound students, television provides a better substitute for live classroom experiences than radio or the telephone, or assignments sent home by the teacher.

Educational television has other limitations. Except in the case of closed circuit telecasts, programs must be watched on schedule. The teacher must adjust all plans to this schedule or miss occasional performances. Also, many useful programs appear early in the morning, at night, or on weekends, so that the audience is scattered and partially uncontrolled. Discussions have less meaning; preparatory work is difficult.

Another limitation of educational television is the lack of opportunity for previewing programs, a practice commonly followed in the use of educational films. However, this limitation, as well as that of timing, can to some degree be overcome by the use of printed program guides. These are furnished by program agencies, television stations, or networks. They are also listed in newspapers and weekly television magazines, occasionally with brief program descriptions.

One must not underestimate the power of television as a supplement to education, for the scope of experiences gained can be deeply penetrating and long lasting. It is certainly a challenge to live teaching. Students might accept television as an educational substitute, if their direct school program is uninspiring.

It is possible through proper planning that educational television programs may be as profitably utilized as high quality sound films. There is no question of the great, lasting significance of out-of-school educational television for parents, pre-school children, all children during after-school and week-end hours, and for teachers in remote communities.

RADIO

The need for developing children's communication skills gives added significance to audio-visual aids. With proper scheduling of radio broadcasts in the school room, children can learn how to listen to and evaluate what they hear. Through radio, pupils can be helped to grow in understanding the world in which they live; they can develop a greater interest in and appreciation of music, art, literature, script writing, civic affairs, drama, news reporting, and life in general.

Teachers can determine in advance what programs will be available locally and make plans for their use. Local radio station managers are usually willing to cooperate in the development of suitable school programs. Other major sources of information and potential cooperation are: the educational department of major radio networks; the National Association of Radio and Television

Broadcasters, 1771 "N" Street, N.W., Washington, D. C.; the National Association of Educational Broadcasters, 1201 10th Street, N.W., Washington, D. C.; most colleges and universities; the U. S. Office of Education, Radio and Television Section, Department of Health, Education, and Welfare, Washington, D. C.; and the National Education Association in Washington, D. C.

PROGRAM TAPES

Radio and television programs are frequently recorded or kinescoped and can be replayed or shown in the classroom or at public meetings. For information, one might contact the Indiana University Film Library, Bloomington, Ind., which distributes the Educational Television and Radio Center kinescopes and tapes; state departments of education; libraries of large educational systems or cities; and commercial libraries such as the A-V Tape Libraries, 730 Fifth Ave., New York 19, N. Y. and the Tempo Record Co. of America, 8540 Sunset Blvd., Hollywood, California. Many schools have their own tape recorders which are used for this purpose as well as for various classroom and art activities such as the preparation and rehearsal of puppet show scripts and making special sound effects for subsequent artistic interpretation.

Because of the projective value of puppetry, speech therapists and the art teacher can aid speech improvement by permitting children to record on tape the dialogue of the puppets as well as the background sounds and music.

RECORD PLAYERS

Every art room should be equipped with a good quality, multi-speed record player. Recorded music, stories, plays, and historical news events can be used effectively to stimulate artistic expression in clay, paint, and other media.

Recorded background music is useful for studio activities. It has been found that many students tend to concentrate more deeply upon their work while listening to music than when they engage in conversation. On the other hand, individuals who prefer absolute quiet while engaged in art activities should be provided with proper space, facilities, and supervision.

Long-playing records are usually desirable since they require less frequent changing and cause fewer interruptions in students' thinking. Each school should have a record collection which can be shared by interested students, teachers, and, to a limited extent, community residents. The purposes of the art program are usually best served by high quality, non-verbal classical and modern music. However, students should be given an occasional opportunity to select their own mood music.

The music and art departments can aid one another in the selection of appropriate music for the art room and appropriate pictures for the music room.

FILM

Opaque projectors. Each art room should be equipped with an opaque projector. It is well suited for enlarging small objects, pictures, and book pages by projecting an exact color image of them on a screen. Fine quality but small-sized color reproductions which are available at most art museums at nominal cost can be projected into life size by means of the opaque projector. In this way a ten-cent color postcard of an art masterpiece can be used in lieu of a twenty-dollar color print or two-dollar color slide of the same work. None of these alternatives, however, can be considered adequate substitutes for the original work.

Slide and filmstrip projector. Every art room should have available a projector which uses glass and cardboard mounted 2″ x 2″ slides. 2″ x 2″ slide and filmstrip projectors are convenient, low priced, and efficient. Projectors should be tested on approval prior to purchase, since some of them bend cardboard-mounted slides, rip the bindings of glass-mounted slides, overheat, or do not operate easily. For schools which have already established collections of 3¼″ x 4″ slides, or in cases where art teachers prefer these over certain 2″ x 2″ slides, it is possible to secure well-designed 3¼″ x 4″ slide projectors with 2″ x 2″ slide adapters. In schools where art teachers simultaneously compare slides in the analysis of art works, two projectors should be available. Under ideal conditions, the art room would have two built-in projectors installed side by side at the proper projection distance from a permanent, beaded screen.

Suggestions for the use of slides, filmstrips, and films. Film materials are among the most flexible and versatile of all teaching aids. Through their proper use, the rate of students' learning can be expedited and its permanence increased. Film materials can deeply enrich our knowledge and can stimulate our imaginative and creative powers.

1. It is essential that the teacher preview and study film materials in advance of possible class use.

2. Students must be prepared for film material which is to be shown. They need to know why it is being shown and what to see.

3. Film material is usually shown in conjunction with a unit of study, before small groups in a darkened art studio or classroom rather than in a large auditorium.

4. Follow-up discussions are essential. Art teachers may prepare discussion and study guides after they have personally previewed film materials. These may be modified after subsequent showing of the same films and after discussion periods.

The use of slides, filmstrips, and films for classroom instruction has become widespread. Art teachers who have made extensive and intelligent use of these materials have found it possible to extend the scope of their pupils' learning experiences as well as to intensify them. The months of preparation and work which went into such a film as "Birth of a Painting," for example, make it possible to demonstrate a process which would otherwise take weeks or might even be impossible to accomplish in a school studio. A series of films including the aforementioned, "The Titan," "Renoir," "Matisse," "Braque," "Alexander Calder, Sculpture and Construction," and others would make it possible to compress years of preparation into the educational experiences of a single semester, without unduly infringing upon the time needed for students' direct participation in studio activities.

There are several hundred excellent art films, many thousands of slides, and numerous filmstrips available on practically any subject in the broad fields of art and art education. Each art teacher should maintain his own art film catalog. Since new films are constantly being produced and since film prices and sources change from year to year, it is suggested that printed film data be clipped out of publicity from film distributors and be pasted on 5" x 8" file cards or loose-leaf notebook sheets and be filed alphabetically by title. As soon as a film listing is changed or superseded, the card or sheet may be easily removed.

A really superior art education program in a secondary school could use as many as five 10 or 15 minute art films per week, necessitating an annual budget allocation for this purpose of about $1,000.

Chalk and crayon board

Chalkboards are produced in green as well as black. White boards are also available, on which one may write, letter, or draw with specially prepared colored crayons which erase with a damp cellulose sponge.

If chalk or crayon boards are used wisely and efficiently, they will enhance pupils' interest and attention. Illustrations and instructions placed on the board should be neatly and clearly reproduced with not too much material appearing at one time.

White chalk for black or green boards, or black crayons for white boards should be used for regular work, with colored chalk or crayons reserved for contrasts or special illustrative work. The board, trays, and erasers (or sponges) must be cleaned each day.

A 6′ length of chalk or crayon board is adequate for most art rooms. When preferred, it can be located on the reverse side of a revolving bulletin board panel.

DISPLAY BOARDS

Several display boards may be located in each art room. Others, properly illuminated, can be installed in adjacent corridors. On these may be shown pupil work as well as reproductions of paintings, newspaper clippings, photographs, assignments, and announcements of school activities. Display boards can be effectively used in connection with almost every school situation as a means of motivating interest and enriching learning.

Material placed on display boards should be correlated with topics of current interest and should be changed at least once every two weeks. This not only creates interest in a variety of subjects, but provides opportunities for student participation in arranging displays on the board.

Boards should be placed in well-illuminated areas at a horizontal center height corresponding generally with the eye level of the students. The specific location of boards within the art room as well as the color they are to be painted should be determined on the basis of an overall interior design plan.

Neatness is one of the most important requirements of a well-arranged display board. Items placed on the board should be straight and secured firmly with thumbtacks, pins, or staples at each corner so they will not flutter or fall. Better design can be achieved by placing the tops and/or sides of several items in line. Items should not be placed diagonally or sideways on the board, since legibility and readability are paramount. Lettering, particularly, should always be placed horizontally and should be simple in style, easy to read.

Many materials are suitable for use as display boards. They should be soft enough for pins, thumbtacks, or staples to be easily inserted, yet strong enough to hold them in place. While cork is best, other possible materials are: soft wood upon which can be stretched burlap or other woven fabrics; Celotex; Homosote; and building board. Special wire spring clips make perforated hardboard useful as a display board, in addition to its many other functional and attractive applications.

MUSEUMS

Purely creative as well as correlated art experiences can be intensified and broadened by means of carefully planned museum visits. The subtle color relationships and powerful designs of Indian ceremonial objects, for example, can be usefully studied to develop one's sensitivity to art principles as well as to learn more about Indian culture. But above all, museums and art galleries should be frequently visited as a means of developing the deepest possible, first-hand knowledge of modern and historic art objects.

An interesting and valuable educational experience is the establishment of a school art museum. A variety of items can be secured for it from pupils' homes, industrial establishments, chambers of commerce, forest commissions, fairs, exhibitions, and established museums. For assistance in establishing and developing a school museum, teachers and administrators might contact organizations such as the American Association of University Women, the Association of the Junior Leagues of America, the American Museum Association, the American Federation of Arts, the National Art Education Association, the state historical society and various individual museums. A school art museum can become a never-ending source of interest to children, teachers, parents, and the general public, provided careful attention is given by those guiding its development to the collection of significant objects of lasting educational value and not a mere collection of souvenirs. (See also "art galleries and museums" section in chapter 8, pp. 285-286.)

EXHIBITS

School art exhibits familiarize students, teachers, administrators, and community residents with the art activities of the school and with what is being done in the art programs of other schools. Children are always interested in seeing what their classmates and pupils in other communities are doing. Exhibits also help to keep visitors, especially parents, informed of the progress being made by their children.

Student art exhibits. Although special exhibits such as art work from foreign lands are popular among student groups, there is no type of exhibit which draws more attention than an exhibition of students' own work. Such exhibitions held periodically may in the course of a school year include the work of every student. In addition to exhibitions in the school building, art works might be shown in clubs, churches, community buildings, theater lobbies, and at county and state fairs.

Exhibits in local stores. Students enjoy arranging exhibitions of their art work, or traveling exhibitions which have appeared at their school, in local store windows or interior display areas. Exhibitions of paintings, house models, or other art products of interest to the general public necessitates cooperative planning between the students in charge and store personnel. The social contacts involved are important parts of a total learning experience, and must not be handled exclusively by the teacher.

Exchange exhibits. To broaden the horizons of students, teachers, administrators, and other residents of the community, it is helpful to import exhibitions of works by other students and teachers as well as professional artists. The student chairman of a local exhibition committee might, through his art teacher, contact the art department of a nearby school. With the guidance of their respective art teachers, exhibit chairmen can decide on the number and types of works they would like to exchange. Even sculpture and other three-dimensional works can be exchanged, since they can be transported in private cars, station wagons, or school buses. On a national basis, an exchange of works might be arranged through regional or national art teachers' organizations. On an international basis, the National Art Education Association in cooperation with the International Red Cross has established channels to facilitate the exchange of art works by students throughout the world.

Selecting material for circulating exhibitions. Any exhibit of children's art work, together with a brief, clearly lettered statement of the educational objectives involved, should honestly represent the character of work achieved by all of the children in a given class or school instead of limiting it to the gifted few. In addition to the names of children who did the work, labels should also give their age, grade in school, the title of the work, and the medium in which it was executed. Children should participate in the selection of art works for exhibition in their own or other schools, provided they are mature enough.

Preparing exhibitions for circulation. Mounting pictures or other flat pieces helps to unify an exhibit in size and shape, in addition to making it more attractive. The colors of mounting boards should harmonize with the colors of art works which are to be placed upon them. Provided they are related in hue, intensity, and proportion, several mounting board colors and sizes may be used in the same exhibit. To do this effectively, it is usually necessary to experiment with various color and shape combinations prior to mounting and hanging the actual exhibit. Captions and labels need to be brief, with lettering large and clear enough to be read easily from a distance of four or five feet.

One of the basic factors to be considered in preparing an exhibition is the ease of handling and shipping. Pictures must be securely placed in simple and easily hung frames or mats. Large envelopes or re-usable wrappings may be used as protective coverings on flat works. Three-dimensional objects should be individually wrapped and packed, although several may occupy the same crate. All works, as well as the cartons or crates in which they are shipped, must be clearly labeled and numbered with corresponding figures so that each object may always be repackaged in its original container. Properly designed crates will eliminate any movement of the enclosed objects. Hinged and locked crates are preferable to those which are nailed or screwed together.

The originator of a circulating exhibit should be spared the responsibility and cost of having it returned after each use. Exhibitors are usually held responsible for receiving the exhibit and forwarding it to the next-scheduled institution.

Securing exhibitions. A number of fine exhibits can be secured for the cost of transportation from one school to the next. For others, a small rental fee may be charged. Major exhibitions of original art works may cost as much as several hundred dollars, plus transportation. But even in the latter case, the cost would amount only to several cents for each person viewing an otherwise unavailable exhibition of important art works.

Information and literature regarding exhibitions may be secured by writing to any of the following:

American Childhood Education
1200 15th St., N.W.
Washington, D. C.

Art for World Friendship
Friendly Acres
Media, Pennsylvania

American Federation of Arts
1083 5th Ave.
New York 28, N. Y.

Arts and Activities magazine
Illinois State Normal University
Normal, Illinois

American Junior Red Cross
Washington, D. C.

(Annual national art exhibition
   for children.)

Committee on Education
U. S. Chamber of Commerce
Washington, D. C.

International School Art Program, sponsored jointly by
American National Red Cross
and
National Art Education Association, N.E.A. building,
Washington, D. C.

Japanese Art Exchange
School Arts magazine
400 Woodland Drive
Buffalo 23, New York

Louisiana Art Commission
Baton Rouge, Louisiana
(Many states have comparable
services.)

Museum of Modern Art
11 West 53rd St.
New York 19, N. Y.

National Art Education Association and
National Education Association
1201 16th St., N.W.
Washington, D. C.

National Association of Museum
Directors
Smithsonian Institute
Washington, D. C.

World Affairs Council
Wanamakers
Philadelphia, Pennsylvania

Organizations, such as:

Art Schools

Chambers of Commerce, local

Church Schools

Colleges and Universities

Public and Private Schools

State Departments of Education

Consulates and Embassies in
New York and Washington,
D. C.

DEMONSTRATIONS

Art students and teachers can perform an important educational service by giving demonstrations of various art activities and processes. Students can present demonstrations at open houses or exhibit nights, at church group meetings, or in department store windows. Among the art activities which lend themselves well to demonstration are painting and sketching, interior and architectural design, paper sculpture, puppet making, clay modeling, and sculpture in wire, wood, or stone.

8: Improving the School Art Program

THE ABILITY TO IMPROVE is one of our most important needs. In art education it calls for teachers who are alert to the characteristics of individuals in a changing society, teachers who are willing to spend time and effort doing the best work of which they are capable.

SURVEYING THE PRESENT PROGRAM

Preliminary to any plan of improvement should be a carefully organized survey of existing conditions.* For example:

---

* In the case of a beginning teacher, this would have to be done concurrently with the first year of teaching. Experienced teachers, however, might survey their local situation as part of a graduate study course.

Ceramic sculpture is one of the more p o p u l a r art activities among secondary school students, who are finding increasing opportunity to secure art instruction t h r o u g h required classes, electives, or extra-curricular activities.

COURTESY BALTIMORE
PUBLIC SCHOOLS,
PHOTO BY JACK ENGEMAN

276

1. During a period of two or three weeks, obtain an overview of the entire school-community situation. Look beyond everyday details to see major patterns in the curriculum, the underlying philosophy of the staff, and characteristics of the community.

2. Gather facts and organize them into appropriate categories. Study existing literature on the local situation as well as related professional writings.

3. Evaluate compiled information and data.

4. Write up results of the survey, amplifying generalizations with quotations of fact. Use photographs and drawings to explain and validate written information.

5. Submit survey material to the proper administrative authorities, and request an appointment to discuss it in making plans for the future.

Helpful in accomplishing step 1 above would be a study of recent literature in the field of education in general and art education in particular. If time is available, it would also be helpful to visit other schools, including conferences with teachers and observations of classes in session.

Step 2 may be accomplished in a variety of ways. The chart below may be used for this purpose. Steps 3, 4, and 5 will evolve on the basis of information gathered in 1 and 2. The organization of material in the chart may suggest a form for the final writeup. A brief, chartlike summary is often more effective than a lengthy treatise.

The material which follows has been used to set up or evaluate art programs in the United States, Canada, Hawaii, and Israel. Although it is intended primarily as a conference or discussion guide, it has been successfully used as a checklist. It is planned as an art program evaluation guide for all educational levels.

How good is your art program?[*]

Nearly every public school art program needs to be restudied. Changes and improvements in art teaching philosophies and practices within the past few years have been numerous and rapid. We believe it is important, therefore, for art teachers and administrators to take a few minutes to restudy their art program—however broad or limited it may be—in the light of the criteria set forth here.

---

[*] Based on: "How Good is Your Art Program?" by Howard Conant and Clement Tetkowski, *National Elementary Principal*, Vol. XXX, No. 5 (April, 1951), pp. 11-17; and "Which Type of Art Program is Yours?" by Howard Conant and Clement Tetkowski, *School Arts*, Vol. 53, No. 2 (October, 1953), pp. 8-9.

WHICH TYPE OF ART

TEACHER-DIRECTED

Children show only passive interest in art activities in the elementary school and do not wish to take more courses in art, since they have been convinced that they are not talented.

Teacher confines art activities to scheduled lessons in specified periods, ignoring or minimizing relationships of art to other classroom activities, and contributions to extra-curriculas.

Teacher selects the subject matter and the art media to be employed, often repeating the same lesson at the same time every year with very little modification for individuals.

Teacher demonstrates one definite way of working, in a step-by-step procedure, and makes it clear that each child is judged on how well he follows the method of the teacher.

Teacher limits art activities to two-dimensional seatwork at individual desks, and restricts materials and tools to those which may be passed out quickly, cleaned up promptly.

Teacher limits talking to questions directed to him after a proper raising of hands, and discourages any activity or use of tool which would result in noise or any informality.

Teacher plans or selects prepared subjects for seasonal window decorations and other displays in the classroom and halls, to be copied or imitated.

Teacher plans, constructs, and paints stage scenery and all props, if there are any, and limits the work of children to chores such as filling in areas outlined by him.

Teacher plans all displays of children's work, carefully selecting only that work which he regards as best or which may show off to advantage with administrators and others.

Teacher regards the completed work as more important than the experience in developing it, as if the product desired was on the paper itself and not in the child's personality.

Teacher gives letter grades based on conformity to rigid standards and teacher aims, promoting competition between children to discover and attain objectives he has in mind.

PROGRAM IS YOURS?

PUPIL-DEVELOPED

Children show great enthusiasm for art in the elementary grades and are eager to take additional art courses when given an opportunity to do so in the junior and senior high schools.

Pupils may use art whenever it is applicable and meaningful in any area within the general school program, integrating it with other subject fields and extracurriculars.

Pupils have a choice in the selection of subject matter and materials to be used, and may select activities according to individual backgrounds, needs, and timely interests.

Pupils are shown various ways of using any new tools and materials found successful by others, but are encouraged to develop their own concepts and ways of working with materials.

Pupils can work in a variety of materials and processes in both two-dimensional and three-dimensional activities, either individually or as members of groups working together.

Pupils are free to move about the room to secure materials and tools, and to discuss their work with others in a casual manner, without any restrictions on normal working sounds.

Pupils plan seasonal exhibits and other displays, and develop them as normal children's work, with a great deal of variety in color, size, shape, and individual expression.

Pupils participate in planning, constructing, and painting original stage scenes or backdrops for both school assembly programs and other dramatic activities in the classroom.

Pupils have a part in planning exhibitions of their own work, and every child has an opportunity to be represented without competing with false standards or other children.

Pupils are not led to believe that the completed work is more important than the creative experience in making it, and receive many personal benefits from the activity itself.

Pupils realize that, if their work is evaluated at all by the teacher, it will be on the basis of individual growth with due regard for differing abilities and personalities.

The specific art needs of each school community vary considerably, depending on a number of socio-economic and educational factors. For this reason we have not set up a formal curriculum in art, but have attempted to derive from the most recent developments in the field of art teaching the most essential aspects. They are offered in concise form, hoping they will be helpful in achieving a better art program.

Some questions, suggestions, and facts

If you are an art teacher:
• Have you kept up with the field of art and education by taking refresher courses and by regularly attending national and regional as well as state and local conferences?
• Have you discussed with your administrator and classroom teachers the broad educational values of art for children?
• Have you frequently visited other art classes in action?

If you are a classroom teacher:
• Are summer school courses in art teaching recommended for you, or have arrangements been made with a nearby college or university to offer a local extension course?
• Are you provided with adequate equipment and supplies?
• Are you encouraged to set aside part of your room as an art activity area?
• Are you encouraged to integrate art throughout your programs?
• If these recommendations, provisions, or encouragement are not provided by others, what have you done to provide pupils with needed art materials and creative guidance?

Your art program can foster better school-community relations:
• By offering courses in art as a part of adult education program.
• By inviting local artists and craftsmen to give demonstrations or to discuss their specialties in school assemblies or as part of a special "art night" for the community.
• By borrowing or renting films and works of art from local museums, artists, and collectors, for school exhibitions.
• By having the art teacher explain the art program to P.T.A. or other local groups.
• By exhibiting child art with accompanying explanations to help parents understand their children better.

• By encouraging a community beautification program with the school serving as central headquarters and the school children playing an active role in the program.
• By offering assistance to local civic, church, and farm groups in preparing decorations, posters, and scenery for their special events.
• By exhibiting child art in stores, churches, and club meeting places.

Art can be used as a means of enriching children's general educational development:

• By providing an opportunity for the expression of the children's originality, individuality, and creativity.
• By enabling children to use materials and tools geared to their abilities and interests and to see visible results of their resourcefulness.
• By making the understanding of other subjects more vital and interesting.
• By developing self-confidence through building pride in individual differences.
• By stimulating an interest in future hobbies or possible occupations.
• By learning to appreciate the work of artists and craftsmen through first-hand experiences in similar media.
• By developing a sensitivity to beauty in nature and in man-made things.
• By showing them the functions of art in everyday life.

If you are an administrator you should set up long-range plans for your art program:

• By seeking the services of a person conversant with the most recent developments in art education to help you, your art specialist, and the classroom teachers in setting up overall plans for your art program.
• By including in future building or remodeling plans: (1) well-lighted art activities rooms; (2) work activity areas in each classroom with easels, work benches, storage space, sinks; (3) exhibition space.
• By planning to purchase equipment such as additional storage bins, work benches, kilns, looms, and specialized tools as the art program progresses.

• By coordinating the elementary art program with the high school art program.

Do you know that:

• Many leaders in the field of education have said that creative art activities should form an *essential* part of all education.

• Many small communities have secured the services of an art teacher by sharing the cost of salary and materials with neighboring school districts until such time as they can each afford a full-time art program.

• An increasing number of school administrators have arranged for their teachers to receive in-service art education two or three afternoons a month. This is accomplished by dismissing school early and having the art specialist give demonstrations and lead discussion on subjects related to children's art activities.

• Today's art teacher is more concerned with total child development than with the development of drawing and painting skills in a limited number of talented children.

• Leaders in early childhood and handicapped child education are among the strongest supporters of creative art education.

• Creative art activities contribute positively to emotional stability and mental growth.

• Some of the best, most creative art activities utilize discarded newspapers, wood and metal scraps, driftwood, and other free or inexpensive materials.

On the basis of what you have just read, how good is your school art program?

• Why not use this chart as a basis for a conference with other teachers and with administrators?

IMPROVING ART TEACHING PERFORMANCE

The foregoing chart may prove helpful in studying the local situation and in suggesting means for improving the art education program. The quality of art teaching is probably the most important factor in the entire program of art education. The best-furnished art room and the most generous budget for materials and supplies mean little otherwise.

Assuming that the art teacher is effective, creative, has a personality conducive to teaching (see "Some desirable characteristics in an art teacher," pages 30-41), and can overcome any physical and economic shortcoming revealed in the survey suggested above, here are some means by which the quality of art teaching may be further improved.

1. **On the basis of a careful survey of the local situation, choose one important area shown to be deficient and concentrate upon improving it.** Prove to yourself, as well as to other teachers and school administrators, that you can accomplish things by beginning with one thing and doing it well.

Having a good philosophy about ideal art education programs has value for all of us, but seldom are ideal programs born in finished form. They are developed step by step, over a period of time.

2. **Study carefully the objectives and methods of creative teaching and put them into practice.**

3. **Read, extensively and regularly, books and magazine articles in the fields of art, art education, and education, plus occasional works in the fields of music, literature, science, and social studies.** Art teachers, like specialists in any profession, need to be well informed. They should subscribe to major art and art education magazines and purchase important books in their professional field.

4. **Preview educational films.** A steadily increasing number of excellent films on art and art education are being produced. These, together with many fine films already on the market, provide the viewer with an excellent source of information on improved art teaching, new processes and techniques, and background information on art and education. Films may be previewed at art conventions as well as in one's own school through arrangements with film rental companies who are usually happy to provide "preview" films which may subsequently be rented for classroom use.

5. **Attend regularly and participate in professional conferences on art, art education, and education.** Here many new ideas are brought forth and previously introduced concepts are crystallized. Creative thinking among professional groups often provides a stimulus for improved teaching which cannot be paralleled in one's local situation.

6. **Enroll in graduate courses and in-service workshops in art, art education, and education.** Education is a continuous life-long process. College and university graduate courses provide a source of valuable information on recent professional developments. Refresher courses should be taken every few years by all teachers, including those who have had many years of experience. Most school systems conduct in-service workshops, led by local teachers or invited specialists.

7. **Study art education programs in other schools.** As often as possible, but certainly no less than once a year, art teachers should take advantage of the provision made by most schools to spend a full day visiting other schools for the purpose of self-improvement in teaching. They should visit schools with outstanding programs so as to profit as fully as possible, instead of making a social visit or merely fulfilling an administrative requirement. Preliminary inquiries concerning the location of outstanding art education programs can often be made through art education departments in colleges and universities, through the officers of art teachers' professional organizations, or through the state director of art.

Overview the entire art education program of the school being visited, including philosophy and practices; the physical plant; location, condition, and sources of furniture, supplies, and equipment; and other items suggested in the evaluation chart presented earlier in this chapter. Visiting and evaluating someone else's teaching situation provides an excellent source of periodic comparison to one's own art education program, and is likely to result in improved art education in both one's own school and the school being visited.

8. **Seek the advice and guidance of local, regional, and state school administrators.** Directors and supervisors of various educational departments in the school, region, and state are appointed for the primary purpose of advising and guiding teachers in order that children's educational opportunities may be continually improved. Art teachers should seek assistance from these capable persons in attempting to solve complex educational problems.

9. **Share the professional responsibility for preparing future art teachers by offering your school as a student teaching center.** After consulting your principal or superintendent, invite the director of a nearby art teacher education center to consider you as a "cooperating teacher" for work with student teachers. Ask him, or his representative, to visit your school in order that he may fully understand why your school should become an art student teaching center.

Student teachers, as well as their college supervisors (often prominent art educators) can help cooperating teachers in a variety of ways ranging from assistance in handling supplies, records, and various details to suggestions for more effective teaching. In addition, cooperating teachers' responsibilities for the guidance of undergraduate student teachers tend to make them more aware of their own strengths and weaknesses and thus increase their rate of self-improvement.

10. **Learn more about your pupils' needs, interests, and back-**

In order to see and study contemporary paintings, such as Robert Eshoo's *Evolution of a Day*, art teachers must regularly visit art galleries and museums.

grounds by meeting their parents. By means of P.T.A. meetings, conferences, art fairs, and other co-curricular activities, as well as occasional home visits, art teachers should make themselves acquainted with as many of their pupils' parents as possible. Through informal conversations as well as by means of question and answer sessions at P.T.A. meetings, teachers may become aware of much new information concerning their pupils' backgrounds, needs, interests, and potentialities.

11. **Regularly visit art galleries and museums.** Art teachers need to be well informed on recent trends in painting, sculpture, architecture, photography, and the graphic arts, as well as the nature of child art and adult amateur art. Vacation, business, and professional trips to or through cities with important galleries or museums should include visits to art exhibitions as part of the itinerary.

The broadened understanding of trends in various contemporary professional, amateur, and child art forms gained through frequent visits to exhibitions will contribute directly to the improvement of art education in the school. For this reason, many colleges and universities (as well as superior elementary and secondary systems) have established a sabbatical leave program whereby teachers who have completed a certain number of years of service may apply for several months' salaried leave to travel, to produce art work, to visit museums, to write, or to use the time in some other professionally profitable way.

Helping Others Develop an Interest in Art Education

A sincere desire to assume responsibility for certain aspects of the art education program will arise among some classroom teachers, parents, and administrators if they are encouraged. This desire may often be fostered by urging participation on the following basis:

1. Teaching art is an *enjoyable* experience, both for pupils and teachers. But even the most competent, creative art teacher requires certain assistance from classroom teachers, parents, and others, if pupils' varied and extensive art needs are to be met.

2. Self-rewarding competence, sufficient for the assumption of partial responsibility in elementary art education, can to a surprising extent be gained by the classroom teacher or parent through participation in art workshops, in-service art courses, adult education programs, and graduate study.

Busy participants and interested spectators such as these are typical of the amazing creative spirit engendered by art workshops.

COURTESY C. D. GAITSKELL, ONTARIO, CANADA, DEPARTMENT OF EDUCATION

An increasing number of school systems regularly conduct art workshops for elementary classroom teachers. A valuable by-product of the workshops is the deep interest which many teachers develop in art as a hobby or avocational pursuit. These teachers are developing original compositions for tempera paintings.

COURTESY CHICAGO PUBLIC SCHOOLS

3. Art activities enrich children's learnings in other subject areas, make the teaching of these subjects easier, and provide a splendid source of constructive leisure time or recuperative activity.

4. Classroom teachers and parents who help guide children's growth through art activities find that new doors of understanding are opened which more clearly reveal the nature of children, their ways of working, their products, and their concepts.

Art workshops. In-service art workshops or courses are an excellent means of developing increased competence for guiding children's growth through art activities.

The art workshop idea has been widely implemented in recent years; hence there are numerous varieties ranging from an informal one-hour discussion to an intensive six-week lecture-activity-discussion course. The chart on pages 288-289 indicates some of the workshop formats effective for the needs of various groups.

For teachers, parents, and administrators who have never attended an art workshop, it is difficult to explain the feelings of enjoyment and accomplishment which this activity provides. It is interesting to watch newcomers as they begin an art workshop experience. In almost every case they soon overcome their reluctance toward personal expression and enter into the creative spirit of the workshop. A typical comment made by a participant upon the completion of a three-day art workshop was, "I had absolutely no idea that I could enjoy myself so thoroughly or that I could produce art work I would be proud of! I can hardly wait to get back to try out what I learned with my class."

The participation of school administrators in art workshops for teachers or parents emphasizes the value of the enterprise. Beyond their administrative support, they will thoroughly enjoy the art activities, and subsequently will have a much better understanding of the functions and importance of art in the educational program.

Why Held and For Whom	To develop confidence of classroom teachers, art teachers, parents, administrators, and others in leadership of children's art activities. To provide participants with knowledge of various art activities from which they may later choose a hobby for more constructive use of their own leisure time.
Leader	Local art teacher, art consultant, or art supervisor. Local classroom teacher or administrator who has had previous art workshop experience or has taken numerous art education courses in college. Instructor from nearby college or university. Upper-classman art education students from nearby college or university. Workshop teacher-representative from art materials company.**
Length of Each Session	1 hour (possible, but not recommended). 1½ hours (better). 2 hours (satisfactory). 2½ hours (ideal). 3 hours (ideal, with coffee break). 3½ hours (satisfactory, with coffee break). 4 hours (too long).
Duration of Workshop	1 session per day for one day (possible, but not recommended). 2 sessions per day for one day (better). 2 sessions per day for two days (satisfactory). 2 sessions per day for three days (good). 2 sessions per day for four days (good). 2 sessions per day for five days (good). 2 sessions per day for 2-6 weeks, in summer session (excellent). 3 sessions per day, (AM, PM, Night) (too much).
Frequency of Workshops	Once every 2 years (for 2-4 day workshops of 2 sessions per day) (satisfactory). Once a year (for 2-4 day workshops of 2 sessions per day) (good). Twice a year (for 2-4 day workshops of 2 sessions per day) (excellent).
Time of Workshops	For art teachers, classroom teachers: After school in afternoons, evenings, or on week-ends (unsatisfactory). During regular school hours (classes excused; no salary lost; ideal). During days prior to or following regular school year, with salary paid (prior to: ideal; following: satisfactory). As part of graduate study in summer session (ideal, if supplemental to in-service work in local school). For parents and others interested in children's art education: During school hours (satisfactory, for those with children in school). In evenings, Monday through Thursday (satisfactory for most).
Location of Workshops	In art room of local school (ideal). In classroom or shop where large tables and sink are available (satisfactory). In classroom with individual desks bolted to floor and no sink (unsatisfactory). In church basement, community recreation center, etc. (satisfactory if tables and sink are available).

* Based on a portion of *Art Workshop Leaders Guide*, edited by Howard Conant, Worcester, Mass.: Davis Press, 1958.

** Art workshops are provided free of charge by a few major art supply companies. These art workshops and the people who conduct them should be used as supplements to art-teacher-led workshops or college courses rather than as substitutes for them. Obviously, an art teacher or college professor who better understands the local situation, the individual needs of participants whom he comes to know well over an extended period of time, and who has no commercial obligations to a sponsoring company is best suited to conduct art workshops.

Cost of Workshops	Free: no tuition, all materials provided by school (ideal, for in-service workshops).
	Tuition, plus cost of individual's materials (satisfactory, for college credit workshops).
	Cost of materials, no tuition charges (satisfactory, for parents' or parent-teacher workshops).
	Free: no tuition, all materials provided by art materials company (satisfactory, if no commercial strings are attached).
Workshop Curricula	Art activities which can be enjoyed by participants on their ability and interest level, yet which can be adapted for later presentation to children (such as pasted paper construction, crayon batik, crayon etching, linoleum block printing, stencilling, and clay modeling).
	Discussions and lectures on the importance of creative activities for children and adults.
	Illustrated talks, showing typical work of age group under consideration.
	Illustrated talks and discussions on the arts of painting, sculpture, and graphic arts, using original professional works or reproductions as examples.
Workshop Credit	College credit, when workshop is offered by accredited institution of higher learning and participants pay tuition fees.
	In-service credit, when school board offers participants credit for participation toward salary increment and/or tenure.
	Certificate of accomplishment or completion, awarded by local school board or art materials company, sometimes credited toward salary increment and/or tenure, but in any case an excellent record of participants' growing professional interest.
	No credit or certificate, where workshop is held only for purpose of personal and professional growth on a voluntary or experimental basis.

INTEGRATION THROUGH ART

All significant forms of art expression are based on life experiences. Consciously or unconsciously, people react through art to various stimuli. All art is, to a degree, integrated with other modes of expression, attitudes, experiences, and subjects.

What must concern us, then, is how to help people better integrate their various life experiences. Through creative teaching in art, we have one of the most valuable means of fostering the highest and most desirable types of significant, personal integration. By helping a person express creatively his reactions to a subject or

COURTESY HAZEL PETERSON, JACKSON SCHOOL, HEMPSTEAD, N. Y.

Three-dimensional map making is an excellent means of fostering deepened understanding of geography and other social studies. Papier mâché has great tactile appeal for many pupils.

event, we are helping him to relate, and unify, many aspects of a single subject. The role of the teacher in fostering integration has been well described by an elementary school art supervisor:

It is the teacher who will make the subject matter dry facts or who can make it come alive. She can help the child visualize by making the printed page come to life. It is not enough to say, "Draw a picture of Columbus." The story of Columbus should be made so vivid that the child may identify himself with it. The integrated art experience of the story of Columbus will, therefore, be different for each individual according to the type of self identification which takes place in each pupil. One may identify himself with the joy of the sailors when land was sighted, while another's experience may be focused upon the fears that possessed the sailors through their ignorance of the world. The way in which all these experiences are expressed and organized in art media is intensely personal. Such integration cannot take place when teacher merely says, "Children, let's draw about Columbus." It can only take place if the child becomes completely absorbed by his subject.*

Genuine integration is far more personal than the "illustration" of social studies or science topics. Victor D'Amico, Director of the Department of Education of the Museum of Modern Art in New York, has differentiated clearly between "curricular" integration and that which is individually based:

Integration is a highly personal matter involving perceptions, emotional reactions, aptitudes and skills that must perforce differ with each child, because each child is different. The great value of creative experience is that it provides for and develops personal integration, because the child selects his own motivation and expresses himself in terms of his own needs and aptitudes. The sensitive art teacher guides the child into experience most suited to his ability and most satisfying to his individual concepts, at a rate of learning natural to him.

The curriculum approach is apt to destroy personal integration because the motivation comes from subject matter, such as social studies or science, allowing little expression for emotional needs or creative concepts. Too often it is this kind of motivation, begun by the social studies or the science teacher and involving such evils as copying or poor design, that the art teacher finds she must continue in order to preserve the peace. Emphasis is also inclined to be put on the finished product rather than on creative experience because the mural on brotherhood, the model of a medieval town, the map showing the natural resources of the country, must be finished in time for the Parent Teachers' meeting, or for the principal or superintendent to view. Sometimes the art teacher finds herself prodding a child to undertake a project beyond his powers, or urging a group to finish something long after their interest has died.

---

* Virginia French, "Correlation Can Be Creative," *Art Education*, Vol 7, No. 5 (June, 1954), pp. 3-4.

The greatest danger of the integrated studies approach is the possible destruction of the creative act through imposition of subject matter, use of poor design and emphasis on skill or what amounts to sheer child labor.

The integration of art with other studies has, of course, distinct values, especially to the other studies. It often gives purpose and vitality to studies which inherently lack them. It makes the art teacher feel needed and establishes a prestige which she ordinarily does not enjoy. A constructive solution may be achieved if the planners of all the studies involved agree upon fundamental values as their guide, and if the children have opportunity to choose expressions most suited to their creative needs. In such cases the art teacher must have the responsibility of taking part in the planning at the early stages to propose and promote projects that offer rich creative possibilities, to be sure that no projects are devised which demoralize the creative experience of children. At best, however, integrated projects are limited in their capacity for personal expression. Therefore special art classes should be continued in any case in order to allow for the development and guidance of individual creative growth.*

Not only has D'Amico perceived and spoken courageously about the dangers inherent in curricular integration; he also was one of the first to see possible threats to art education in programs where the art consultant idea excluded the actual teaching services of specially prepared art teachers. It is likely that no one in the art education profession has done more to preserve the quality and intensity of creative, aesthetic experiences for the boys and girls in our schools than Victor D'Amico.

The "self-identification" theory of integration through art has been thoughtfully developed by Lowenfeld, who says:

In total integration the single elements lose their identity and unite to a new entity. In art education integration takes place when the single components which lead to a creative experience become an inseparable whole, one in which no single experience remains an isolated factor.

Integration means neither correlation with nor interpretation of other subject matters, outside of art. This, to my knowledge, represents the greatest misunderstanding of the meaning of integration. Teachers often think if history is illustrated, or interpreted in the art lesson, integration of two subject matters takes place. This is by no means true. In such a superficial situation neither history is explained, nor does a creative experience become meaningful.

. . . Integration does not occur from the outside; integration is not "made" by "assembling" two subjects; integration happens from within. That says clearly that integration can only take place by self-identification. The integrated art experiences of the settlers who landed

* Victor D'Amico, "Are We Jeopardizing the Child's Creative Growth?", *Bulletin* of Eastern Arts Association, Vol. 10, No. 4 (April, 1953), pp. 5-6.

on our shores will, therefore, be different for each individual, according to the type of self-identification which takes place in each individual.*

EXTRA-CURRICULAR ACTIVITIES

Students' preference for the informality and excitement of extra-curricular activities is shown by the many clubs and other organizations to which they belong, plus the fervor with which they work. We know that many of the same learning experiences which draw negative reactions from students in regular classes are enjoyed enthusiastically in an informal setting. In addition, extra-curricular activities afford opportunities for cooperative group experience which are sometimes not available in the formal curriculum. The semi-parliamentary structure of activity organizations causes individuals to work on committees and other groups where their leadership abilities are exercised beyond the usual limits. Thus in some schools is found an extra-curricular program more diversified than the curriculum itself.

Organizing extra-curricular activities. Occasionally a group of students will form a club and request that it be recognized by the school. More frequently, however, extra-curricular groups are implemented by teachers who recognize a need. For instance, the art teacher might ask one or two potential leaders: "What do you think of organizing an art club where advanced students like you and John and Mary might meet once a week to sculpt, sketch, and paint?" or, "Why don't you people organize a stagecraft club? Then you could really design the kind of sets you seem to think this school needs!"

In schools where the extra-curricular program has been very limited, it may be necessary to make an approach through the administration. One student might be told, "You know, Jim, I think some of our more responsible students like you, Peter, Joan, and Carol should have a chance to apply your art knowledge to the appearance of our school. Why don't you get these other people together and see our principal? I believe that if you told him some of the ideas I've heard you discussing here about circulating framed reproductions among the classrooms and corridors, he would be happy to have you organize some sort of art service club."

In similar fashion teachers are able to encourage existing organizations by making such suggestions as, "Your organization is doing a fine piece of work. What do you think of including exchange exhibits with other schools in your activities?"

---

* Viktor Lowenfeld, "The Meaning of Integration for Art Education," *Research Bulletin* of Eastern Arts Association, Vol. I, No. 1, (April, 1950), p. 4.

Nearly every extra-curricular organization decides to charge dues, ranging from a few cents per meeting in elementary school groups to several dollars per year in adult groups. Dues help defray the organization's operating expenses, but even more important, they give the members a sense of belonging, even of ownership, which deepens interest.

A warning may be necessary here: There are probably more potential extra-curricular activities in the field of art than in any other subject area; most art teachers possess a zeal which too often prevents them from saying "no" to additional activities which they are expected to advise; and the assumption of too many responsibilities often results in unsatisfactory results. *It is important for the art teacher to maintain a workable balance of curricular and extra-curricular responsibilities.*

The activities listed in the chart page 294 and described in the pages which follow have not been categorized according to age. In most cases they are suited for or can be modified to suit any age level.

Assembly programs

Periodic assembly programs on art subjects are desirable. On the secondary school level they serve as a direct source of art education for students who do not elect enough art courses to provide them with an adequate background. On the elementary school level they supplement art classes, and provide a source of entertainment.

Art films. Interesting movies are always appreciated by school audiences. Hundreds of films on art topics are available at very reasonable cost. For purposes of economy and ease in scheduling, it is usually more desirable to show three or four short movies (10-15 minutes each) consecutively than to present them in separate showings. For example, a combination like *The Loon's Necklace, Making a Mask,* and *Totems* provides an interesting related film program for elementary or secondary grades which might, if desired, be used as a general stimulus for subsequent art activities. Another possible combination, especially for use on the secondary school or college level, would be a film like *The City* (30 min.) followed by a shorter film such as *Making A Model House* (15 min.).

Where seating capacity permits, interested parents should be invited to attend. One might also include occasional groups of pupils from neighboring schools. This may lead to reciprocal assembly exchange. In areas where budgets are low and feature length art films are expensive, this would be economically as well as educationally and socially desirable.

Extra-Curricular Art Activities

ASSEMBLY PROGRAMS	CLUBS	EXHIBITS	FESTIVALS
Art films	Art club	Student art exhibits	Art festival
Professional artists' lectures and demonstrations	Art service club	Exhibits in local stores	Art bazaar
	Art squad		Art week
Panel discussions	Poster club	Exchange exhibits	
Fashion parades	Stagecraft club	Seasonal displays	
Chalk talks	Sketch club		
Theatrical productions	Art teachers of tomorrow club		
Art career days			

FIELD TRIPS	SOCIAL EVENTS	PUBLI-CATIONS
Art interest spots	Dance & party decorations	School newspaper
Art galleries and museums	Art games: group sequence pictures;	School year book
Department store & factory displays	art charades; creative costumes;	Literary quarterly
Examples of contemporary architecture	commercial games	School newsletter or magazine
Neighboring schools, colleges, & universities		Club newsletter or magazine

(See detailed descriptions of many of these activities on following pages.)

Professional artists' lectures and demonstrations. Painters, sculptors, architects, photographers, jewelry designers, and other professional artists may be called upon occasionally to give illustrated talks to school audiences. Through interesting and educational assembly programs at schools and other community centers, the artist is often able to foster improved public understanding of the arts.

Panel discussions. "Modern Art" or "Careers in Art" are panel discussion topics which are effective on the secondary school level. All-student, all-faculty, student-faculty, or student-faculty-outside guest combinations are possible. In most cases, the more varied the backgrounds of panel members, the more interesting the panel presentation will be. When possible, slides, film strips, recordings, films, or charts should be used to supplement the panel topic.

Fashion parades. People are fashion-conscious from nursery school through old age; hence a "fashion parade" assembly program or any program format on a clothing design topic, is likely to be well received. Students whose interest in good clothing design is recognized can show contemporary trends in male and female clothing and accessory designs. A student or faculty member can point out various features of each participant's dress, grooming, and accessories by means of a public address system. Prior to the fashion parade, participants should be given instruction in stage poise, particularly with regard to the way to walk, turn, and point out various features of their attire.

Chalk talks. Audiences of all ages are fascinated by speakers who can illustrate their subject as they speak, or who tell a story while an artist illustrates it. Many media have been successfully used for this purpose, although colored chalk is the most popular because of the speed with which it can be used as well as the bright colors, which can be seen throughout an auditorium.

Chalk talks might be used to present stimulating educational topics, such as "What is Modern Art?" An art teacher might, for example, illustrate the basic composition of several modern paintings or pieces of sculpture on display by drawing with colored chalk on large pieces of paper. Also effective is the actual creation of a painting before an audience, although it is difficult for most artists to produce works of art under these conditions. It might also be possible to prevail upon several advanced secondary school art students to demonstrate their procedure in making a painting or piece of sculpture before a school audience.

Theatrical productions. Plays, operettas, and skits are highlights of the extra-curricular program. Many aspects of these productions involve art, including the design of sets and costumes, lighting, participants' positions on stage, and the writing of original scripts, music, and lyrics.

Since there is practically no limit to the amount of time and effort which may be expended on theatrical productions, it is important for the art teacher, the dramatics teacher, classroom teachers, and students to plan carefully the amount of time they can afford to spend in these endeavors, and decide which portion of it will be curricular and which part extra-curricular. In schools where administrators, the board of education, the public, and some of the non-participating teachers have come to expect Broadway quality school productions, it may be necessary to discuss the purposes of the entire extra-curricular program before making any further commitments.

Art career days. At least once a year, art career days should be held for high school students and interested junior high school students in order that all possible careers in the arts may be considered. Representatives from college and university art education departments as well as professional art schools may be invited to explain the requirements, curricula, and placement opportunities in each field. Following their general presentations to the career day audience, the school representatives need to be available to meet with small groups of specially interested students to provide more details and to answer questions.

In most schools, guidance counselors are responsible for planning and managing career days. The special responsibility of the art teacher is to see that the counselor adequately represents the various art professions on panels of career day speakers. In schools where there is no guidance counselor or where the guidance counselor does not adequately represent this area, it is the art teacher's responsibility to plan art career days.

CLUBS

Art clubs are important on every educational level, from the

Art Service Club Aids Members In Career Choice

The Art Service Club of New Rochelle High School is preparing its members for careers in commercial art.

NEWSPAPERS GIVE SUPPORT

Under the direction of Paul Schmall, a student, the members practice lettering by making posters advertising school dances and other school activities. Other community organizations have also availed themselves of the club's services by having posters made free of charge.

---

intermediate grades through college and adult education. The art club provides an informal, social experience in which students are likely to grow personally, socially, and artistically; it serves the total educational program, in that its agenda often includes art activities which contribute to the beauty and efficient operation of the school.

Art clubs. A broadly designated title such as "art club" is satisfactory for smaller schools, or those in which a wide variety of extra-curricular activities are not feasible. Nearly every activity listed under the following club headings might be considered appropriate for an art club.

Art service club. The purpose of an art *service* club is to render art services to the school, whereas the usual art club functioning in the same school would provide opportunity for personal art activities such as sketching and modeling in clay.

Art service functions might be the preparation of posters for school and community events (see description of functions of "poster club," pages 298-299); assisting in planning dance and party decorations and games (see details under "Dance and party decorations," page 308); arranging bulletin board displays, selecting and placing flowers and decorative plants in corridors and offices; and hanging pictures and exhibits throughout the school.

Great care must be taken to prevent members of an art service club from assuming more work than they can adequately handle in the out-of-class time available. Classroom teachers, art teachers, administrators, fellow students, and community residents are always eager to request art services for their parties, dances, exhibits, and other social functions. Their well-meant requests might swamp an extra-curricular group unless a work schedule had been carefully arranged in advance.

Art squad. Sometimes called the art squad, art helpers, or art workers, students in the upper middle grades, as well as junior and senior high school, enjoy banding together to form a club which renders physical plant improvement services. In one school the art squad designed, constructed, painted, and installed slanting bookshelves for art magazines; painted the interior of the art room as well as certain pieces of equipment; and performed other services combining art and physical performance. This group was made up of high school boys who were considered by many teachers to be trouble makers, yet under the skillful guidance of the art teacher they assumed many important responsibilities, gained a reputation among their peers as an exclusive group, and drew praise from school officials.

297

Helpful in carrying out the program of any club such as the art service club or art squad is a room where they may hold private meetings and work at the jobs they have undertaken. In most cases, the art room is used, after classes have been dismissed or during lunch hour; but a separate room such as the art supply room or a basement work room is desirable for construction activities. When other space is not available, the club group should be given a corner or end of the room in which to meet and work privately.

Another function of the art squad might be the assumption of responsibility for checking in new orders, making inventories, passing out supplies to classes, and even guiding cleanup operations at the end of the class. This sort of activity is particularly effective for youngsters who need to assume greater responsibility and authority but who have not previously found constructive channels.

Poster club. A poster club for students who have developed reasonable skill in layout, lettering, and general design offers a potential solution to the problem raised by requests for signs, charts, and posters. It should be clearly understood, throughout the school and community, that *students* make the posters.

It is important for the poster club to have its own president and other officers. The club president should be a person with whom the teacher can plan, suggesting conditions of service, as below.

POSTER SERVICE CONDITIONS

Posters may be made for recognized school organizations (and certain community organizations, if time permits) provided the organization:

1. Submits requests with complete information at least one month in advance of the date posters are desired, during October, November, and January through May, only.
2. Limits requests to two poster jobs per organization per school year if only one or two original works are desired or if layout design is to be reproduced by a commercial printer.
3. Limits requests to one poster job per organization per year if poster club is to silk screen (maximum 25) or otherwise reproduce the poster.
4. Permits poster club members to decide matters of design, lettering styles, and how much content to include.
5. Pays the cost of materials used or a fixed rate per poster (dependent upon size, complexity, reproduction process used, and school policy), and agrees to pick up and pay for completed posters at a specified time.
6. Agrees to remove posters from display the day following the event.

Conditions of service such as those just suggested might be circulated to all faculty members, to club and organization presidents, and to community leaders (in cases where such an extension of services is possible and felt desirable). In this way, poster club members are able to limit and schedule their work in order that it may be completed on time, without interfering with other work.

An active poster club can readily improve the over-all appearance of a school, which is often defaced by poorly designed objects on display. Posters should be art products, designed for easy communication as well as attractiveness. Posters for school or community display should be produced by students who have superior art ability. Only the exceptional beginner's work in poster making merits public display. Membership in a poster club is usually honorary, and might be accomplished through the recommendation of the art teacher or an examining board of club members.

In cases where requests for poster making exceed one or two per year, the organization which makes the request can be referred to a commercial designer who specializes in this field. Names, addresses, and price ranges of reliable commercial designers in the locality might be listed on the "Conditions of Service" sheet. Poster designers are in business for the purpose of designing high quality posters for mass production. School poster clubs should not be in competition with them. Rather, the poster club becomes the proving ground from which professionals of the future can receive their basic preparation.

Stagecraft club. A stagecraft club provides a source of specialized learning for students interested in designing sets, costumes, and lighting effects. Under the guidance of an art and/or drama teacher who has had special preparation in stagecraft, students may develop skills which will provide a source of immediate pleasure and service as well as a background for participation in future amateur or professional theatrical productions.

Sketch club. A sketch club might take the place of an art club in a smaller school, or might serve as a center of specialized learning in a larger school. Meeting after school, or on week-ends, the sketch club affords members an opportunity to visit interesting scenic spots for sketching and painting. Because of widespread interest in drawing and painting among non-art groups, membership in such a club should be open to any interested student. At least once a year, the sketch club, accompanied by the art teacher, should be permitted to go on a half or full day field trip during regular school hours, as a special incentive.

Art Teachers of Tomorrow club. Beginning in the fifth or sixth grade, art teachers, classroom teachers, guidance counselors, and school administrators can be on the lookout for students who show unusual interest in various subjects, including art, and who may be able to develop professional skills. Students who have an unusual interest, are able to produce personally satisfying art work, who have pleasant personalities, and who enjoy working with others may be potential art teachers.

Interested students should be told of the advantages and pleasures inherent in art teaching and the means by which they might best prepare for the art teaching profession. Occasionally, a representative of a college or university art education department may be invited to speak with them and provide scholarship information, application blanks, and school catalogs.

One means of promoting recruitment is to stimulate the formation of an Art Teachers of Tomorrow club, beginning as early as junior high school. Here students can interest many others in the profession of art teaching as well as participate in activities which will better prepare them for their intended life's work. Among some of the more desirable of these activities would be: setting up a program whereby members of the club would assist their art teacher in presenting lessons to classes; helping individual pupils with problems they are attempting to solve; helping to issue and collect art materials; engaging in art activities; taking field trips to exhibitions of art works at galleries and museums; and reading books on art and art education.

A series of frequently-changing school art exhibits should fill school foyers, corridors, and classrooms throughout the year. Wide varieties of subject matter interpretation and ability, as shown, indicate creative teaching.

An opportunity to participate in exhibitions of student work is an important part of learning. However, care should be exercised in its design and construction to show the exhibits to their best advantage. This excellent display was created by advertising design students in a professional art school.

Public displays of this type are important educationally and should be scheduled in different stores on a year-round basis. National Art Week provided the "card of introduction" to a local merchant, which resulted in this downtown store window display of work by members of a college art department.

Student participation in the selection of art works for classrooms and corridors is highly desirable. This activity deepens their interest in art, and extends the democratic process to a significant level of operation. Shown here is a class gift committee viewing colored reproductions of famous modern paintings with the help of an art museum staff member.

In schools where there would not be a sufficient number of students to form an Art Teachers of Tomorrow club, a regional organization might be formed, with one, two, or several members from each school meeting at one of the cooperating schools on a rotating basis. Also possible would be affiliation with an existing organization such as the Future Teachers of America.

Exhibits

As a rule, exhibits are looked upon as a part of the regular school program. But exhibition activities may effectively be extended on an extra-curricular basis. The exhibition committee may eventually develop into an all-student group, under faculty guidance.

Exhibits of art work, like poster designing, must, if they are to be attractive and effective, be prepared by persons who have an art background. After they have learned the basic factors underlying exhibition techniques, students might decide to form another art club, and could, under the guidance of their art teacher, assume responsibility for student, professional, and exchange art exhibits in the school, local stores, and community centers.

301

The classrooms and corridors of every school should contain examples of significant art works, either in original or reproduced form. A portion of the annual school budget should include funds for this purpose, just as each year books, films, and recordings are added to the school library. Student participation in the selection of work is frequently desirable, although a person of mature artistic judgment should act as consultant.

Seasonal displays. As far as community residents, non-art teachers, administrators, and many students are concerned, seasonal displays of art work are superior to regular exhibits. Although most art teachers do not share this opinion, due to the stereotyped nature of seasonal displays, they frequently find themselves giving aid to students preparing displays at Christmas, Easter, Halloween, Thanksgiving, and other special holiday periods. There is no sound reason why seasonal exhibits should continue to be routine and repetitious, such as bells and holly for Christmas and a horn of plenty for Thanksgiving. Through careful and stimulating teacher guidance, students may come up with new, refreshing, and significant ideas. Since there is a favorable attitude on the part of the school as a whole and the public in general toward seasonal displays, art teachers and their students often want to take advantage of the situation to present their best creative efforts. On the other hand, neither art teachers nor their students should be coerced into seasonal activity participation.

FESTIVALS

An effective means of bringing an art program to the attention of the entire school and community is an art festival. It also brings many participants before the public, providing them with social as well as art experiences. An art festival, art fair, art bazaar, or art week might take any of many forms and last anywhere from an hour to several weeks. The chart below presents a variety of ideas which have been developed in a number of different communities. From these, interested teachers and students might establish the framework for an art festival in their own school and community setting.

Suggested Activities For An Art Festival

PLANNING: Form committee with representatives from:
　　　　　　　faculty
　　　　　　　student groups
　　　　　　　community organizations
　　　　　　　professional artists in area

Choose dates for festival months—even a year—in advance, checking with program planners of other groups and civic headquarters in community to be sure festival dates do not conflict with already-planned school and community events.

PUBLICITY: Provide illustrations and descriptions for school and community newspapers.

Circulate printed or mimeographed handbills.

Place advertising posters in local store windows, on school bulletin boards, and send copies to neighboring schools and communities for display.

Place "bumper cards" (varnished or shellacked for waterproofing) on automobiles of "volunteers."

Ask each student and faculty member to be responsible for bringing at least one "outside" acquaintance to the festival.

FEATURES: Exhibits of two- and three-dimensional art work by local students (every student should, if possible, be represented by at least one piece of work). Exhibits can be hung on school or playground fences, snow fence, from strung rope or wire, or placed on folding tables.

Exhibits of work from other schools, from community art groups, from professional artists living in area.

Exhibits of well-designed furniture or industrial design objects selected by student groups from interested local stores.

Demonstrations of various art activities and processes by students, teachers, adult amateur artists, and local professional artists.

Portrait sketching and painting by students, teachers, local amateurs, or professionals.

Auctions or sales of drawings, paintings, pieces of sculpture, jewelry, ceramics, and other creative products produced in the school and community.

Movies on art subjects.

Speakers or panel discussions on art subjects.

"Gallery Tours" of exhibits led by advanced students, teachers, or local professionals who would attempt to offer introductory explanations of the works.

Art game demonstrations (see section on Social Events, pages 308-309) on stage or platform so visitors may be entertained while they learn new activities for their children or for adult parties.

Displays of "Suggested Art Materials for the Home"; "Hopes for the Future" (showing art room furniture or equipment which is hoped for in future budgets, works of art which would look well in the local school and community, and illustrations of well-designed art rooms).

A field trip must be carefully planned as an educational experience. Before leaving on the trip, or while in transit, students may be given suggestions on what to look for or what to do, so as to derive full benefits from the venture.

Either the teacher or an experienced guide should point out significant aspects of the objects or places being observed, encouraging questions and comments.

Shortly after the trip has been completed, a follow-up discussion is important. Plans for improving future experiences of a similar nature might also be discussed.

Outdoor art activities. Every community has subjects likely to appeal to students interested in sketching, painting, photography, or merely observing for subsequent art expression. Among these are:

> views from the art room or classroom windows
> the school building and grounds
> interestingly shaped trees
> interesting cloud formations
> old houses or stores
> perspective views of residential or business streets
> stone quarries
> lakes, ponds, rivers, creeks
> boats, docks, fishermen, shanties
> industrial scenes
> factory interiors
> farms
> railroad yards

Art galleries and museums. Within a field trip's distance of nearly every school is an art gallery or museum worth visiting. It is just as important to take a group of students to a distant city to visit an art gallery as it is to take them on athletic field trips or to county fairs and industrial centers. There is no substitute for original works of art seen in gallery and museum settings.

In all major cities and many smaller communities, there are galleries, art museums, art institutes, art clubs with exhibition galleries, colleges, universities, and art schools with exhibition galleries, or other places where art works are displayed regularly. In most cases, admission to these institutions is free. Many of the larger museums which charge a small admission fee on certain days of the week will provide special school rates or free admission for school groups. In all cases, it is wise to make arrangements in advance to be sure the gallery or museum will be open on the day

Reniassance masterpieces such as *The Miracle of the Loaves and Fishes* by Tintoretto (1518-1594) are too large to be sent about the country in traveling exhibits. Color, texture, and, most important, scale cannot be fully appreciated or understood in reproductions. Field trips to see art masterpieces in major museums should be included in the itinerary of every school.

a school group plans to visit, and that a visiting group can be accommodated at that time.

Names and locations of various galleries, museums, colleges, universities, and art schools which have art galleries are listed regularly in *Arts* and *Art News* magazines. Also included in these useful publications are the titles as well as critical reviews of exhibitions currently on display at galleries throughout the United States and Canada.

Because of the size of the art collections in larger museums, as well as the number of art galleries and museums in larger cities, art field trips to these cultural centers are often scheduled by high school, college, and art school groups for several days in succession.

Department store and factory displays. Nearly every community has often-untapped sources of inspiration and interest for art students in its department stores and factories. In these commercial and industrial settings may be found well-designed objects which

Class visits to well-designed industrial or commercial displays, such as this *Kitchen of Tomorrow*, are often responsible for students' grasping clearly the importance of art in their lives.

might otherwise be unavailable for close observation and on-the-spot discussion.

Among the many commercial products of interest to art students are:

automobiles	glassware
ceramics	hand tools
clothing	jewelry
dishware	kitchen appliances
draperies	lighting fixtures
floor coverings	tableware
footwear	toys
furniture	wallpaper

To locate stores and factories which include well-designed objects of art interest among their merchandise, the art teacher and/or several advanced art students should scout the town. After they have made a list, they should request permission from the managements to bring a student group to visit on a certain day at an agreed time. In some cases two or three stores or factories can be visited in a single day.

Examples of contemporary architecture. Within every community are examples of well-designed contemporary architecture. These provide an excellent source of study and inspiration for students from the upper grades through college and adult education. It is of utmost importance for students to learn the merits of well-designed contemporary architecture. This knowledge will help increase the demand for up-to-date, well-designed homes, churches, schools, offices, factories, and communities.

Of particular importance, if available, would be visits to homes and other buildings designed by architects such as Frank Lloyd Wright, Edward Stone, Richard Neutra, Philip Johnson, Craig Ellwood, Eero Saarinen, Walter Gropius, and Mies van der Rohe.

Also of great importance, although examples are unfortunately few, are planned communities where beauty, safety, economy, health, recreation, and many other human needs have been carefully considered. Some well-planned communities are located at: Greenbelt, Maryland, near Washington, D. C.; Greenhills, Ohio, near Cincinnati; Greendale, Wisconsin, near Milwaukee; and New Rochelle, N. Y. (Bayberry) near New York City. Students need to realize that in their hands rests the power to shape new communities of the future and to remodel already established communities into designs for good living.

Nearly every community has outstanding examples of modern architecture. The General Motors Technical Center near Detroit, designed by Eero Saarinen, is one of these.

Neighboring schools, colleges, and universities. Limitless sources of interest and inspiration are available through visits to elementary and secondary schools, colleges, universities, and art schools. Students of art, whether they be elementary school children or college men and women, should occasionally visit schools on their own educational level to compare what they are doing with the work and environment of others. They should also visit schools which are on other educational levels. Upper elementary and secondary school students should visit colleges, universities, and professional schools to see art exhibitions, examples of architecture, and to "get the feel" of a college campus, which may partially induce them to enter an institution of higher learning. College-age men and women should visit elementary and secondary schools, where they may possibly develop further interest in a teaching career, and where they may see examples of children's and adolescents' art work. Whenever possible, a visit to another school should be highlighted by a talk by one of the school's art teachers, or, where appropriate, an art demonstration or gallery tour. Descriptive literature should be issued when this is available.

A variety of social events present opportunities for extra-curricular art services which, when properly guided into student activity channels rather than faculty assignments provide numerous educational benefits. Since students entertain their friends at parties and dances, and will continue to do so after they have completed their formal education, it is desirable that they learn means of bringing their knowledge of art into functional use for social events.

Dance and party decorations. Classrooms, corridors, gymnasiums, or cafeterias are often well designed for their daily uses, but when they are used for parties or dances they may seem too large and bare, and do not lend themselves to party atmosphere. An imaginative art teacher can help pupils choose and direct their installation of simple yet effective decorations and lighting effects which will transform the chosen area into a pleasant social setting. Such materials as crepe-paper sheets and strips, large cardboard pieces from mattress boxes, old sheets, colored cellophane, and a variety of other materials the students will think of can be inexpensively secured and easily utilized.

The time spent on school dance or party decorations, should be carefully balanced between school, after-school, and Saturday time, and limited to a certain number of hours. Otherwise, more time than is really necessary may be consumed in this extra-curricular activity.

Art games. Intelligently-planned and interesting games can make a party educational as well as entertaining, whether it is for children, teen-agers, or adults. A number of art games fall into this category and, because they have been so little used in the past, are almost always new to everyone present and are certain to be effective morale boosters.

Group sequence pictures are made in several ways. The most popular is the method whereby a piece of paper is folded accordion style, numbered in the upper corner of each rectangular space thus created, then unfolded. The first person draws an imaginative head, folds it under, and hands it to the next person. Trying not to see what has been drawn previously, successive participants draw sequential body parts (neck, chest and upper arms, etc.), fold them under, and pass them along until the last person draws the feet. Afterward the paper is unfolded and displayed, revealing, as a rule, a humorously related series of body parts. Another method is to draw, in sequence, various lines, shapes, or parts of the face on a large sheet of paper or a blackboard. One person begins by making a line, shape, part of a face, etc.; the next person may add another line, shape, etc., until everyone has participated. Again, the results are usually a source of considerable interest as well as amusement.

Art charades is an approach to an old parlor game. The demonstrator performs in non-verbal pantomime before guests. He attempts to describe by gesture and symbol a famous artist, a famous work of art, an art style, or some other mutually agreed-upon category. Art charades might occasionally be used in the classroom to emphasize subject matter which would otherwise seem routine.

Creative costumes may be made in several ways. Groups may be divided into pairs where one person drapes rolls of 2-inch crepepaper, or safety-pins pieces of cloth, on his partner, seeing who can create the most interesting, attractive, or humorous costume.

PUBLICATIONS

One of the most important extra-curricular activities is the field of school publications. If used in its proper perspective, the school publications program can make tremendous contributions to interested students' educational growth through participation in the production. Other values include faculty members' and students' increased enjoyment of school life, the development of leadership, and over-all public relations of the school. Layout and type design, illustration, and many graphic art procedures contribute to the art education of students who participate. But few if any contributions to students' and teachers' educational and social growth will result if publications are permitted to dominate their daily life.

School newspaper. Like every school publication, the school newspaper should be designed, written, and printed (if possible) by students. Selected faculty members act as advisers or guides, without directly participating in the publication activity, since this deprives students of important educational experiences to which they are rightfully entitled. The school newspaper reflects the age levels, interests, and abilities of the students who produce it. A junior-high school newspaper, for example, need not resemble a city daily, a local weekly, or even a senior high school newspaper in content, layout, or general quality. It should be a unique and true reflection of the students who produce it. Like posters, school newspapers are designed to communicate to all students, teachers, and administrators in the school, plus certain residents of the community. Teachers can play an advisory role in helping students to understand the importance of selecting writers, layout designers, and artists for the school newspaper who are interested and qualified.

By encouraging the editor, art editor, and staff artists to study the illustrations and layout of outstanding publications, and by offering instructional suggestions concerning professional as well as student newspapers, the art teacher can make far-reaching educational contributions. Students can learn how publications might be enriched with linoleum print or lithographic reproductions, cartoons which are genuinely humorous at the age level of the intended audience, and layouts which show imagination, have eye appeal, and are functional in design.

School yearbook. Although the process of producing a yearbook is unusually extensive and complex, it is educationally sound to have students participate as fully as possible in the total procedure. In light of the extreme limitations of time which must be imposed upon students' and teachers' participations, and the cost of production equipment needed, writing, research, photography, design, and art work offer the best avenue for student expression. It requires skilled and experienced personnel to set the type, print, and bind a book that is expected to be treasured by all students the rest of their lives. So actual production is best done by an outside printer and binder.

Because it is dominantly an art activity, the yearbook offers many opportunities for art student participation. In addition to the art editor a fairly large art staff is usually required. The art editor and staff may be responsible for designing the yearbook cover and section separators; organizing photographs and copy into layouts; drawing, painting, or clay modeling (for later photographing) illustrations, and designing advertisements, (if any are used).

Literary quarterly. A growing number of schools include among their activities the publication of a literary or arts quarterly which serves as an outlet for students interested in writing and illustrating short stories, poems, and art reviews. Here, again, are needed students with art ability and interests to serve as editor, art editor, or art staff members. Ideally, students would assume responsibility for writing, illustrating, possibly printing and binding, distributing, and keeping a financial record of the publication.

9: Art in the Community

IN THE MODERN CONCEPT OF EDUCATION, *the school:*

1. Is the center of community educational and certain social activities.

2. Draws heavily upon community resources for field trips, sources of unit studies, guest speakers, and volunteer teacher-assistants.

3. Contributes generously to community growth and improvement. As one of the most important community enterprises, the school purchases many products in the local community. It produces future community leaders and workers by offering appropriate curricular specializations.

COURTESY FUNSTON ELEMENTARY
SCHOOL, CHICAGO, ILLINOIS

This elementary school class is using art media to add personal touches to the Christmas gift basket idea.

COURTESY PRIMARY ANNEX,
SOUTHLANDS SCHOOL, VANCOUVER, B. C.

Children who learn to enjoy creative art activities are more apt to accept art in every aspect of living.

How ENVIRONMENT AFFECTS ART EDUCATION

The following chart lists some of the elements of human and physical environment which affect art education. The remainder of the chapter is devoted to discussions and illustrations of the ways some of these elements may contribute to the betterment of art in the community which is a composite of these environmental elements.

Various elements of our environment make contributions to our art education. However, these contributions may be positive or negative, as indicated below.

ELEMENTS OF ENVIRONMENT WHICH FOSTER ONE'S ART EDUCATION	ELEMENTS OF ENVIRONMENT WHICH HINDER ONE'S ART EDUCATION
Functionally designed, contemporary home.	Poorly designed, unimaginative home.
Home is designed as an artistic unit around the family's needs.	A clutter of poorly designed pieces of furniture, drapes, and rugs.
Significant paintings and pieces of sculpture in original or reproduced form are included as part of interior design.	Gaudy pictures, bric-a-brac, carnival statuettes, some antiques, and souvenirs decorate walls, shelves, and table tops.
Family members and friends are selective in dress and grooming.	Some family members and friends show little aesthetic judgment in selection of clothing and personal grooming.
Extensive, creative art activities are available from nursery school through adult education in both public and private schools.	A scarcity of art activities in elementary schools. No art classes in secondary schools and adult education programs.
Local community has gallery where diverse but significant art works may be seen.	Local art gallery facilities are limited or non-existent.
Other art galleries are within commuting distance for occasional visits.	Other art galleries are not easily accessible.
Community has good library where important art books may be borrowed, where educational and art exhibits are held.	Few important art books are included in community library; or community has no library.
Community is functionally and artistically designed for beauty, safety, economy.	Community is poorly planned, unsightly, unsafe.
Local colleges and art galleries offer frequent lectures to public on art subjects.	Public lectures on the arts are seldom available locally.
Mass communication media realize and assume their responsibility for improving public understanding in areas such as art, and regularly offer features of genuine educational value for interest groups on all age levels.	Mass communication media conform to, or lower, public taste; and do not offer enough public service features of genuine educational value.
The general economic level of the community makes it possible for most youngsters to enter colleges and technical schools where additional or specialized art courses are available.	The general economic level of the community causes youngsters to terminate their education with high school, if not sooner.

Reasons for the many aesthetically undesirable elements in to-day's environment might be suggested,* yet those who read this book are likely to be more concerned with, "What can we do about them?" without reviewing the familiar details of slums, architectural eyesores, traffic jams, smogs, and other social detriments.

Among the possible channels through which art may be developed and improved in the community are:

elementary and secondary schools
colleges, universities, and
    professional art schools
adult education programs
art galleries, libraries, and museums
recreation programs and camps

youth groups
art associations
civic organizations
business-sponsored art programs
government-sponsored art
    programs
mass communication media

Some of the contributions which each of these agencies and institutions may make to the growth of art in the community are discussed further, below. In many cases, these discussions represent established community practices worthy of further adoption.

ELEMENTARY AND SECONDARY SCHOOLS

Of all the possible channels through which art in the community may be developed, elementary and secondary schools are among the most important. During the five-to-eighteen year age range, pupils are a receptive audience to whom art and other essential curriculum areas may be presented in a well-organized, extensive, and effective manner.

If the learning experiences which are offered to children in these grades are assimulated, there is a likelihood that art will eventually flourish in our communities. We have learned that in order to be *effective*, learning experiences must be *desired* by those to whom they are offered. Similarly, to become effective, suggestions for the improvement of our communities must be welcomed by a significant percentage of the populace. Suggestions for extending and enriching the arts will be accepted only by people who know some of the satisfactions and values inherent in them. The best place for the majority of our fellow community residents to become familiar with these values is in school.

*Those interested in these reasons and in the improvement of cultural conditions will wish to read Lewis Mumford's *The Culture of Our Cities* and *The Brown Decades,* Marshall McLuhan's *The Mechanical Bride,* and *Mass Culture,* edited by Rosenberg and White.

COURTESY ELLENSBURG PUBLIC
SCHOOL SYSTEM,
ELLENSBURG, WASHINGTON

Making monoprints, an activity easily adapted to related subject areas, is most valuable for its rewarding aesthetic pleasures.

In one sense, elementary and secondary schools are probably more important than colleges, universities, art schools, art museums, and adult education programs simply because they affect more people over a longer period of time, at a time of their lives when they are most receptive to new learning experiences, and before they are established in routine patterns of thinking. Therefore, let us consider some of the specific means of developing children's art awareness, interest, and ability which are likely to carry over into adult life.

CONSUMER ART COURSES

In secondary school, consumer art courses should be made available to *all* students. Such courses may combine study and practice. They should be related to activities which will develop the individual's ability to use art in his everyday life: the improvement of his personal appearance; the planning and designing of his own

Consumer education in the arts has taken on a new importance in modern education. Many schools have established "art centers" where well designed objects can be viewed regularly by students. Bowl designed by George Federoff of Sitka, Alaska.

314

The public school foyer, or a room located near the main entrance, is ideally suited for the establishment of a school-community art gallery. Both pupils' and professional art work may be exhibited. Some w o r k s may be priced for sale.

room, apartment, or home; the planning and improvement of his community; his understanding and purchase of the work of professional artists; and his selection of well-designed, handmade and manufactured objects.

Many aspects of consumer art courses may be offered in unit studies in elementary and secondary schools, and in programs of adult education. Individuals might build cardboard models of an ideal community, redesign their own communities in three-dimensional form, or plan and build well-designed model "dream" homes. By suggesting to children that they consult with their parents and seek their advice about such projects, explaining what they have learned about architectural and interior design in school, learning experiences are extended to the entire family. If parents approve, the actual redesigning of the child's room or some other part of his home is educationally valuable.

It is important to share the art knowledge pupils have gained with as many people as possible. This may be done by displaying completed model communities, home plans, and interior designs in store windows, public libraries, home shows, and at community meetings, as well as in the school itself.

Extra-curricular activities. Many of the extra-curricular activities described in Chapter 8 serve as channels for the art interests of community residents. Such activities as art bazaars and art auctions present important learning experiences in a lively atmosphere for people of all ages.

School-community art gallery. Especially important in communities which do not have an art gallery are exhibitions in the foyer, lobby, corridor, or a room of the local school. Exhibits such as landscape gardening plans, model houses, model communities, paintings, sculpture, well-designed handmade and manufactured objects, and clothing designs are of great value to those who create and arrange them as well as to visitors from the community.

Art teachers' services. If possible, community services should form a part of the art teacher's regular daytime schedule.

• Speaking and/or demonstrating before various community groups on such subjects as community planning, architectural design, interior design, industrial design, clothing design, painting, sculpture, photography, and the graphic arts.

• Working with civic officials in planning exhibitions at fairs and special community occasions. Of special importance here is the art teacher's knowledge of the need for well-rounded exhibitions representative of as many of the exhibitors as possible rather than stressing prizes (especially with reference to children's exhibits, but applicable also to the work of adult amateurs).

• Teaching classes or leading workshops on art subjects for parents, teachers, administrators, businessmen, or other interested community groups. One of the most important results is that they become more sympathetic to their children's art interests, and encourage them to grow into more art-minded adults.

COLLEGES, UNIVERSITIES, AND PROFESSIONAL ART SCHOOLS

Colleges, universities, and professional art schools possess a high potential for developing art in the community. The conferences, exhibitions, non-credit courses, consultant services, and scholarship art classes for pre-college high school students which they sponsor can vastly extend the scope and increase the quality of community art activities.

The Wisconsin Idea. Several years ago the University of Wisconsin originated and put into practice an idea which has since become widespread. "The Wisconsin Idea" implies that the University considers its boundaries of service to be those of the state, rather than the traditional limits of the campus. Articulation is very strong. An important aspect of the University of Wisconsin's state-wide program has been its activities in the field of art, some of the highlights of which are: the employment of a nationally known artist-in-residence who produces creative work in the campus setting and helps develop leadership in art groups throughout the state; the production of radio and television art programs for schools throughout the state; the encouragement of rural art through exhibitions, lectures, and workshops;* an anual state-wide exhibition of profes-

---

*See *Rural Artists of Wisconsin* by John R. Barton, University of Wisconsin Press, Madison.

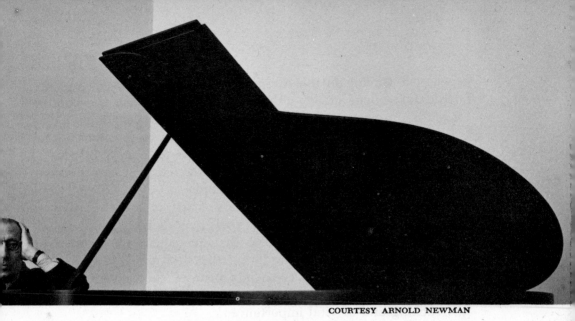

An art teacher may be called upon to offer artistic criticism on photographs by local amateurs and professionals, or of recognized masters such as Steiglitz, Cartier-Bresson, and Arnold Newman who made this sensitive portrait of *Igor Stravinsky*.

sional art work; and the preparation of teachers of art to serve schools and adult programs throughout the state.

College-community art gallery. Colleges, universities, and professional art schools are often in a better position than elementary and secondary schools to develop art galleries which can serve the community as well as the student body. A number of them have established excellent reputations for the quality of national, regional, or state painting, sculpture, and industrial design exhibitions which they sponsor.

Community teaching services. Many colleges, universities, and art schools encourage their students to offer voluntary educational services to the community. Those who participate sometimes receive college credit or part-time pay. Students teach art to small groups in agencies ranging from nursery schools to homes for the aged. They often begin as leaders' assistants but soon become fullfledged community art teachers. Some of them may even plan and direct art workshops for groups of parents or teachers, panel discussions on art subjects for interested community groups, and lecture-demonstrations on various art topics.

Extension classes. Many institutions of higher education schedule classes in late afternoon, evening, or Saturday hours when people who are working part or full time can take advantage of them. Some college faculty members travel to an outlying community to teach a class to save twenty or thirty students the time and expense of coming to the campus. Extension courses are usually offered for college credit, although many adults take the courses for self-improvement on a non-credit basis. Among the more popular courses are those which are similar in content to the high school consumer art course suggested earlier in this chapter.

Preparing artists and art teachers. Although their contributions may seem less direct than those of people in other areas of community service, the artists and teachers of art prepared by colleges, universities, and professional art schools may do more for the community and individuals within it than an equivalent number of trained social workers. Considering the vast numbers of people with whom art graduates come into contact, the influence of the teaching they experience during their professional preparation is far reaching and of vital importance.

ADULT EDUCATION PROGRAMS

Adult education gives promise of becoming one of the major means of disseminating important art information to large numbers of people. It is especially important for art teachers to serve communities in which they teach by sharing in the development and improvement of adult education programs.

Adults are capable of changed attitudes toward art; but their preference for contemporary trends usually grows at a slower rate than that of children whose beliefs and preferences have not become so deeply fixed. Many adults, of course, will never develop a pref-

It takes much work and art ability for a young person to become a professional book illustrator. By intensive study and regular consultation with the instructor, a student can sometimes develop and ultimately reach such an objective.

COURTESY COOPER UNION, NEW YORK

318

Adult education art classes provide stimulating and enjoyable leisure time activities.

erence for the contemporary arts, yet an understanding of this area will at least help them to be tolerant of it and willing to have others, including their own children, enjoy it if they wish. It is fairly common today to find young people planning homes with contemporary furniture, even though they have been brought up in traditional homes. This is often due to the attitudes of intelligent, open-minded parents who want their children to make decisions for themselevs, and are willing to endorse young people's preferences for newer styles in art.

Adults in many communities have shown that they are interested in keeping up to date on the arts as well as other areas of living. They may ask that art courses in subjects of interest to them be offered as part of an educational program in the late afternoon and evening hours. Probably one of the most important and popular of these courses would be similar in content to the secondary school consumer art course described earlier in this chapter. Here adults could study and experiment in painting, sculpture, home planning, interior design, landscape design, clothing design, and a variety of related art areas. A consumer art course serves as an excellent introduction to specialized courses.

Adults derive many benefits from their participation in art activities. They gather useful information about art in the design of homes and communities. They find great satisfaction and enjoyment in art activities, which in turn contribute to emotional stability and constructive social relationships. Perhaps most important is the fact that art activity participation teaches people to think creatively. The sophistications of adult life have caused many of us to think and react in stereotyped patterns. Creative thinking pays dividends in many areas of life, and can be developed by anyone who makes the effort.*

---

*See Alex Osborne's *Your Creative Powers; Wake Up Your Mind;* and *Applied Imagination: Principles and Procedures of Creative Thinking.*

Broad, introductory courses in understanding the arts are becoming increasingly popular. Original works by major artists of the past and present, such as the etching *Two Women in Profile*, by Georges Rouault, are excellent for instructional purposes.

Creative thinking is not fostered by the use of patterns or by copying the work of others. For this reason it is especially important for art teachers to volunteer their services in adult education as well as their regular teaching level. To effectively carry out this additional responsibility, they will need the moral support of the adult education administrator as well as determination to work slowly but surely toward the goal of creative expression in all students.

This chart represents a sampling of human intellectual behavior over a period of nine years. It contains the profiles of intellectual success and failure. Only about 5% of the population achieve intellectual success; the rest fail for lack of motivation, inadequate understanding of their abilities and how to use them, and, in many cases, because of mediocre or low native intelligence. The majority reach their peak of curiosity and intellectual growth in high school, college, or early adult life, and then cease to grow and begin to decline.

Why do so many fail to achieve their potential? It is becoming increasingly clear that it is not because of poor heredity or inadequate native ability but because they fail to discover that if they choose they are able to make more of their lives. How to prevent

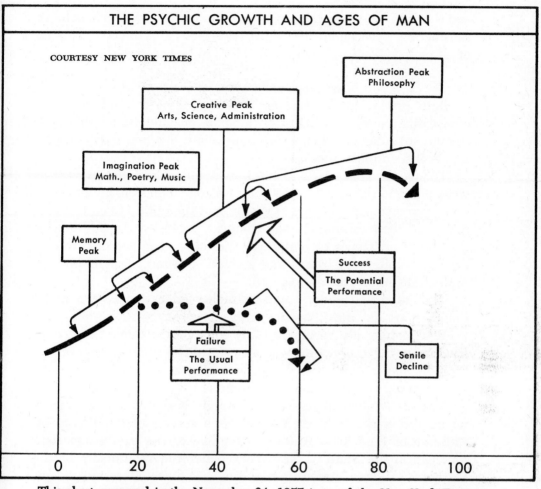

THE PSYCHIC GROWTH AND AGES OF MAN

COURTESY NEW YORK TIMES

Abstraction Peak
Philosophy

Creative Peak
Arts, Science, Administration

Imagination Peak
Math., Poetry, Music

Memory
Peak

Success

The Potential
Performance

Failure

The Usual
Performance

Senile
Decline

| 0 | 20 | 40 | 60 | 80 | 100 |

This chart appeared in the November 24, 1957 issue of the *New York Times* in an article written by Dr. Joseph W. Still, M.D., M.P.H., Washington, D. C.

these failures constitutes one of the great problems facing our society.

Art educators recognize that virtually everyone can achieve success to his own satisfaction in any one of several art activities,

Many benefits, such as constructive use of leisure time and emotional satisfaction, are derived by adults participating in creative art activities. This lady is completing a piece of clay sculpture modeled directly from life.

COURTESY UNIVERSITY OF MICHIGAN AND
SCHOOL ARTS

321

and that a much larger than expected number of people can achieve satisfaction, even eminence, in art expression. Continuous planning at all periods of life is essential if this is to be accomplished.

ART GALLERIES, LIBRARIES, AND MUSEUMS

Both private and public art galleries, libraries, and museums offer extensive services. Most of them are available to all who wish to take advantage of their exhibitions, films, lectures, gallery tours, art classes, and loan services.

Today, art museums and libraries maintain evening as well as week-end and daytime hours. They welcome children, adults, amateurs, professionals, the casual visitor, and the critic. Even the very nature of their exhibitions has changed markedly. In addition to paintings and pieces of sculpture, one finds examples of furniture design, architectural plans and models, clothing design, photography, and industrial design.

The extension-service trend in higher education is also to be found in art galleries, libraries, and museums.

Bookmobiles are becoming fairly common throughout the country. They, together with regional, centralized library services, are bringing more and better books and magazines (many of which deal with art subjects) to more people.

The art equivalent of the bookmobile is the artmobile, one of which serves the State of Virginia as a service of the Richmond Museum of Fine Arts. Another artmobile carries exhibits to communities in the State of New York under the sponsorship of the State Art Teachers' Association and several other interested groups.

A number of public and private libraries now have special sections where art books and magazines are available. Many of them sponsor art exhibitions, discussions on art subjects, and courses in art.

RECREATION PROGRAMS AND CAMPS

Each year more children and adults participate in recreation programs during late afternoons, evenings, week-ends, and summers. With leisure time increasing, it is important that a wide variety of creative activities be included in such programs. To be effective, art experiences need to be frequent and consistently high in quality.

YOUTH GROUPS

Closely allied in nature and importance to recreation programs and camps are youth groups such as the Y.M.C.A., Y.M.H.A.,

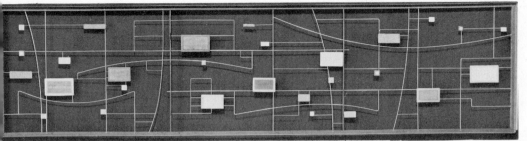

This decorative panel by Willard Rosenquist, made of brass wire and small brilliantly colored enamel plaques, has many aesthetic uses, such as a room divider or wall decoration.

Y.W.C.A., Y.W.H.A., the C.Y.O., "Teen Clubs," Boy and Girl Scouts, Cub Scouts, Camp Fire Girls, Brownies, Blue Birds and Boys' clubs. Youth group leaders often permit stereotyped, time-filling art activities. However, they are usually willing to receive suggestions which will enable their youngsters to produce personally satisfying and tangible, yet creative, art works which they can take home. The Girl Scout organization has recently made a concerted effort to emphasize creative activities in its extensive program. Its stimulating and idea-packed film, "Adventuring in the Arts," illustrates the plan, as does its National Educational Television network series, "Adventuring in the Hand Arts," kinescopes of which may be rented from the Indiana University Film Library at Bloomington.

ART ASSOCIATIONS

Through their activities, art clubs and associations contribute to community art growth. For example, the Ithaca, New York, Art Association exhibits its members' works in downtown store windows. Another organization assigns each member a space in a

Creative art activities such as paper sculpture and tempera painting should be used in recreation programs and summer camps. "Something to take home" can just as well be the product of a creative activity, need not dull art sensitivity.

PHOTO BY DEWEY EKDAHL

Like many smaller cities throughout the world, New York has its community art groups with annual exhibitions of members' work which occasionally uncovers talent and provides opportunity for unknown artists to present their accomplishments. Shown here is a p o r t i o n of the semi-annual Washington Square Art Exhibit in Greenwich Village.

NEW YORK UNIVERSITY,
PHOTO BY WILLIAM SIMMONS

local hotel lobby where he regularly hangs his most recent work. Both the hotel and the art association have found this arrangement to be very satisfactory. Larger, professional art groups have long-range and complex systems whereby contributions are made not only to their members' growth but to their communities as well. (See Chapter 4, pages 104-119 for more details.)

Civic organizations

Although the functions of civic groups are widely varied, such organizations as Parent-Teacher Associations, Rotary, Kiwanis, Lions, women's clubs, the Red Cross, Junior League, and labor unions often sponsor art activities which bring direct benefits to the community. A description of one activity may serve as an example.

P.T.A. members of the Stratford Avenue School in Garden City, N. Y., organized a "Thrift Shop" to provide funds for the purchase of original art works and suitable-for-framing reproductions to be hung in the school. One day a week, from 1-4 P.M., members took turns selling used (cleaned or washed) clothing to community residents. Seventy-five percent of the purchase price was returned to the person who brought in the clothing, and the remainder went into an art purchase fund. Included in the art works purchased for the school were paintings produced by local high school students, as well as works by adult amateurs and professionals.

Business-sponsored art programs

An increasing number of business organizations sponsor art exhibitions and develop art collections. Probably none has done more in this field than Gimbels of Milwaukee, through the leadership of manager Charlie Zadok, which sponsored a yearly series of art competitions from which works were purchased, exhibited, circulated, and later donated to public institutions. They have also commissioned murals for institutions of higher learning, concerning which Gimbels said it wished to:

1. Encourage the integration of the arts with architecture in public buildings.

2. Aid in exposing the public, and particularly the youth in our colleges, to the art of our times in order to encourage their own appreciation of the arts and speed their initiation into the enrichment that culture brings into their lives.

3. And above all—to offer the painter the opportunity for full expression in a monumental medium and to win for him as permanent and wide a showing for his work as any artist can achieve.

Another Wisconsin firm, the Meta-Mold Aluminum Company of Cedarburg, arranged for periodic exhibits of artists' works in its office building. It invited the public to attend these exhibits and arranged for non-commission sales of work even to the extent of financing purchases on a 25% down payment plus installment plan. Inspiration for this project was initially provided by board chairman Otto Spaeth, whose interest and enthusiasm soon spread to other executives, employees, and eventually to residents of the community at large.

GOVERNMENT-SPONSORED ART PROGRAMS

Much has been said for and against government sponsorship of the arts. There seems to be general agreement, however, that certain aspects of the arts might properly and successfully be sponsored by international, federal, or state governments.

On the international level, UNESCO has undertaken many art projects. One of these is the UNESCO publication *Education and Art*, which includes contributions from artists and art educators representing many member nations. This book was the first international venture of its kind. Valuable mimeographed lists of recommended books and other teaching aids, with entries from many countries, have been circulated more recently.

On the national level, the Works Progress Administration Art Project of the United States Government is widely acknowledged as having been successful. Many prominent American artists received preparation, encouragement, or professional employment during the W.P.A. art project of the 1930's.

Thousands of men and women, previously unfamiliar with the pleasures and values inherent in art activities, may be reached in one of the rapidly growing programs of the armed forces. This soldier is making a piece of self-designed jewelry in a supervised and well-equipped army craft shop.

U. S. ARMY PHOTOGRAPH

Little sponsorship of the arts has been noted on the state level, except through departments of education. The Vermont Department of Education is somewhat unique in that it offers an arts and crafts service through which it:

- Calls on craftsmen in their homes to help with craft problems and asks shops to sell craft work.
- Acquaints craftsmen with current craft news, trends, and exhibits, by publishing bulletins.
- Helps craftsmen by advising them on sources of materials, improvement of their work, and available markets.
- Organizes adult craft classes in silk screen printing, rug making, weaving, stenciling.
- Publicizes the work of Vermont craftsmen.
- Sponsors several craft exhibits annually both in and out of the state.
- Offers the use of a lending library of craft books and magazines.
- Publishes biennial reports of the work for information of legislature, directories of Vermont craftsmen and shops, and other pamphlets.
- Lends to Vermont craftsmen small amounts of money for three month periods, toward the purchase of supplies where a definite order is pending.
- Cooperates with other craft and community groups interested in raising standards and developing crafts in the state.
- Provides a supplementary, and in some cases a full-time income for many Vermonters through their craft work.*

Several excellent art programs are sponsored internationally by

* "Arts and Crafts Service," State Education Department, Montpelier, Vt., not dated.

the armed forces. Uniformed men and women, plus civilian employees in almost every military installation, may enroll in a variety of art courses, where they receive competent instruction from specially trained personnel. These programs should receive full professional support because of their vast potential for so many people.

MASS COMMUNICATION MEDIA

Television, radio, newspapers, magazines, and books reach audiences on every social and economic level. They include programs, articles, or full texts on art, ranging from painting and sculpture to interior design and architecture.

When the mass communication media deal with bonafide examples and descriptions of the arts, they can effect rapid and continued improvements in general understanding. These public services have already had pronounced effects upon increased consumption and production of the arts. As a direct result of such information, thousands of home interiors have been redesigned and literally millions of adults have begun to participate directly in the arts, especially painting.

Regularly scheduled television programs carried on major networks, frequent and well-illustrated newspaper and magazine articles such as those found in the New York *Times, The Christian Science Monitor,* and *Life* magazine, and books such as the pocket-size *7 Arts* series and the superbly printed and well-illustrated Skira volumes have all shared in what may eventually become a worldwide art renaissance. This desirable cultural condition can be hastened by television and radio station managers and newspaper, magazine, and book publishers who devote themselves sincerely to the widespread dissemination of legitimate and constructive information on the arts. A steadily increasing number of these people realize the educational responsibility of mass communication media, and are trying sincerely, often courageously, to do more than provide what their least intelligent consumers prefer.

DEVELOPING A PLAN FOR COMMUNITY IMPROVEMENT THROUGH ART

Art in the community may someday become a reality rather than a dream of art educators. In fact, it did become a reality in the city of Owatonna, Minnesota, in the early 1930's. Largely due to the inspiration of the late Melvin Haggerty, Dean of the School of Education of the University of Minnesota, coupled with the enthusiasm and industriousness of other members of the faculty, a philosophy of art as a "way of life" was put into practice.

A University of Minnesota faculty committee, sponsored by the Carnegie Corporation, hoped:

"first, to find out to what degree art entered into the daily activities of the people who lived there [the community to be selected for the experiment]; second, to arouse in these people an interest in the further use of art in their everyday lives; and third, to develop a school program in art based on their needs and their requirements."*

This plan for community improvement through art preceded one of the most important experiments in the history of art education.

The success of the Owatonna project is widely recognized and it should be studied by everyone interested in art education. The entire midwest, in which the Owatonna project was developed, seems to be on the threshold of a cultural renaissance. Beyond university-sponsored and business-supported art programs are many interesting sidelights such as a grocer in Eau Claire, Wisconsin, who for a short time provided room and board for several artists whose works produced during that period were later displayed in his supermarket. Not only was the community made more art conscious, but the artists sold a number of their works and the store's grocery sales are reported to have increased by one-third during the exhibition period.

In Cedar Rapids, Iowa, more than 600 original paintings are owned by local residents and displayed in their homes. Several factors have encouraged art consciousness in this community, among them the fact that the famous regional painter Grant Wood lived there; and that Coe College sponsored a six-day arts festival as part of its centennial celebration.

To help future teachers prepare for the improvement through art of communities in which they will teach, an "Artopia"** assignment is recommended. After studying community planning and the development of art programs, students can be encouraged to give their imaginations free reign in describing an ideal community in which art permeates every aspect of daily life. This type of assignment is best described by example, one of which follows. It was written by a freshman student of art education:

*Ziegfeld, Edwin, and Smith, Mary Elinore, *Art for Daily Living*, Minneapolis: University of Minnesota, 1944, p. 6.
**The term "Artopia" was coined by Professor Clement Tetkowski of the State University College for Teachers at Buffalo, New York.

ARTOPIA[*]

The community of Artopia has a population of about 3,000 persons and consists of groups of houses and apartment buildings surrounded by large parks. These parks separate the residential areas from main boulevards and industries, and border the area where the shopping center, schools, social centers, and public service buildings are centrally located. Each of these divisions serving the public is also separated by huge lawns traversed by sidewalks. A large boulevard encircles the central area. From this large boulevard, streets radiate to public centers by means of clover-leaves. These streets do not go any farther than the public center they serve so that only persons for a particular public center, such as the educational center, will use that street. All streets and boulevards, except cul-de-sacs, are within safety zones. These zones consist of wide bands of lawns and greenery on either side of the pavement that are fenced off from the rest of the community. Many wide sidewalks also go from the residential areas to the public centers and instead of intersecting the highways, go underneath them. It is possible to drive to each individual house, but all streets within residential areas that are not surrounded by safety zones are cul-de-sacs. The numerous canals throughout Artopia also serve as a minor means of transportation.

The educational center is the largest of the public divisions. This area includes the following:

Nursery School	Combination Art Dept. and Gallery
Kindergarten Building	Large Auditorium
Primary School	Small Auditorium
Elementary School	Three Gymnasiums
Junior High School	Two Swimming Pools
High School	Library
Music Building	Clinic

There are approximately 700 children from Artopia and about 800 from the surrounding agricultural areas attending these schools during some part of the day. Parents can leave their small children in the nursery for no more than half a day. This convenience provides the parents shopping time or time for any other business that needs their full attention.

. . . Since the adults of the community have a 4-day working week, persons graduated from high school attend some department of the educational system a half day each week. Consequently all undergraduates attend school 4½ days a week. Supervised playgrounds and sport activities are provided for children while their parents are in school.

For this educational system a huge faculty is required. It is possible to maintain a large staff because Artopia exists in a world of peace where the money that is now used for war is used to shorten man's working week, raise his standard of living, finance research centers, improve communities, pay educators well and provide tax-financed education not only for elementary and secondary school students, but also for adults.

---

[*] By Sally Williams, State University College for Teachers, Buffalo, 1952.

Once a week a speaker is brought from outside the community to the huge auditorium within the educational district. After the lecture, panel discussions are held on different subjects. High school students are encouraged to participate. The following week, before the lecture, conclusions from the various panels are reported to the entire audience. These panels discuss not only problems of Artopia, but also world problems. An average of 60% of the adult population attend the lecture and panel discussions weekly.

Every Saturday the Art Department is open to the public for free instruction. Those participating may come and go whenever they wish, since it is run like the workshops held at our college.

There are also several musical organizations within the community, including both school and community bands, orchestras, and choral groups. In addition to these large groups, there are several smaller instrumental and choral ensembles.

Music appreciation and art appreciation courses are provided within the adult educational system. A large percentage of the adult population (about 90%) attend some division of the art and musical programs and many attend both. These groups are an important part of the community life.

The people of Artopia are broad-minded individuals and are patriotic to their own community without being so at the expense of other communities. They are as much interested in the betterment of communities far removed from them as they are in their own. To promote this idea, each year a group of students and adults visits other communities of the world. They are selected for their abilities in different fields and for their ability to convey their ideas to the people of the communities they visit. In return, they bring back to Artopia new ideas they have obtained from these communities.

"Artopia" assignments often elicit idealistic responses such as that reproduced above. Yet most of the world's major social, political, and religious reforms have been brought into being by philosophic idealists, people who were seeking perfection and were not satisfied with the status quo. The cultural facilities described by the freshman girl are actually available on most large college campuses today. Community planning simply has not advanced that far.

If the condition of art in only one community is improved as a result of the thought and action of a student who has received his first stimulus through an "Artopia" assignment, the practice of including this activity in programs of art teacher education is amply justified. The condition of art in scores of communities has been improved by teachers able to draw upon the reservoir of information remembered from their days as a college student of art education.

330

BIBLIOGRAPHY

AESTHETICS AND CRITICISM

Arnheim, Rudolf, *Art and Visual Perception,* University of California Press: Berkeley, 1954.

Baur, John I. H., *Nature in Abstraction,* Macmillan: New York, 1958.

Beam, Philip C., *The Language of Art,* Ronald Press: New York, 1958.

Bernier, Georges and Rosamond, Editors, *The Selective Eye,* 1956-57, Reynal & Co.: New York, 1956.

Edman, Irwin, *Arts and the Man,* Norton: New York, 1939.

Faure, Elie, *The Spirit of the Forms,* Harper & Bro.: New York, 1930.

Fleming, William, *Arts and Ideas,* Henry Holt and Co.: New York, 1958.

Focillon, Henri, *The Life of Forms in Art,* Yale University Press: New Haven, 1942.

Fry, Roger, *Vision and Design,* Chatto and Windus: London, 1920.

Gardner, Helen, *Understanding the Arts,* Harcourt, Brace and Co.: New York, 1932.

Ghiselin, Brewster, Editor, *The Creative Process: A Symposium,* University of California Press: Berkeley, 1952.

Goldwater, Robert, in collaboration with Rene d'Harnoncourt, *Modern Art in Your Life,* The Museum of Modern Art: New York, 1949.

. . . . , and Marco Treves, *Artists on Art:* 3rd edition, Pantheon Books, Inc.: 1945.

Jenkins, Iredell, *Art and the Human Enterprise,* Harvard University Press: Cambridge, 1958.

Kepes, Gyorgy, *Language of Vision,* Paul Theobald: Chicago, 1945.

. . . . , *The New Landscape in Art and Science,* Theobald: Chicago, 1955.

Kuh, Katherine, *Art Has Many Faces,* Harper: New York, 1951.

Malraux, Andre, *Voices of Silence,* Doubleday: New York, 1953.

Moholy-Nagy, Laszlo, *The New Vision,* Wittenborn: New York, 1947.

. . . . , *Vision in Motion,* Paul Theobald: Chicago, 1947.

Mumford, Lewis, *Art and Technics,* Columbia University Press: New York, 1952.

. . . . , *Technics and Civilization,* Harcourt, Brace and Co.: New York, 1934.

Munro, Thomas, *The Arts and Their Interrelations,* Liberal Arts Press: New York, 1956.

Myers, Bernard S., *Problems of the Younger American Artist,* The City College Press: New York, 1957.

. . . . , *Understanding the Arts,* Henry Holt: New York, 1958.

Ozenfant, Amedee, *Foundations of Modern Art,* Dover: New York, 1956.

Panofsky, Erwin, *Meaning in the Visual Arts,* Doubleday & Co.: New York, 1955.

Read, Herbert, *Art Now,* Faber: London, 1948.

Saarinen, Eliel, *Search for Form,* Reinhold: New York, 1948.

Santayana, George, *The Sense of Beauty,* Dover Publications: New York, 1957.

Weitz, Morris, *Problems in Aesthetics,* The Macmillan Company: New York, 1959.

Bayer, Herbert; Gropius, Walter; and Gropius, Ilse, editors, *Bauhaus, 1919-1928*, The Museum of Modern Art: New York, 1938.

Behrendt, Walter C., *Modern Building*, Harcourt, Brace & Co.: 1937.

Faulkner, Ray, *Inside Today's Home*, Henry Holt: New York, 1954.

Giedion, Siegfried, *Architecture, You and Me*, Harvard University Press: Cambridge, 1958.

. . . ., *Space, Time & Architecture*, 3rd edition, Harvard University Press: Cambridge, 1954.

Gropius, Walter, *The New Architecture and the Bauhaus*, The Museum of Modern Art: New York, 1937.

. . . ., edited by Ruth Nanda Anshen, *Scope of Total Architecture*, World Perspectives, Vol. III, Harper & Bros.: New York, 1955.

Hilberseimer, Ludwig, *The New Regional Pattern*, Theobald: Chicago, 1949.

Hitchcock, Henry-Russell, and Drexler, Arthur, *Built in U.S.A.: Post-War Architecture*, The Museum of Modern Art: New York, 1953.

Kaufmann, Edgar Jr., *What is Modern Interior Design*, The Museum of Modern Art: New York, 1953.

Le Corbusier, *The City of Tomorrow*, Payson & Clark: New York, 1947.

Mock, Elizabeth, *Built in USA—Since 1932*, The Museum of Modern Art: New York, 1944.

Mumford, Lewis, *The Brown Decades*, 2nd revised edition, Dover Publications: New York, 1957.

. . . ., *The Culture of Cities*, Harcourt, Brace: New York, 1938.

. . . ., *Roots of Contemporary American Architecture*, Reinhold: New York, 1952.

Nelson, George, *Storage*, Whitney Publications: New York, 1954.

Neutra, Richard, *Survival Through Design*, Oxford University: 1954.

Peter, John, *Masters of Modern Architecture*, Braziller: New York, 1958.

Pevsner, Nikolaus, *An Outline of European Architecture*, reprint, Penguin: Baltimore, 1957.

Richardson, Albert Edward, and Corfiato, Hector O., *The Art of Architecture*, Philosophical Library: New York, 1956.

Rudofsky, Bernard, *Behind the Picture Window*, Oxford University Press: New York, 1955.

Sullivan, Louis H., *The Autobiography of an Idea*, Dover Publications: New York, 1956.

. . . ., *Kindergarten Chats*, Lawrence, Kansas, 1934, distributed by Wittenborn & Schultz: New York, 1947.

Wright, Frank Lloyd, *An American Architecture*, Edgar Kaufmann, editor, Horizon Press: New York, 1955.

Alschuler, Rose H., and Hattwick, LaBerta W., *Painting and Personality*, University of Chicago Press: Chicago, 1947.

Bannon, Laura, *Mind Your Child's Art*, Farrar, Strauss, and Cudahy: New York, 1952.

Barkan, Manuel, *A Foundation for Art Education*, Ronald Press: New York, 1955.

Bland, Jane Cooper, *Art of the Young Child*, The Museum of Modern Art: New York, 1957.

Cane, Florence, *The Artist in Each of Us*, Pantheon Books: New York, 1951.

Columbia University, Teachers College, *Art Education Today*, Bureau of Publications: Teachers College, Columbia University, New York, 1935-43, 1948, 1949-50, 1951-52.

Conant, Howard, ed., *Art Workshop Leaders Planning Guide*, Davis Publications, Inc.: Worcester, Mass., 1958.

Curriculum Bulletin Number Two, *Art for Elementary Schools: A Manual for Teaching*, Board of Education of City of New York: 1951-1952.

D'Amico, Victor; Wilson, Frances; and Maser, Moreen, *Art for the Family*, The Museum of Modern Art: New York, 1954.

. . . ., *Creative Teaching in Art*, revised edition, International Textbook Co.: Scranton, Pa., 1954.

deFrancesco, Italo L., *Art Education, Its Means and Ends*, Harper: New York, 1957.

Denver, Colorado Public Schools, *Creative Arts in the Elementary Schools*, Board of Education: Denver, 1949.

. . . ., *Creative Arts in the Secondary Schools*, Board of Education: Denver, 1957.

Dewey, John, *Art As Experience*, Minton: New York, 1934.

. . . .; Barnes, Albert C.; Buermeyer, Lawrence; Mullen, Mary and de Mazio, Violette, *Art and Education*, 3rd edition, The Barnes Foundation Press: Merion, Pa., 1954.

Eastern Arts Association, *Eastern Arts Association Yearbooks* (Annuals: 1944-50, Biennials: 1952-Present), Eastern Arts Association: Kutztown, Pa.

Erdt, Margaret Hamilton, *Teaching Art in the Elementary School*, Rinehart: New York, 1954.

Faulkner, Ray; Ziegfeld, Edwin; Hill, Gerald, *Art Today*, 3rd edition, Henry Holt & Co.: New York, 1956.

Gaitskell, C. D., and Margaret, *Art Education During Adolescence*, Ryerson Press: Toronto, distributed by Harcourt, Brace: New York, 1954.

. . . ., *Art Education for Slow Learners*, Ryerson Press: Toronto, 1953, distributed by Chas. A. Bennett Co., Inc., Peoria, Ill.

. . . ., *Art Education in the Kindergarten*, Ryerson Press: Toronto, 1952, distributed by Chas. A. Bennett Co., Inc., Peoria, Ill.

. . . ., *Arts and Crafts in Our Schools*, 7th revised edition, Ryerson Press: Toronto, 1956, distributed by Chas. A. Bennett Co., Inc., Peoria, Ill.

. . . ., *Children and Their Art: Methods for the Elementary School*, Harcourt, Brace: New York, 1958.

. . . ., *Children and Their Pictures*, Ryerson: Toronto, 1951, distributed by Chas. A. Bennett Co., Inc., Peoria, Ill.

Gezari, Temina, *Footprints and New Worlds*, Reconstructionist Press: New York, 1957.

Gregg, Harold, *Art for the Schools of America*, 2nd edition, International Textbook Co.: Scranton, Pa., 1947.

Haggerty, Melvin E., *Art, A Way of Life*, The University of Minnesota Press: 1935.

Hartley, Ruth; Frank, Lawrence; Goldenson, Robert, *Understanding Children's Play*, Columbia University Press: New York, 1952.

Harvard University, *Report of the Committee on the Visual Arts at Harvard*, Harvard University Press: Cambridge, 1956.

Highet, Gilbert, *The Art of Teaching*, Vintage Books: New York, 1957.

Huxley, Aldous, *They Still Draw Pictures*, Oxford University Press: New York, 1939.

Kainz, Luise C., and Riley, Olive L., *Exploring Art*, Harcourt Brace & Co.: New York, 1948.

Keiler, Manfred L., *Art in the Schoolroom*, 2nd revised edition, University of Nebraska Press: Lincoln, 1955.

Knudsen, Estelle H., and Christensen, Ethel M., *Children's Art Education*, Chas. A. Bennett Co., Inc.: Peoria, 1957.

Lindstrom Miriam, *Children's Art*, University of California Press: Berkeley, 1957.

Logan, Frederick M., *Growth of Art in American Schools*, Harper: New York, 1955.

Lowenfeld, Viktor, *Creative and Mental Growth*, 3rd edition, The Macmillan Co.: New York, 1957.

. . . ., *The Nature of Creative Activity*, Routledge and Kegan: London, 1952.

. . . ., *Your Child and His Art*, Macmillan: New York, 1956.

MacDonald, Rosabell, *Art As Education*, H. Holt & Co.: New York, 1941.

Mathias, Margaret, *Beginnings of Art in the Public School*, Scribner: New York, 1924.

Mendelowitz, Daniel M., *Children Are Artists*, Stanford University Press: Stanford, 1953.

Munro, Thomas, *Art Education: Its Philosophy and Psychology*, The Liberal Arts Press: New York, 1956.

National Art Education Association, *National Art Education Association Yearbooks* (Biennial: 1949, Annuals: 1951-present), National Art Education Association: Washington.

National Society for the Study of Education (40th Yearbook) *Art in American Life and Education*, Public School Publishing Co.: Bloomington, Ill., 1941.

Naumburg, Margaret, *Studies of the Free Art Expression of Behavior Problem Children and Adolescents as a Means of Diagnosis and Therapy*, Coolidge Foundation: New York, 1947.

Pearson, Ralph M., *The New Art Education*, revised edition, Harper: New York, 1953.

Perrine, Van Dearing, *Let the Child Draw*, Frederick Stokes Co.: New York, 1936.

Progressive Education Association, Victor D'Amico and others, *The Visual Arts in General Education*, Appleton-Century-Crofts: New York, 1940.

Randall, Arne, *Murals for Schools*, Davis Press: Worcester, Mass., 1956.

Read, Herbert, *Education Through Art*, Pantheon Books: New York, 1945.

. . . ., *The Grass Roots of Art*, Wittenborn: New York, 1946.

Reed, Carl, *Early Adolescent Art Education*, Chas. A. Bennett Co.: Peoria, 1957.

Richardson, Marion, *Art and the Child*, University of London Press: London, 1948. Distributed by Chas. A. Bennett Co., Inc., Peoria, Ill.

Schaefer-Simmern, Henry, *The Unfolding of Artistic Activity*, University of California Press: Berkeley, 1948.

Schultz, Harold A., and Shores, J. Harlan, *Art in the Elementary School*, 5th printing, University of Illinois Press: Urbana, 1952.

Tannahill, Sally, *Fine Arts for Public School Administrators*, Teachers College, Columbia University: New York, 1932.

Tomlinson, R. R., *Children As Artists*, Penguin Books: Baltimore, 1943.

. . . ., *Picture and Pattern Making by Children*, revised edition, The Studio: London and New York, 1950.

334

UNESCO, *Teaching of Arts in Primary and Secondary Schools,* UNESCO Publications Center: New York, 1955.

Viola, Wilhelm, *Child Art,* 2nd edition, Chas. A. Bennett Co., Inc.: Peoria, 1944.

Wickiser, Ralph L., *An Introduction to Art Education,* World Book Co.: Yonkers-on-Hudson, New York, 1957.

Winslow, Leon, *The Integrated School Art Program,* 2nd edition, McGraw-Hill: New York, 1949.

Ziegfeld, Edwin, editor, *Education and Art: A Symposium,* United Nations Educational, Scientific and Cultural Organization: Paris, 1953.

Ziegfeld, Ernest, *Art in the College Program of General Education,* Bureau of Publications: Teachers College, Columbia University, New York, 1953.

DESIGN

Bassett, Kendall T., and Thurman, Arthur B., in collaboration with Victor D'Amico, *How to Make Objects With Wood,* The Museum of Modern Art: New York, 1951.

Betts, Victoria Bedford, *Exploring Papier Mâché,* Davis Press: Worcester, Mass., 1955.

Duncan, Julia Hamlin and D'Amico, Victor, *How to Make Pottery and Ceramic Sculpture,* International Textbook Co.: Scranton, Pa., 1947.

Emerson, Sybil, *Design: A Creative Approach,* International Textbook Co.: Scranton, Pa., 1953.

Herdeg, Walter, editor, *Graphis Annual,* Hastings House: New York.

Johnson, Pauline, *Creating With Paper,* University of Washington Press: Seattle, 1958.

Kaufmann, Edgar Jr., *What Is Modern Design,* The Museum of Modern Art: New York, 1950.

Long, Lois Culver, *Ceramic Decoration,* American Art Clay Co.: Indianapolis, 1958.

Lord, Lois, *Collage and Construction,* Davis Publications: Worcester, Mass., 1958.

Lynes, Russell, *The Tastemakers,* Harper: 1954.

Mattil, Edward L., *Meaning in Crafts,* Prentice-Hall: Englewood Cliffs, New Jersey, 1959.

Nelson, George, editor, *Display,* Whitney Publications: New York, 1953.

. . . ., *Chairs,* Whitney: New York, 1953.

Neutra, Richard J., *Survival Through Design,* Oxford University Press: New York, 1954.

Newhall, Beaumont and Nancy, *Masters of Photography,* George Braziller, Inc.: New York, 1958.

Pollack, Peter, *Picture History of Photography,* Harry N. Abrams, Inc.: New York, 1958.

Read, Herbert, *Art and Industry,* Horizon: New York, 1954.

Riley, Olive L., *Masks and Magic,* Studio Crowell: New York, 1955.

Struppeck, Jules, *The Creation of Sculpture,* Holt: New York, 1952.

Teague, Walter Darwin, *Design This Day,* Harcourt, Brace & Co.: New York, 1949.

UNESCO, foreword by Jean Cocteau, *Stage Design Throughout the World Since 1935,* UNESCO Publications: New York, 1956.

Van Doren, Harold Livingston, *Industrial Design,* McGraw-Hill: New York, 1954.

Winebrenner, D Kenneth, *Jewelry Making As An Art Expression,* International Textbook Co.: Scranton, Pa., 1953.

DICTIONARIES, ENCYCLOPEDIAS, GLOSSARIES, HANDBOOKS AND PORTFOLIOS

American Federation of Arts, Dorothy B. Gilbert, editor, *American Art Directory,* R. R. Bowker Co.: New York, 1955.

Daniel, Greta, editor, *Useful Objects Today: Teaching Portfolio No. 4,* Museum of Modern Art: New York, 1955.

d'Harnoncourt, Rene, editor, *Modern Art Old and New: Teaching Portfolio No. 3,* Museum of Modern Art: New York, 1950.

Lake, Carlton; Maillard, Robert, published under the direction of Fernand Hazan, *Dictionary of Modern Painting,* Paris Book Center Inc.: New York, 1955.

Landon, Edward, *Picture Framing: Modern Methods for Making and Finishing Picture Frames,* American Artists Group: New York, 1946.

Mayer, Ralph, *The Artists Handbook of Materials and Techniques,* revised edition, Viking: New York, 1957.

McCausland, Elizabeth, *Careers in the Arts, Fine and Applied,* John Day Co.: New York, 1950.

. . . .; Farnum, Royal B.; and Vaughan, Dana P., editors, *Art Professions in the United States,* Cooper Union Art School: New York, 1950.

Myers, Bernard S., editor, *Encyclopedia of Painting,* Crown Publishers: New York, 1955.

Osborn, E. C., editor, *Modern Sculpture: Teaching Portfolio No. 1,* Museum of Modern Art: New York, 1947.

. . . ., *Texture and Pattern: Teaching Portfolio No. 2,* Museum of Modern Art: New York, 1949.

Ott, Richard, *The Art of Children* (Portfolio), Pantheon Books, Inc.: New York, 1952.

Praeger Picture Encyclopedia of Art, Praeger: New York, 1958.

Seuphor, Michel, *Dictionary of Abstract Painting,* Tudor Publishing Co.: New York, 1957.

Thieme, U. and F. Becker, *Allgemeines Lexikon Der Bildenden Künstler Von Der Antike Bis Zur Gegenwart (General Dictionary of Artists from Antiquity to the Present),* Leipzig, Germany, 1907-1950.

Vollmer, H., *Allgemeines Lexikon Der Bildenden Künstler Des XX Jahrhunderts (General Dictionary of Arts of the 20th Century),* Leipzig, Germany, 1958.

Wolf, Martin L., *Dictionary of the Arts,* The Philosophical Library: New York, 1952.

DRAWING AND GRAPHIC ARTS

Albert, Calvin and Seckler, Dorothy, *Figure Drawing Comes to Life,* Reinhold Publishing: New York, 1957.

Heller, John, *Print Making Today,* Holt: New York, 1958.

Nicolaïdes, Kimon, *The Natural Way to Draw,* Houghton Mifflin Co.: Boston, 1941.

Peck, Stephen Rogers, *Atlas of Human Anatomy for the Artist,* Oxford University Press: New York, 1958.

Sachs, Paul J., *Modern Prints and Drawings,* Knopf: New York, 1954.

Schider, Fritz, *An Atlas of Anatomy for the Artist*, 3rd edition, Dover Publications: New York, 1957.

HISTORIES OF ART

Barr, Jr., Alfred H., editor, *Masters of Modern Art*, The Museum of Modern Art: New York, 1954.

Baur, John I. H., editor, *New Art in America*, New York Graphic Society: Greenwich, 1957.

.... *Revolution and Tradition in Modern American Art*, Harvard University Press: Cambridge, 1951.

Texts by Marcel Brion and others, *Art Since 1945*, Harry N. Abrams, Inc.: New York, 1958.

Cahill, Holger, and Barr, Jr., Alfred H., editors, *Art in America*, Reynal & Hitchcock: New York, 1935.

Cheney Sheldon, *A New World History of Art*, Viking: New York, 1956.

.... , *A Primer of Modern Art*, Liveright: New York, 1956.

.... , *The Story of Modern Art*, Viking: New York, 1951.

Gabo, Naum, *Gabo*, Harvard University Press: Cambridge, 1958.

Gardner, Helen, *Art Through the Ages*: 4th edition, Harcourt, Brace: New York, 1958.

Gombrich, E. H. J., *The Story of Art*: 6th edition, Phaidon: New York, 1954.

Hauser, Arnold, *The Social History of Art*: Volumes I and II, Vintage Books (paperback), Alfred A. Knopf: New York, 1958.

.... , *The Social History of Art*: Volumes III and IV, Vintage Books (paperback), Alfred A. Knopf: New York, 1958.

Larkin, Oliver W., *Art and Life in America*, Rinehart: New York, 1949.

McCurdy, Charles, editor, *Modern Art*: *A Pictorial Anthology*, Macmillan Co.: New York, 1958.

Mondrian, Piet, *Plastic Art and Pure Plastic Art*, Wittenborn Schultz: New York, 1948.

Rewald, John, *The History of Impressionism*, The Museum of Modern Art: New York, 1946.

.... , *Post-Impressionism*: from Van Gogh to Gauguin, The Museum of Modern Art: New York, 1956.

Riley, Olive L., *Your Art Heritage*, Harper and Brothers: New York, 1952.

Ritchie, Andrew Carnduff, *Abstract Painting and Sculpture in America*, The Museum of Modern Art: New York, 1951.

.... , editor, *German Art of the Twentieth Century*, The Museum of Modern Art: New York, 1957.

.... , *Sculpture of the Twentieth Century*, The Museum of Modern Art: New York, 1954.

Schaefer-Simmern, Henry, *Sculpture in Europe Today*, University of California Press: Berkeley, 1955.

Upjohn, E. M.; Wingert, P. S.; and Mahler, J. G., *History of World Art*: 2nd edition, Oxford: New York, 1958.

The Unesco World Art Series: *Volumes I thru XV*, New York Graphic Society: Greenwich, Conn.

Wilenski, R. H., *The Modern Movement in Art*, Faber & Faber: London, 1957.

HISTORIES OF PAINTING

Barker, Virgil, *American Painting*: *History and Interpretation*, Macmillan: New York, 1950.

Barr, Jr., Alfred H., *What is Modern Painting?*, revised edition, The Museum of Modern Art: New York, 1956.

Brown Milton W., *American Painting From the Armory Show to the Depression*, Princeton University Press: Princeton, 1955.

Cairns, Huntington, and Walker, John, editors, *Great Paintings from the National Gallery of Art*, Macmillan: New York, 1952.

Duthuit, Georges, *The Fauvist Painters*, Wittenborn Schultz: New York, 1950.

Hess, Thomas B., *Abstract Painting: Background and American Phase*, Viking: New York, 1951.

Janson, H. W. and D. J., *The Picture History of Painting*, Harry N. Abrams: New York, 1957.

Soby, J. T.; and Barr, Jr., A. H., editors, *Twentieth Century Italian Art*, The Museum of Modern Art: New York, 1949.

Myers Bernard S., *Mexican Painting in Our Time*, Oxford: New York, 1956.

. . . . , *Modern Art in the Making*, McGraw-Hill: New York, 1950.

Raynal, Maurice, *History of Modern Painting: Volumes I, II, and III*, Skira: New York, 1949-1950.

Selz, Peter, *German Expressionist Painting*, University of California Press: Berkeley, 1957.

INDEX